PRESENTS

THE 2ND GIANT BOOK OF GAMES

BY THE EDITORS OF GAMES

TIMES

BOOKS

All of the games that appear in this work were originally published in *Games,*
Games World of Puzzles, Pencilwise Extra, or *Games Premium Puzzles* magazines.

ISBN 0-8129-2614-5

Printed in the United States of America on acid-free paper
12

First Edition

INTRODUCTION

Since its launch in 1977, GAMES Magazine has prided itself on publishing puzzles of the highest quality and greatest variety found anywhere. Our dedicated staff and talented contingent of freelancers—including top wordsmiths, logicians, illustrators, and photographers—strive constantly to find fresh ideas that break new ground, and to raise the art of puzzlemaking to new levels.

This book contains a selection of our editors' favorite puzzles, games, quizzes, and other features from the past few years. All the material in this book originally appeared in GAMES, GAMES WORLD OF PUZZLES, PENCILWISE EXTRA, or GAMES PREMIUM PUZZLES.

Technology has changed dramatically since the first *Giant Book of Games* appeared in 1991, and GAMES has taken full advantage of advances in electronic digital imaging. In the color section of this volume, you'll find stunning examples of puzzles that were created by means of computer 3-D modeling, electronic retouching, and other special effects that would have been impossible to achieve just a few years ago.

For making this book a reality, special thanks are due to Don Wright and Ronnie Shushan for redesigning the material; to Suzie Elliott for managing the project; to Megan Denver for handling production; and of course to all the GAMES staff members and contributors whose collaborative efforts cannot be acknowledged in bylines.

So sit back, relax, and let us take you on a leisurely journey through the pages of GAMES. Enjoy!

R. Wayne Schmittberger
Editor in Chief
GAMES Publishing Group

CONTENTS

1
WARM-UP CALISTHENICS TO STRETCH YOUR MENTAL MUSCLES

2
LOOK HERE! VISUAL PUZZLES TO TEST YOUR EYE-Q

3
THE WONDERFUL WORLD OF WORDS

4
A COLORFUL JOURNEY THROUGH THE PAGES OF GAMES

1 WARM-UP CALISTHENICS TO STRETCH YOUR MENTAL MUSCLES

MORE BUTTONS

BY BOB STANTON

M Hugh Solvitt has cordially invited you to one of his fiendish puzzle parties. And, as usual, he's rewired the control panel of the elevator to his apartment. Beside the panel of 16 buttons (shown below), you read the following note:

"Welcome. The buttons represent the 16 floors in the building.

"If the buttons all showed their correct numbers, you'd see that they're arranged in sequence. Button 1 is (horizontally or vertically) next to button 2, which is next to button 3, and so on to button 16.

"To keep things interesting, only half the buttons are numbered, and to make it really interesting, exactly half of those numbers are wrong.

"Pressing button 15 will get you to the party. Pressing any other button will result in two minutes of elevator music and a trip to the wrong floor. Come on up!"

Can you find button 15?

ANSWER, PAGE 173

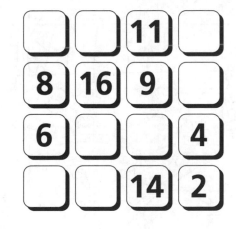

SQUARE DANCE

BY TOM BLOOM

Each of the squares at the bottom of the page is identical to one of the squares in the hoedown scene above it. Some of the squares, though, have been turned sideways or upside-down. How many of them can you find?

ANSWERS, PAGE 173

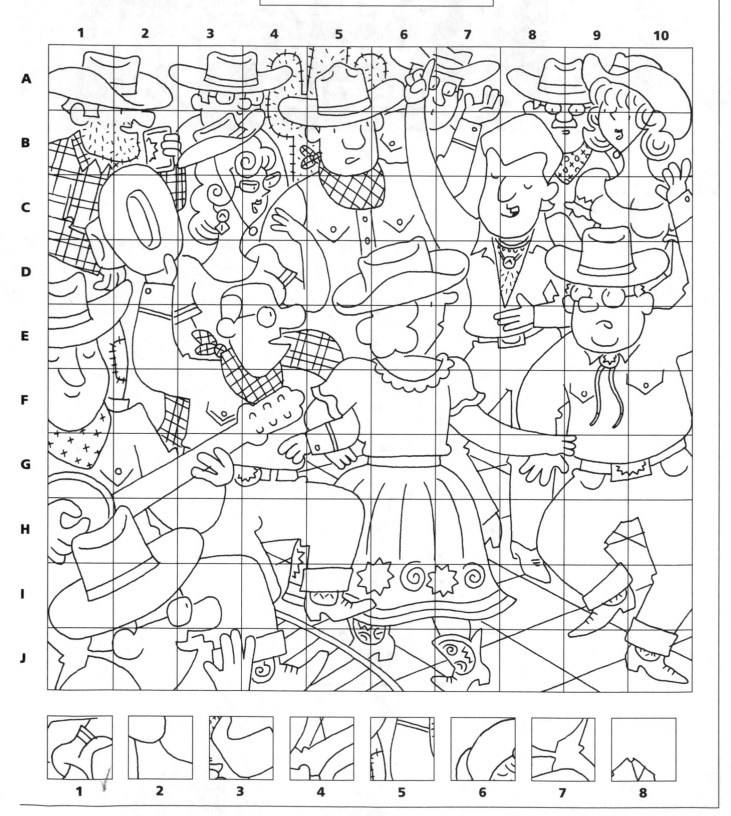

Sum OF THE Parts

BY LINDA SHEPARD

They say the whole can be more than the sum of its parts—but sometimes some things are really just *some* parts. Pictured below are items that belong in groups of three, based on how they can represent parts of a whole. For example, BOW (A), BRIDGE (D), and CABIN (J) suggest parts of a ship. Each item is used only once. Our assumption is that only some of you will somehow identify all six groups and their corresponding wholes—if you do, consider yourself awesome!

ANSWER, PAGE 173

STEVE MELLOR

FILM DIRECTION

BY BOB STANTON

Here's your chance to direct films, right (and left) in your own home! This word search has all the information you need built into the movie titles you're looking for. Each of the 36 film names below tells you how it's hidden in the grid; for example, if RAISING ARIZONA were in the list, you would find it reading vertically from bottom to top. Answers appear horizontally, vertically, and diagonally, as usual, and a few other ways as well—just follow the directions in the titles themselves. Words such as RIGHT or SOUTH generally indicate the direction in which the entry travels in the grid, rather than its location. If you need a little help in your film-directing foray, just "Cut!" to the end of our last reel.

ANSWER, PAGE 173

```
J J G H E L E E G A N T U B Y A T O P P E R L C L I F F
U A F G C D N D O E S G L O D W C I H W Y A E R D S T H
A T L N E D A I I N O O N H G I H L I K E A F V I L M A
T O Y I X O B H N A V E U A B E G I E A S T O F E D E N
N N I I N G A M S I D E S D O T H E R I G H T T H I N G
W D N L E A N D O A N E G N D B T H E T H U T N O T N E
E E G C E S N R U T E R N A M T A B S S I A R I L Y I R
S N D T I L H A T T O R I D S E K T F A R D K C A B R I
T S O V B T O E H V E N S S P S S I E L T Y N I B E C V
S R W E G O L I N T E R I O R S A S T A T E D N P E O E
I O N R P L O E E H A V R E F O L P R G O T T E E N D R
D W T H O O W M A T O T E L L A A S T T O R Y S T E P S
E S O T O L A R E N U T R O F F O L A S R E V E R I U E
S E R S D L M R O N O T H F L A T L I N E R S A V E S D
T A I M C I A X D D C N L E O R H A N E N W D A N Y T G
O M O O R N E T T H R E M C E A T Y U S U A H L L Y A E
R H A V G E E S D A O R N E A B R P E E D E H T E G H I
Y I N N I H T W I N S N O D L R O W T S E W G T R H W A
T N C E C V T W I N S E R D N U N S T O P S B E G O I N
N T O O F T F E L Y M I N G R E D R O B E H T H E E N D
```

BACKDRAFT	FLATLINERS	MY LEFT FOOT	THE BORDER
BATMAN RETURNS	FLYING DOWN TO RIO	NORTH TO ALASKA	THE DEEP
BOOMERANG	GOIN' SOUTH	NORTHWEST PASSAGE	THE END
BOXING HELENA	HIGH NOON	OLIVER TWIST	THE THIRTY-NINE STEPS
CLIFFHANGER	INTERIORS	ONCE AROUND	TOPPER
CROSSROADS	JAGGED EDGE	REVERSAL OF FORTUNE	TWINS
DO THE RIGHT THING	LEAN ON ME	RICOCHET	WEST SIDE STORY
EAST OF EDEN	MALCOLM X	RISING SUN	WESTWORLD
EVERY WHICH WAY BUT LOOSE	MISSING	RIVER'S EDGE	WHAT'S UP, DOC?

ONE TWO THREE

BY MIKE SHENK

Solve this puzzle as you would a regular crossword except that each space may hold one, two, or three letters. The number of letters in a space is for you to determine from logic and the crossing of words. The answer to 1-Across, C-HO-ICE, has been filled in as an example.

ANSWER, PAGE 173

1 C	2 HO	3 ICE		4	5	6	7		8	9	10	11
12				13					14			
15				16					17			
18			19			20		21				
		22		23			24			25	26	27
28	29	30			31	32	33			34		
35					36				37			
38				39					40			
41			42				43	44				
		45		46	47			48		49	50	51
52	53	54		55		56			57			
58				59					60			
61				62					63			

ACROSS

1 Of special excellence
4 One cause of job stress
8 Food zapper
12 Corn ear covering
13 Book before Proverbs
14 Peepers peep through it
15 Number representing the distance from the X-axis, in math
16 Rule breaker
17 The Tate and the Louvre, e.g.
18 Underhanded tactics: 2 wds.
20 Hungry enough to eat a horse
22 English county on the North Sea
24 Classic alien-shooting arcade game
28 Red shade
31 Polar pioneer Robert
34 Noggin, in slang
35 Spigot output: 2 wds.
36 Collar
37 Parking ticket issuer: 2 wds.
38 Pope's envoy
39 Tribe of western Africa
40 Make amends
41 Plainly exposed
43 Chart anew
45 Dentist visit complaint
48 Expeditiously: 3 wds.
52 Explain satisfactorily: 2 wds.
55 Metal stand for hot dishes
57 Used a stopwatch
58 Got equipped
59 Grinning cat's home
60 Dry hands soother
61 Old Faithful, e.g.
62 Curl
63 *Country* star Jessica

DOWN

1 Guitarist's concern
2 Pioneer of escapism
3 Figure eight maker: 2 wds.
4 Pre-college institutions: 2 wds.
5 Auction
6 Large Indonesian island
7 Put aside for future use
8 Popular watch adorner: 2 wds.
9 One in a line of identical dwellings: 2 wds.
10 Class reunion attendee, for short
11 Flying formations for geese
19 Print shop employee
21 Janet Jackson hit song
23 Balloon
25 Baseball Hall-of-Famer Clemente
26 Company thinker: 2 wds.
27 Slyly derisive
28 Tool used in carpentry and upholstery: 2 wds.
29 Place to clean a Cougar: 2 wds.
30 Procrastinator's promise
32 Mr. Clean wears one
33 Fix old paintings
37 "All the world's a stage," for example
39 Coped: 2 wds.
42 Broken: 3 wds.
44 Sinclair Lewis novel: 2 wds.
46 Major's predecessor
47 Holding dear
49 Cantina snack
50 Dropping in rank
51 Given a makeover
52 Farm measure
53 Buffalo Bill's last name
54 Loosens knots
56 Bride's wear

THE LOST PICTURE SHOW

BY LESLIE BILLIG

A picture may usually be worth a thousand words, but in this case just one will do. Each of the 24 pictures shown here represents a word that belongs in a particular movie title. Those titles are indicated by the 10 sets of blanks and little words below—each picture's word fills in one of the blanks. Got the picture? Then it's off to the movies!

ANSWERS, PAGE 173

1. _____ AND _____
2. THE _____ _____
3. THE _____ THAT _____ THE _____
4. THE _____ IN THE _____ _____
5. _____ OF THE _____ _____
6. _____ _____ _____
7. _____ _____
8. _____ _____
9. _____ _____
10. _____ _____

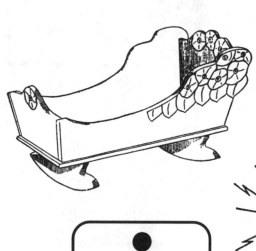

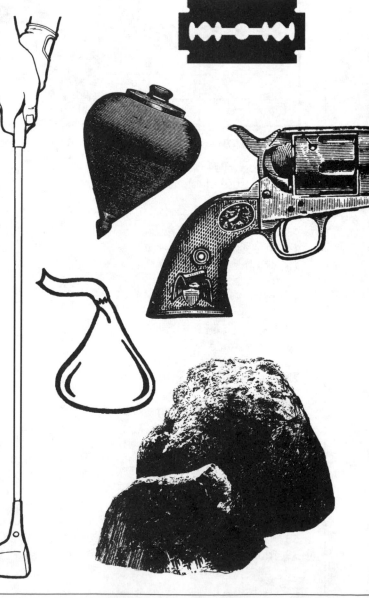

CHANGING CHANNELS

BY AMY GOLDSTEIN

You always know when your favorite TV shows come on—the familiar music, the distinctive title logo. But how easy is it to recognize that unique lettering with a *different* title? We've taken the names of 16 popular shows and drawn each in the style of one of the others. For example, *Coach* is in the style normally used by *M*A*S*H*, while *M*A*S*H* is in the style of another series, and so on. *Cheers* to you if you can match all the shows with their logo styles, but if you need some *Coach*ing, just take a *Quantum Leap* to the answers.

ANSWERS, PAGE 173

C*O*A*C*H

"Northern Exposure"

FAMILY FEUD

QUANTUM LEAP

BONANZA

I LOVE LUCY

SEP CALIFORNIA 92
48 HOURS

CHEERS

Jeopardy!

THE TWILIGHT ZONE

NIGHTLINE

LA LAW

STAR TREK

MASH

THE SIMPSONS

MISSION: IMPOSSIBLE

ANALOGRAMS

BY DAVID VANOVER

In an analogy such as "CAT is to KITTEN as DOG is to PUPPY," the first two items (CAT and KITTEN) bear a relationship that is shared by the second two (DOG and PUPPY). In the puzzle below, we've supplied 20 more analogies, all incomplete. The first two words of each analogy appear at the left. The 40 words that go in the blanks to complete them are arranged alphabetically in the column at the right. Each of the words in the column will be used exactly once, so you may cross them off as you fill them in the blanks. A word of warning: Keep your mind flexible—some of the relationships are completed in unexpected ways.

ANSWERS, PAGE 174

1. SHUTTER is to CAMERA as	_____ is to _____
2. GOLF is to CLUB as	_____ is to _____
3. EAST is to SOUTH as	_____ is to _____
4. RADIUS is to CIRCLE as	_____ is to _____
5. LION is to MANE as	_____ is to _____
6. TANGERINE is to ORANGE as	_____ is to _____
7. BICYCLE is to MOTORCYCLE as	_____ is to _____
8. LIE is to LAY as	_____ is to _____
9. GLOBE is to SPHERE as	_____ is to _____
10. BUN is to BURST as	_____ is to _____
11. GROUT is to TILE as	_____ is to _____
12. FISH is to NET as	_____ is to _____
13. MAGAZINE is to EDITOR as	_____ is to _____
14. KANSAS is to ARKANSAS as	_____ is to _____
15. FLAW is to DIAMOND as	_____ is to _____
16. CROATIAN is to RAINCOAT as	_____ is to _____
17. BASKETBALL is to DUNK as	_____ is to _____
18. CARROTS is to WAIT as	_____ is to _____
19. JOCKEY is to HORSE as	_____ is to _____
20. DIVIDE is to TRAP as	_____ is to _____

ACROSS
ANCHOR
ARRANGE
BECKONED
BOO
BRICK
BROOM
COMB
CUBE
CUCUMBER
DIE
DOWN
ESCALATOR
EYE
FLY
GREEN
IRIS
LATVIAN
MORTAR
NEWSCAST
OURS
PLUG
POOL
RACKET
RANGE
RECORD
ROOSTER
SCRATCH
SINK
SPOKE
SQUASH
STAIRS
SWALLOW
THYME
VALIANT
WEB
WHEEL
WIND
WITCH
WOUND

"B" HIVE

BY WILL SHORTZ

When this puzzle is completed, 30 six-letter words will swarm in circular fashion around the numbers in the beehive. To solve, answer the clues (which all start with the letter B, naturally) and enter each answer word around the corresponding number in the grid. Each answer will begin in the space indicated by the arrow and will proceed clockwise or counterclockwise—the direction is for you to determine. As a small solving hint, we'll tell you that each of the 26 letters of the alphabet will be found at least once in the completed hive. ANSWER, PAGE 174

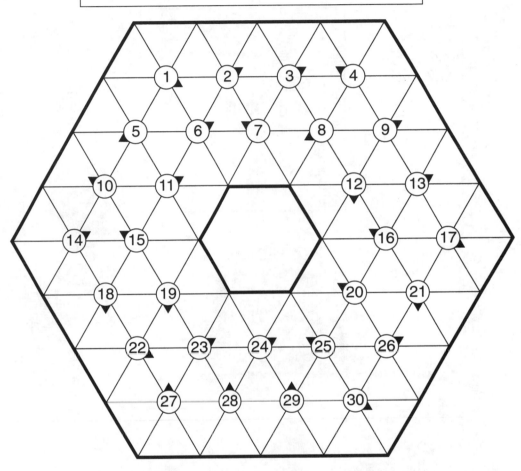

1. Bamboozle
2. Big-name
3. Bordeaux container
4. British Columbia's home
5. Book reviewer, e.g.
6. "Because" for a murderer
7. Boy's or girl's "shooter"
8. Booze made from plums
9. Barbara Bain's hubby, Martin ___
10. Block letters' opposite

11. Bulging with muscles, perhaps
12. Best period of the past
13. Bush's veep
14. Business earnings
15. Building column
16. Beautiful? Not!
17. Bug's antenna
18. Body's middle section
19. Boosts in stature
20. Busy, busy guy
21. Brownie, e.g.

22. Band formed by two trios
23. Briefly washes
24. Bone-chilling horror movie sound
25. Bony
26. Boomer?
27. "Beloved disciple" of Christ (2 wds.)
28. Breathe deeply
29. Begin a fire
30. Building regulations, of a sort

Odds and Ends

BY SUZIE ELLIOTT

Ready for some fun & games? Here's a puzzle you can go at hammer & tongs. The 24 illustrations below can be mixed & matched into pairs to make 12 familiar expressions of the form "this & that." For example, a picture of a ship's bow could be paired with one of a scrape on the knee for the answer BOW & SCRAPE. Work back & forth, try trial & error—and if you can get 10 or more correct pairings, you'll be among the best & the brightest!

ANSWERS, PAGE 174

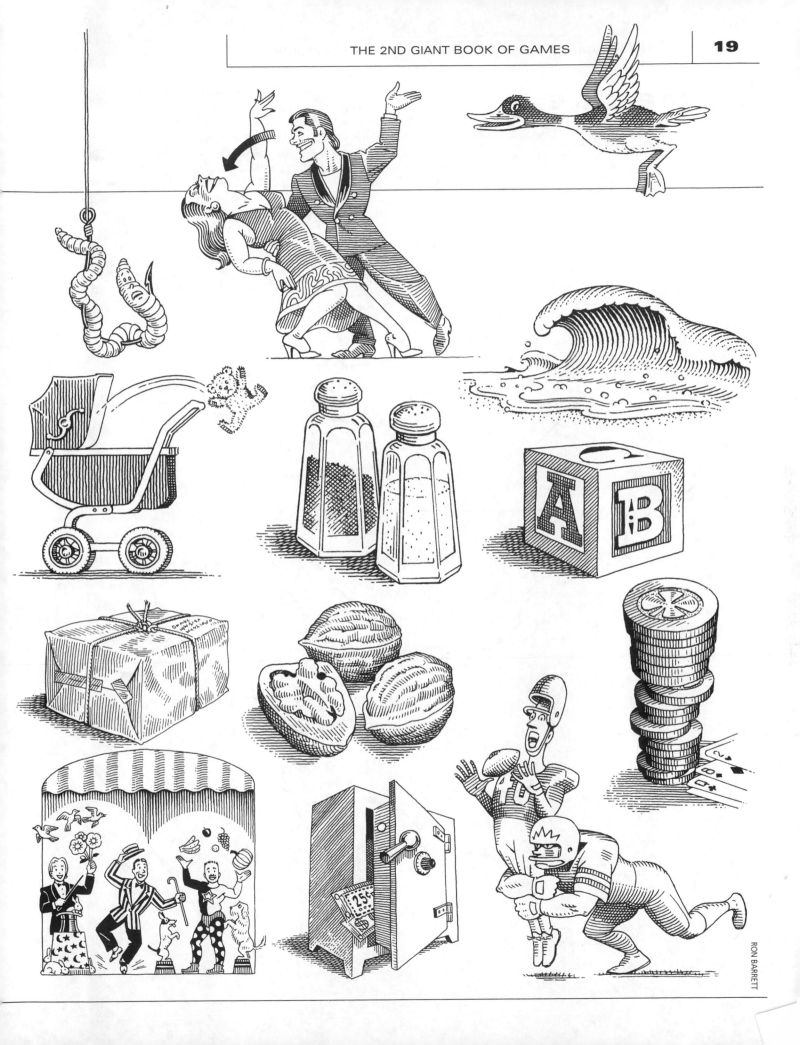

BORDERLINE INSANITY

BY R. WAYNE SCHMITTBERGER

A practical joker in our art department has taken outline maps of 12 different U.S. states, sliced each one into two pieces, and spliced them back together again in new combinations to make 12 unfamiliar-looking "states." She also cut each state's name in two (first removing any spaces between two-word names), then named the new states by giving them a name made up of one piece of each of the component states. The new names are listed at the top of the facing page in alphabetical order. From the shapes and the list of new names, can you determine what the 12 original states were, and identify which states were combined to make each map? All the states are drawn at the same scale, but their component pieces have been rotated in various directions.

ANSWERS, PAGE 174

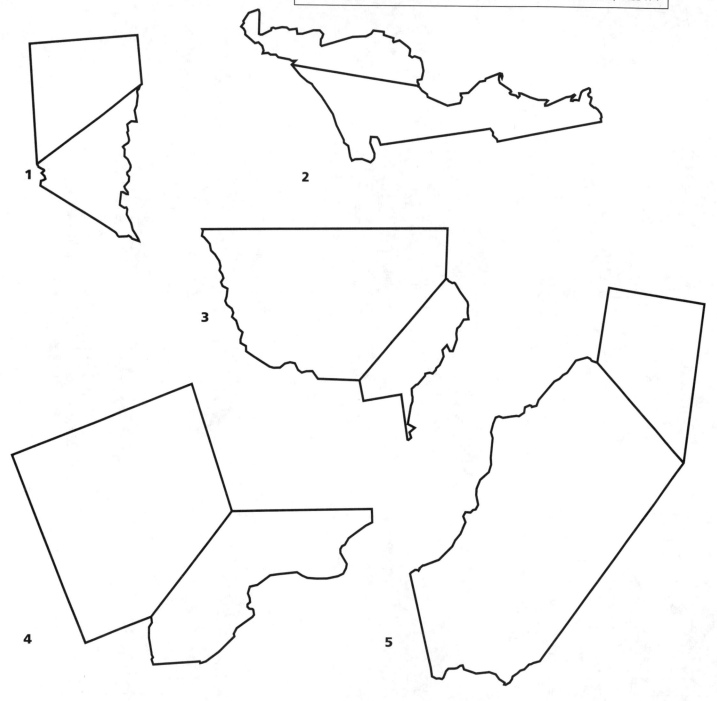

1

2

3

4

5

ALAFORNIA   FLORIANA   NEWEST   OMARK

BAMANIA   INEAH   NEWYOUT   PENNSYLVAID

CALIBRASKA   LOUISIMA   OKLAHAHO   VIRGINIADA

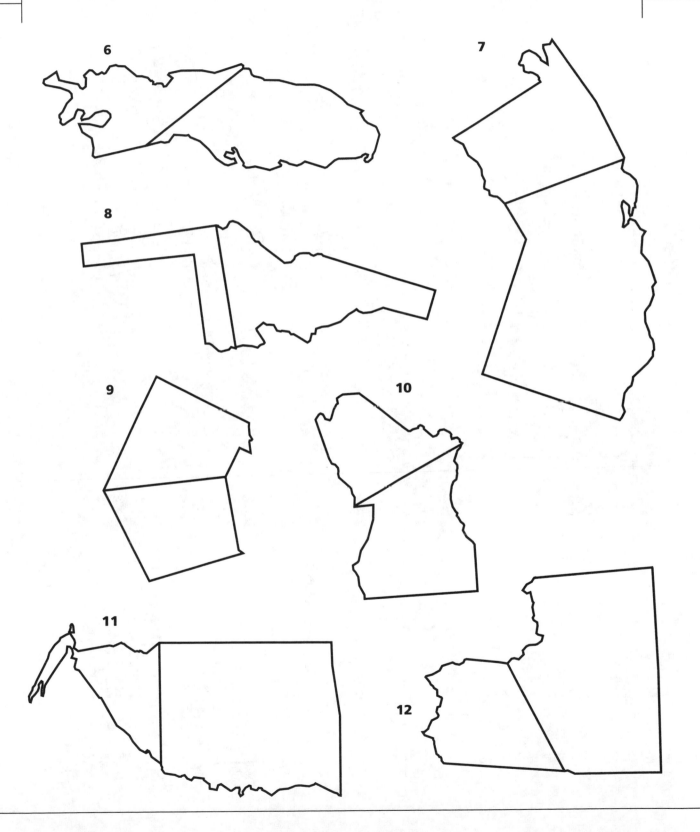

ILLUSTRATED EXCLAMATIONS!

WRITTEN AND ILLUSTRATED BY ROBERT LEIGHTON

Wowie kazowie! Look at all these exciting situations! But wait! Inside each of the exclamation balloons, there should be an appropriate word or sound! Choose the illusration of the correct word (labeled a-j) and place it in the appropriate balloon! Get 10 right and you can exclaim "Bravo" for yourself!

ANSWER, PAGE 174

CHOICES

ONE FOR THE BOOKS

BY AMY GOLDSTEIN

This puzzle isn't exactly by the book—it's both a crisscross *and* a word search. First, fill in the 25 well-known book titles in the list below into the empty spaces in the gray crisscross grid so they interlock in crossword fashion. Each title will be used exactly once. When the crisscross is completed, you'll have a word search grid in which you can find the 25 authors of those books—last names only (the blanks in the title list are for authors' names). Answers may read horizontally, vertically, or diagonally, but always in a straight line. If you're at a loss for a writer's name, you're authorized to check the authors list in the answers. And if every trick in the book doesn't seem to work, you can also find the completed grid, with both filled-in titles and circled authors, on the books in the answers. Okay—hit the books!

AUTHORS LIST, PAGE 176   ANSWER, PAGE 174

```
T H G I   W M O S T   L Y   W E A U T H O R K   U B S M
U S T R   E P U           E F A T O   U R S E
L V E S   W R E H A   V E   T W H   O O I R T   H R E E
G R                 S E   A A T         E M   O V I N
G E X P   E R R I E   N T   L C E   S I E L L   V L E M
A N O U R I L I V E Y S S   O G R   E A T   A   N D M O
V L I N A G T H A W O T Y   V I T             I D O E
S N C T   S H E T E M A N Y   O N E   E V L N S E
H A           S B S   E               E G N
C O A T   R U C L   G H T   U S P A N   D D P O O U
V L N   D           E O D K   A A N D R D
A Z O   O Z L E T   D A N   D A S N T   O L N I W S
H A E   D C O J A   R N D   B               E
A T U   D         E N   A N   D K B R L O
K E N   A N   D R S   E S D   C E   U F E D A A N L D
I L L U T N M I K C   B N I   T
S H E L L   Y N         A T E   D A N D S R E W A
R D E D A N N   D T H U M O B L B   E D I N J S U S T
T H A T W A Y E   V T E R R B E E F   O R E F S C E O T
T F I V O K O B   N T Z B G E R R A       L H D
```

4 LETTERS

BURR _____
EMMA _____

5 LETTERS

GIANT _____
ROOTS _____

6 LETTERS

EXODUS _____
LOLITA _____

7 LETTERS

CANDIDE _____
IVANHOE _____
LORD JIM _____
ULYSSES _____

8 LETTERS

JANE EYRE _____
MOBY-DICK _____
THE TRIAL _____
TOM JONES _____

9 LETTERS

KIDNAPPED _____
NATIVE SON _____
WHITE FANG _____

10 LETTERS

ANIMAL FARM _____
EAST OF EDEN _____
ETHAN FROME _____

11 LETTERS

LITTLE WOMEN _____
STEPPENWOLF _____
WAR AND PEACE _____

12 LETTERS

FRANKENSTEIN _____
THE GOOD EARTH _____

STAMP OF DISAPPROVAL

WRITTEN AND ILLUSTRATED
BY ROBERT LEIGHTON

The Post Office's quality control department regularly recalls stamps for a variety of shortcomings, from printing problems to factual errors. The block of stamps below was pulled at the last minute after careful inspection revealed numerous inconsistencies. Some of these differences, you'll notice, occur between the left and right stamps, others appear between the top and bottom versions, and some appear both ways. (The Post Office, with its tight budget, ignores diagonal differences, and so should you.) Using a straight-edge, draw a line between adjacent stamps connecting these differences. For example, the top left stamp reads "Yeers" where the stamp beside it says "Years," so you should draw a line connecting the second e on the left to the a on the right. (You should also connect the wrong e to the a in the lower left stamp.) The lines you draw will cross out some of the lettered circles. When you've found and connected all the differences, the letters in the circles that remain will answer the question "What problem lurks behind even the most perfect-looking stamp?"

ANSWER, PAGE 174

CRACKING UP

BY TOM ALLEN

This diagramless crossword puzzle is 17 squares wide by 23 squares deep and has regular crossword symmetry. As a starting hint, the location of the first square of the answer is given on the bottom right corner of page 173.

ANSWER, PAGE 174

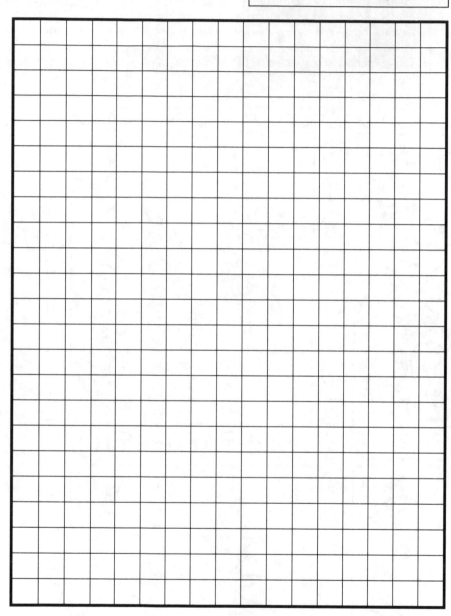

44 Sort
45 PART 2 OF THE RIDDLE'S ANSWER
47 New Deal org.: Abbr.
48 Haig and Hirt
49 Santa's cry of discovery?
50 *Who's Afraid of Virginia Woolf?* playwright
51 Serving of butter pecan
52 Get ___ brass tacks: 2 wds.
54 Jeanne d'Arc, for one: Abbr.
55 Spends time at the mirror
57 Dundee denial
58 Dobbin's favored morsel
60 Film star Farrow
62 *Mayberry ___*
63 Cpl.'s superior
64 Bottom line concerns
66 Actress Russell, to fans
67 Greek vowel
69 PART 3 OF THE RIDDLE
70 Moo
71 Peter or a Wolfe
73 Speedometer units: Abbr.
74 Woman of tomorrow
75 Novel price, once
77 Tatters
78 Tyrannical leaders
82 PART 4 OF THE RIDDLE: 2 wds.
83 Abhorrence
84 Roosted

DOWN

1 Tie up
2 Jellystone Park bear
3 New Year's Eve adjective
4 Manipulated chessman?
5 Collectors' goals
6 Period of rapid economic growth
7 Provided footwear for
8 Worked the garden
9 Give off
10 Purloined
12 Dental covering
13 PART 1 OF THE RIDDLE'S THREE-PART ANSWER: 3 wds.
14 Earthshaking
15 List-ending abbr.
16 Cooked in the microwave, in slang
18 PART 3 OF THE RIDDLE'S ANSWER: 5 wds.
20 ___ Na Na (pseudo-'50s group)
21 Chapel seat
23 Groups of melodious bells
24 Out of kilter
25 "Right?" in Rouen: 2 wds.
27 Flutes and oboes, e.g.
32 Homer's tale of Troy
33 Strike while the iron ___: 2 wds.
35 Blow one's bowler off
37 One making an inquiry
38 Tide types
41 DDE's command: Abbr.
42 Apply lotion
46 Blot
53 Ensnared
54 Tempest
56 Ballpark boo-boos
59 Circumference segment
61 "For what ___ worth ..."
65 Jack-a-dandy
68 Bone-dry
70 Kiss equipment
72 Exclude
74 Prepare (oneself) for action
76 Resound
77 Meander
79 Koppel and Turner
80 *Turandot* tune
81 Racetrack tipster

ACROSS

1 Not ___ long shot: 2 wds.
4 Devout
6 Showy bracelets
8 PART 1 OF A FOUR-PART RIDDLE: 3 wds.
10 Any minute now
11 A handful
13 Bit of gossip
14 Rep.'s Congressional counterpart
17 Fred and Wilma's pet
19 Yes-man's signal
20 Layout
22 Road crew's goo
23 "Silent" president's nickname
24 PART 2 OF THE RIDDLE
26 Gullet
28 Anti-anti vote
29 W. Hem. alliance
30 Ram's ma'am
31 *The Name of the Rose* author Umberto ___
32 Like O. Henry endings
34 Something else April showers bring
36 Western movie brawl setting
39 Abner's appellation
40 Hank of yarn
42 Drunkard's woe, for short
43 Enthusiastic poem

2 LOOK HERE! VISUAL PUZZLES TO TEST YOUR EYE-Q

LEAPIN' LIZARDS!

BY DAVE PHILLIPS

The eminent but absent-minded herpetologist Dr. Dinah Sorris forgot to lock the cages, and now all the Malaysian leaping lizards are loose in the lab. Perhaps you'd be so kind as to help round them up? Just enter the lab through any of the outer doors (but which is the right one?), collect all the lizards, and exit the lab through another door. We should warn you, though, of two important facts: Malaysian leaping lizards are rather large, and they like munching on human legs. Fortunately, the leaping lizard can be easily subdued if you sneak up on it and tickle its stomach. So *never* enter a room by the door closest to the lizard's mouth! Dr. Sorris wants your time in her lab kept to a minimum, so don't retrace any part of your route. You should have no trouble at all rounding up the lizards, right?

ANSWER, PAGE 174

Mental Exercise

BY MARK DANNA

The Olympic athletes pictured below are training for the Summer Games in a rather unusual way. To get in the proper frame of mind for the competition, each is practicing his or her sport without any of the usual equipment involved. As a mental exercise of your own, can you identify the Olympic event or sport for which each athlete is preparing?

ANSWERS, PAGE 175

CARLOS TORRES

Making the Rounds

BY ROBERT LEIGHTON

Look around—many familiar symbols and logos we see every day are based on circular designs. We've cut 12 such round images into thirds and mixed the tops and bottoms on this page. (The middle thirds went into our circular file.) Can you match the tops (1–12) with the bottoms (A–L) and identify the logo or image that each came from? We'd guess that most of these will have a familiar ring, though one or two may throw you a curve.

ANSWERS, PAGE 175

THE TOPS

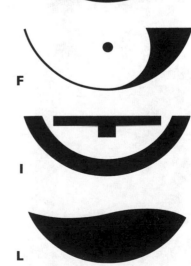

THE BOTTOMS

WHIRLED LEADERS

BY POLLY TITIAN

Politicians are sometimes criticized for distorting the facts. Since turnabout is fair play, we've put a little spin directly on these well-known heads of state, past and present. Can you straighten them out? If you can identify 12 or more, you're a spin doctor supreme!

ANSWERS, PAGE 175

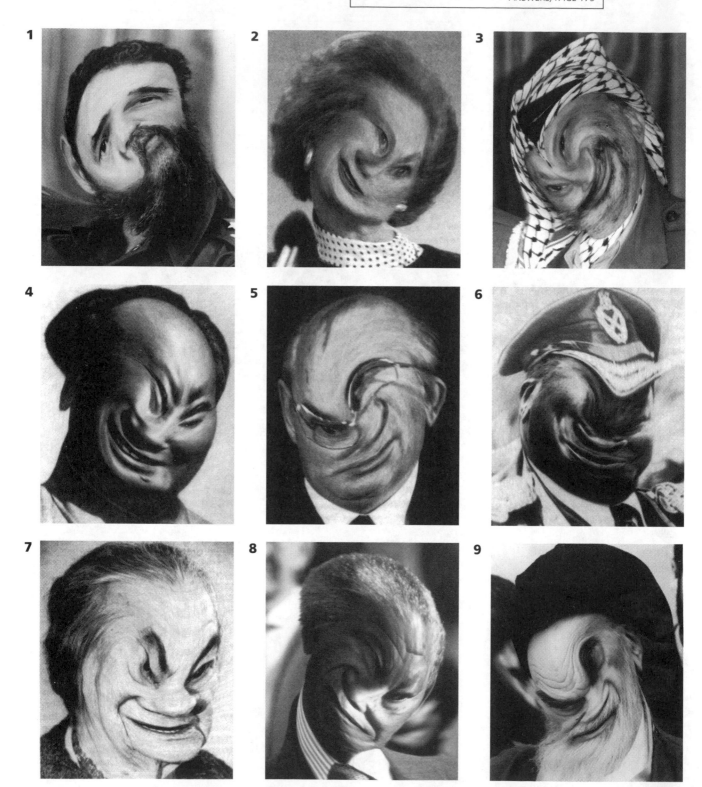

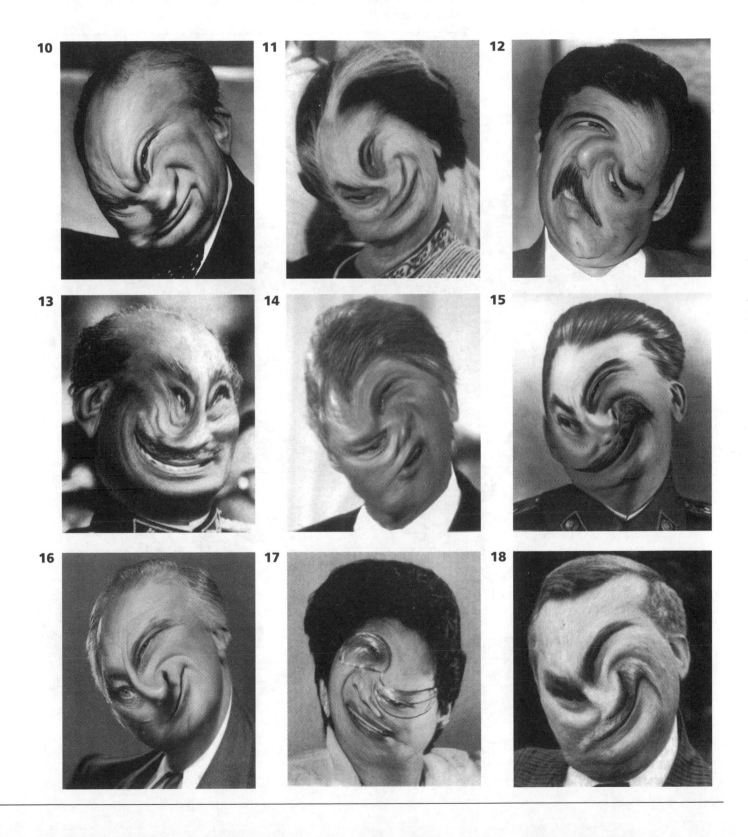

SHADOW PLAY

BY MARGOT SEIDES

On Groundhog's Day, we think of just one weather-sensitive woodchuck emerging from his hole in Punxsutawney, Pennsylvania, to let us know when spring will come. But of course the weather isn't the same everywhere, so naturally there are groundhogs all over the world to serve the local populaces. And when they correspond with each other and want to show off the local attractions, these creatures don't send the usual photographic postcards. Groundhog greetings always feature *shadows* of the local landmarks. Punxsutawney Phil recently received the postcards on these pages from his colleagues around the world. Can you tell what landmark each of these shadowy postcards shows?

ANSWERS, PAGE 175

WHAT'S LOOKIN' AT YOU, KID?

BY RAYMOND ECKE

Of course you know what a bird's-eye view is, but on this page are nine animal-eye views that are *not* for the birds. Can you identify the animals that see these scenes?

ANSWERS, PAGE 175

ARTIFACT— OR FICTION?

BY EMILY COX & HENRY RATHVON

Wealthy business magnate Carnegie Vandermoolah has collected thirteen priceless art treasures, pictured in the room below. You are the new security guard on the Vandermoolah estate, so it's your responsibility to know and protect these valuables. Study them carefully for *two minutes*. Then, to test your observational skills and memory, turn the page. Once you turn, you will not be able to refer back to this page.

RANDY JONES

PARADING YOUR DIFFERENCES

The two Thanksgiving Day parade scenes below may look identical at first glance, but there are actually 21 differences between the top and bottom views. Can you spot all 21 differences?

ANSWERS, PAGE 175

BY ROBERT LEIGHTON

ARTIFACT—OR FICTION? PART II

BY EMILY COX & HENRY RATHVON

Important: Don't examine this picture or read this page if you haven't first followed the instructions on page 35.

One morning as you make your rounds, you notice that the lock has been damaged on the door to this room. At first glance, everything within seems intact. But on more careful perusal, you see that some of the pieces of art don't look quite right. It dawns on you that somebody has stolen the originals and replaced them with forgeries, hoping you wouldn't notice the difference. But if you've done your job well, you'll find 11 errors in the replicas before the police arrive. Can you name all the discrepancies and identify the one piece that turns out to be an original?

ANSWERS, PAGE 175

RANDY JONES

Out of this World

BY JOHN CHANESKI

An eccentric traveler we know has a hobby of visiting places with "heavenly" names. Just back from Cosmos, Minnesota, he recently challenged us to identify these 12 unlabeled map details from his scrapbook. From clues in the maps and your knowledge of geography, can you determine which eight U.S. states and four foreign countries are represented here?

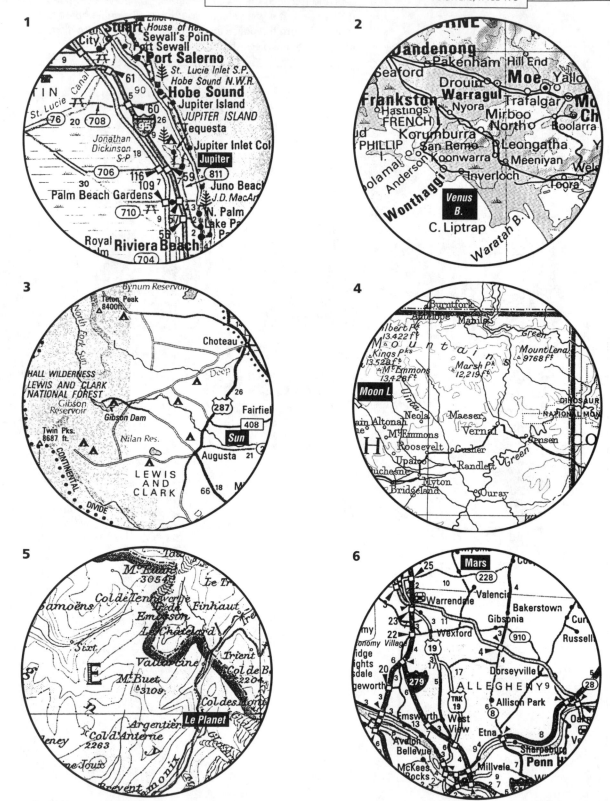

1

Stuart
City
House of Re
Sewall's Point
Port Sewall
Port Salerno
St. Lucie Inlet S.P.
9
77
61
Hobe Sound N.W.R.
90
5
Hobe Sound
76
20
708
60
Jupiter Island
26
JUPITER ISLAND
TIN
St. Lucie Canal
Tequesta
95
Jonathan
Dickinson
S.P.
18
Jupiter Inlet Col
706
Jupiter
811
116
109
7
59
30
Juno Beach
Palm Beach Gardens
J.D. MacAr
710
77
N. Palm
9
Lake P
56
Royal
Riviera Beach
Pa
704

2

RNE
Dandenong
Pakenham
Hill End
Seaford
Drouin
Moe
Yallo
Frankston
Warragul
Trafalgar
Mo
Hastings
Nyora
Mirboo
Ch
FRENCH I
Korumburra
Northo
Boolarra
PHILLIP
San Remo
Leongatha
I.
Koonwarra
Meeniyan
olama
Anderson
Wel
Venus
Inverloch
B.
Togra
Wonthagg
C. Liptrap
Waratah B.

3

Bynum Reservoir
Teton Peak
8400ft
North Fork Sun
Choteau
Deep
HALL WILDERNESS
LEWIS AND CLARK
NATIONAL FOREST
26
Gibson
Reservoir
287
Fairfiel
Gibson Dam
408
Nilan Res.
Sun
Twin Pks.
8687 ft.
Augusta
21
LEWIS
AND
CLARK
66
18
M
CONTINENTAL
DIVIDE

4

Burntfork
Antelope
Mahile
Albert P
13,422ft
Green
Mo
Kings pks
untains
Mount Lena
13,528ft
9768ft
Mt Emmons
Marsh Pk
13,428ft
12,219ft
DINOSAUR
Moon L
NATIONAL MON
Neola
Maeser
Altona
ain
Vernal
Mt Emmons
H
Roosevelt
Gusher
Jensen
Co
Upalo
uchesne
Randlett
Green
Myton
Bridgeland
Ouray

5

To
M. Buet
3054
Le Tr
Col de Tenbavorde
Finhaut
Samoëns
da
Emosson
Fre
Le Châtelord
Sixt
Trient
Vallorcine
Col de B
E
2204
Mt Buet
3109
Col des Mont
Argentier
Le Planet
eney
Col d'Anterne
2263
 line Tour
Brevent
onix

6

25
Mars
228
10
Valencia
Warrendale
4
23
Bakerstown
3
11
Gibsonia
Cur
my
22
Wexford
910
onomy
Village
Russell
idge
19
hts
6
sdale
20
17
Dorseyville
geworth
279
17
5
ALLEGHENY 9
6
28
TRK
19
Allison Park
3
8
Emsworth
West
Avalon
13
View
Etna
Bellevue
Oak
McKees
Millvale
Sharpsburg
Rocks
Penn H
V

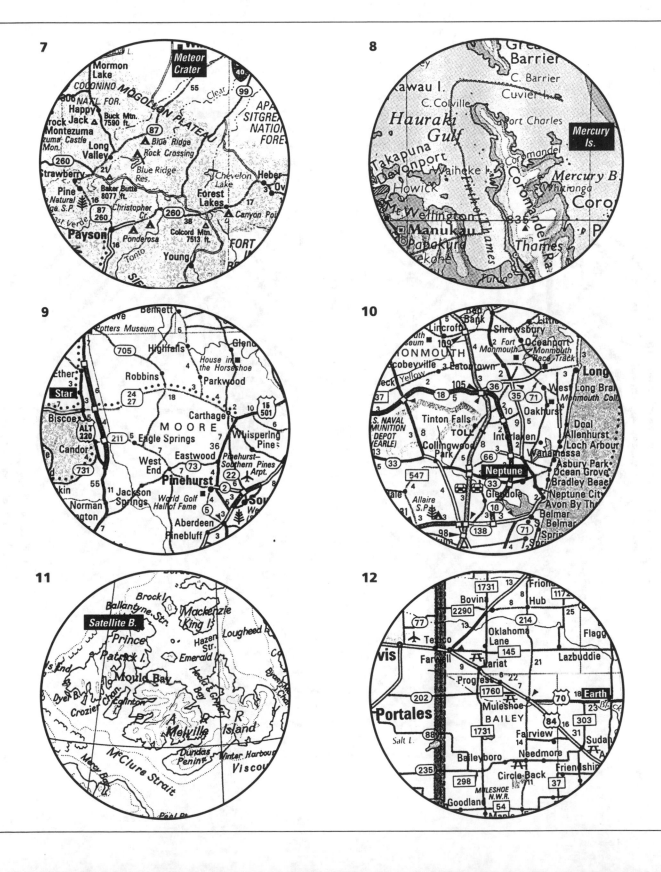

TWICE TWISTED

BY DAVE PHILLIPS

This maze should keep you hopping—from one page to the other. The object, as usual, is to travel from START to FINISH. Whenever you come to one of the numbered chambers, hop to the correspondingly numbered chamber on the other page. Finding any solution is difficult enough, but for maze-loving masochists, we offer an additional challenge: Find the *lowest scoring* route from START to FINISH, adding up all the numbers you pass through. (Count each number only once.)

ANSWER, PAGE 176

Not My Type

BY RICHARD MARSH

We'll bet not many of you know you're reading a paragraph that uses the typeface Frutiger. The name "Frutiger" doesn't tell you much about what the words set in that typeface look like, but many typeface names are more helpfully descriptive. We've taken the names of 27 such appropriately titled typefaces and set each in one of the other typefaces. For example, the name "Giddyup" in the upper left corner appears in the typeface Digital, while the word "Digital" is set in another typeface, and so on. If you get 20 or more, you're a Type A typecaster!

ANSWERS, PAGE 176

GIDDYUP   LEMONADE   Hairpin

Stencil   KELLS   QUAKE

Tigerteeth   ELEKTRIK

Nuptial   Rock A Billy   Shotgun

Countdown   Old German

Mystery Black   DIGITAL   PARISIAN

Arriba-Arriba   POINTILLE

Shanghai   UMBRA   shatter

Paintbrush   Moulin Rouge

Collegiate   Mythos   MESQUITE

AMERICAN TYPEWRITER

3 THE WONDERFUL WORLD OF WORDS

MIX AND MATCH

BY MIKE SHENK

Each set of clues in this puzzle consists of four words. Two of them are synonyms of the two answers that should be entered in the correspondingly numbered row or column of the diagram; the other two are anagrams of two other answers that are defined elsewhere in the puzzle. For example, the first word in Row 1 is RUSTLES; it's defined as STEALS in the clues for Row 1, and is an anagram of RESULTS, listed among the four words at Column 5. Each word will be used exactly once (as either a synonym or an anagram), so you may want to cross off words as you use them. Separating the synonyms from the anagrams and determining the order of the answers in each row or column is part of the puzzle's challenge.

ANSWER, PAGE 176

ROWS

1 CITRUS CLAY MISLEARN STEALS
2 AIDE CASK SCATTERER WORRIED
3 RULES SENATOR SKIERS YOKEL
4 COPIES FIRE SPOTTER TEHERAN
5 CADRE LOOSED RIFTS TENACIOUS
6 CLERIC DOURNESS EDUCE HEAPS
7 HATER LEARNING PRETTINESS SLIGHTING
8 ARDENT BETRAYAL PRECISE SATANISTS

COLUMNS

1 FORMULAS GASP INTERIMS PICKET
2 CAUTIONED SECTIONAL TRAM TWO-SPOT
3 LINK ORES PROCEDURES SHAVER
4 DIALED DINES INVOICES OVEN
5 BRIEFNESS EFFORTLESS PRESENT RESULTS
6 AYES ECHOES FACE TESTAMENTS
7 DISPERSE NUCLEUS SECTION SHORE
8 EASTERN NECTARINES SPOTS VIPER

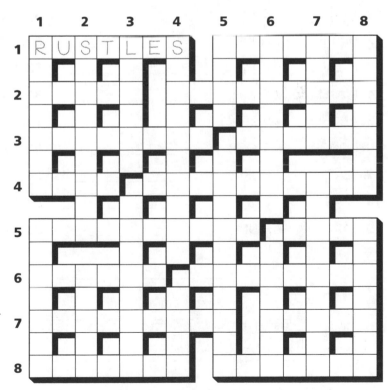

LESS IS MORE

BY STEPHEN SNIDERMAN

In each pair of words below, remove a letter from Word A and a letter from Word B so that the remaining letters, in order, spell a new word. The removed letter may be at the beginning, the middle, or the end of the word. For example, in #1 with the words CONTEMPT and LATHE, you should remove the second T from CONTEMPT and the H from LATHE, leaving the word CONTEMPLATE. Transfer the letters you've removed to the correspondingly numbered and lettered spaces in the quote. In #1, the T from CONTEMPT is letter 1A, and the H from LATHE is letter 1B, and these have been entered onto the dashes of the quote. Do the remaining 37 in this way and you will reveal a quotation followed by its source.

ANSWERS, 176

	A	B	
1.	CONTEMPT	+ LATHE	= CONTEMPLATE
2.	AMOUNT	+ RAIN	= _____
3.	ECRU	+ DEITY	= _____
4.	RESIN	+ FORCEPS	= _____
5.	MASON	+ SCHISM	= _____
6.	TOUT	+ ORNAMENT	= _____
7.	CART	+ ALONG	= _____
8.	ECHO	+ COLLATE	= _____
9.	PRIMER	+ HOSE	= _____
10.	GENRE	+ REALLY	= _____
11.	TRAVEL	+ STAY	= _____
12.	HINGE	+ NUDITY	= _____
13.	PALACE	+ BOY	= _____
14.	MATES	+ TRIO	= _____
15.	ANCHOR	+ VICES	= _____
16.	DONOR	+ STOOP	= _____
17.	SEATS	+ HORSE	= _____
18.	BEAN	+ EARTH	= _____
19.	EASY	+ PLUM	= _____
20.	ACHE	+ MOIST	= _____
21.	SEQUEL	+ NICE	= _____
22.	TORCHES	+ TRAP	= _____
23.	STIR	+ HANGER	= _____
24.	BEGUN	+ TILE	= _____
25.	UNIT	+ FINED	= _____
26.	DEBT	+ RISK	= _____
27.	SOIL	+ HOIST	= _____
28.	FROWN	+ TIGER	= _____
29.	CLAMP	+ ALIGN	= _____
30.	HIDE	+ NOTIFY	= _____
31.	COMPEL	+ VAIN	= _____
32.	PER	+ INMATE	= _____
33.	VAN	+ THEATER	= _____
34.	SNUB	+ TALE	= _____
35.	GAY	+ MONASTIC	= _____
36.	SLY	+ STEAM	= _____
37.	COLA	+ NAKED	= _____
38.	MEN	+ DEMONIC	= _____

T										H								
1A	8A	29A	19A	31B	23A	5B	14B	37A	16A	1B	11B	4A	19B	15A	30B	33A	10B	12B

14A	9B	34B	17A	4B	31A	20B	22B	8B	3A	28A	21B	11A	29B	36A	16B	35B	26B	13A

26A	18A	5A	13B	25A	12A	27A	24A	28B	18B	20A	6A	23B	32A	7A	22A	33B	2A	7B

9A	35A	15B	27B	6B	24B	30A	38A	2B	36B	25B	32B	21A	37B	34A	38B	3B	10A	17B

Sundial

BY PATRICK BERRY

The sun-shaped grid below will contain 20 seven-letter words and phrases when filled in. Each answer begins in the space next to its corresponding number, continues outward, makes a hairpin turn, and ends up in the starting space of the following answer. If you keep at it, all the answers should eventually dawn on you.

ANSWER, PAGE 176

1 Balloonist's ballast
2 "Sledgehammer" singer Peter
3 German city in which Wagner was born
4 Food-grinding part of a bird's stomach
5 TV show that changed the names "to protect the innocent"
6 Popular bowling game

7 Brandy glass
8 Light-receptive parts of eyes
9 Drink made from red wine, juice, and soda water
10 Battle of Britain attack: 2 wds.
11 Blueprint, for example
12 Inventor who received the 1909 Nobel Prize for physics
13 Following the usual sequence: 2 wds.

14 Bureaucratic hassle: 2 wds.
15 Soldier's shoulder ornament
16 Home of the Israel Philharmonic: 2 wds.
17 No-Doz competitor
18 State of complete bliss
19 Servant, for taverns
20 Lots for yachts

CARTOON REBUSES

BY MIKE SHENK

Cartoon Rebuses have always been one of our favorite contests here at GAMES. And they're obviously popular with solvers, too, since we've received over 60,000 entries to the contests over the years. Try your hand at this latest batch.

How to Solve The answer to each rebus is a name that combines any or all of these elements from the cartoon:

- Words or synonyms of words spoken by the characters or found anywhere else in the picture
- Names of prominent objects in the picture
- Isolated letters in the picture
- Words implied by the cartoon's action or scene

These elements are combined phonetically to form the name fitting the category and the number of letters given as clues above the cartoon.

Example The answer to the example cartoon above right is *Vanity Fair*. It's found by combining VAN, pictured in the background; the word IT spoken by the cabbie; the letter E on the van; and the word FARE, suggested by the scene. Put them together phonetically and you get VAN-IT-E-FARE.

ANSWERS, PAGE 176

3. Beverage: 8

4. Bandleader: 3,5

5. Baseball Player: 5,7

9. TV Show: 8

10. Pro Sports Team: 5,3,10

11. TV Character: 5,11

Ex: Magazine: 6,4

1. Country: 8

2. TV Personality: 5,5

6. 1980s Book: 6,5

7. U.S. City: 11,8

8. Fictional Character: 5,7

12. Composer: 5,7

13. Movie Actor: 6,5

14. Food Item: 10

TO THE NINES

BY HENRY HOOK

Answer each clue in this puzzle with a nine-letter word that combines three of the letter triplets beside the grid. (The triplets are used as units; you do not need to rearrange letters within them.) Each triplet will be used only once. When you have found all the words, transfer five letters from each into the grid as indicated by the boxes in the appropriately numbered row. For example, for #1, place the third, ninth, second, fourth, and seventh letters, in that order, in the top row of the grid. When all the boxes have been filled, a quotation will read down the grid column by column. Two of the 35 triplets beside the grid will not be used; when put in proper order, they will spell the name of the quotation's author.

ANSWERS, PAGE 176

1. Stamp collecting _____
2. Dare _____
3. Exhibiting a grand view _____
4. Consider (2 wds.) _____
5. Fined _____
6. Large South American boas _____
7. Underlying principle _____
8. Kinfolk _____
9. Gripe _____
10. Declaration of beliefs _____
11. Ingredient of gunpowder _____

TRIPLETS

ALI	ANA	ARD
ATI	CHA	COM
CON	COW	DAM
DAS	ELY	ENT
FUN	IFE	INT
LAT	LLE	MAN
MIC	NGE	NKO
ORA	PAN	PEN
PHI	PLA	REL
SAL	STO	TER
THI	TPE	VER
VES	ZED	

1	3	9	2	4	7
2	2	5	3	9	7
3	6	8	3	1	9
4	7	5	1	2	6
5	8	2	6	4	3
6	8	1	2	6	9
7	6	3	1	9	2
8	2	8	4	9	3
9	3	5	1	2	9
10	9	6	8	5	1
11	9	5	8	4	6

COMMON STOCK

BY MIKE SHENK

The four answers to each numbered set below have something in common. To discover what, fill in the blanks to complete the words reading across. The letters you put in the blanks, taken in order from left to right, must also spell shorter words. These shorter words will all be members of the same category. For example, the first word in set #1 is POTLUCK, with the shorter word being POLK. The remaining three shorter words in #1 will also be names of presidents. Getting one answer in a set will help you get the others, but breaking into a set can be tricky. A score of four or more sets is excellent. Only word geniuses will solve all six.

ANSWERS, PAGE 176

1. P O T L U C K
   _ E _ _ T R E N _ _ _ _
   S _ E _ D _ A S _
   _ _ _ E _ A K _ _

2. E _ _ _ _ I N A T _
   _ _ _ _ _ I A N C _
   _ R _ D _ T _ O _
   _ E T R O _ E _ _

3. C O _ P _ _ I _ O N
   _ _ _ _ _ _ A T I O _
   C A _ _ R _ O _ _
   _ O L _ _ _ _ I _ N

4. _ _ _ D R _ L _ _ I O N
   P _ _ _ _ A T _ O _
   B _ L L I _ E _ _ N _
   G _ _ _ _ S T O _ E

5. _ _ _ _ _ N G R O _ _ R
   _ _ A G R _ _ _ _ _
   _ M M O R _ _ _ I T _
   I N _ _ I R _ T _ O _

6. E I _ H T F _ _ _ _
   _ L O D H _ _ _ _ _
   _ M P _ _ V I _ G
   _ _ M O N _ _ E

THINK-A-LINK MAZE

BY PAUL KELLY

In this maze, two boxes are linked if: 1) they're adjacent horizontally or vertically, and 2) the words suggested by the pictures together form a compound word or a familiar two-word phrase. For example, a box with a head adjacent to a box with a dress could go together to form "headdress."

The object of the puzzle is to find a path from the upper left corner to the lower right (starting and ending with BOX) that's formed by a chain of consecutively linked boxes. The end of each link will be the start of the next. Thus, from BOX at the upper left you could proceed right to SCORE (to make "box score"), right again to CARD ("scorecard"), and down to CATALOG ("card catalog"). Since none of the pictures adjacent to CATALOG builds out from that word, this path is a dead end. Can you find the one path that goes from BOX to BOX?

ANSWER, PAGE 177

RON BARRETT

BRAGGING RITES

WRITTEN AND ILLUSTRATED BY ROBERT LEIGHTON

All the characters seen here think they're unique—but they've never stopped bragging long enough to listen to anyone else. If they did, they might notice that each of their boasts is duplicated by somebody else on these pages (albeit with a different meaning). For example, in #1 one of the lawyer's boasts is H, "My appeal can't be denied." The ladies' man (#6) can make the same boast, as well as another boast that is, in turn, repeated elsewhere. When all the boasts are filled in (using each one twice), they will create a chain that ends where it began. You'll have the bragging rights if you can get all the bragging right.

ANSWERS, PAGE 177

BOASTS

A. "My plants have grown very rapidly."

B. "Curls are my specialty."

C. "I have record sales every week."

D. "I've had some very long runs this season."

E. "I'm a wise guy."

F. "I know just where to cut."

G. "I can extract very complex roots."

H. "My appeal can't be denied."

I. "I've arranged dozens of hits."

J. "I can put you in some very secure bonds."

K. "I've never mishandled a suit."

L. "All the biggest people submit to me."

M. "I can suggest a great CD."

N. "You'd be amazed at how much I can press in a day."

O. "I'm great at playing the field."

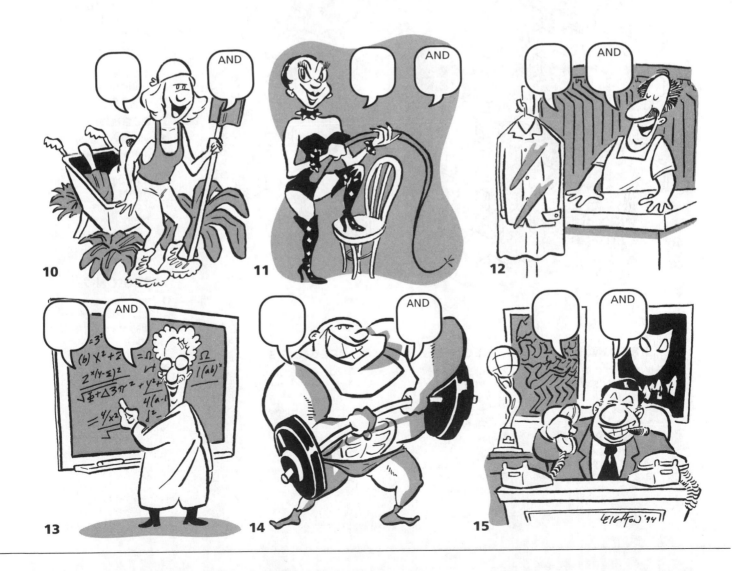

SNOWFLAKE

BY MIKE SHENK

When completed, the grid below will be filled with 42 interlacing words. Six words, all seven letters in length, surround each of the numbered regions of the grid; each of these words reads in a straight line of seven hexagonal spaces running tangent to one of the sides of the numbered region. Clues to the words are given by region, though it's up to you to determine their exact placement and orientation. Answers to the first two clues (LEOPARD and SPIN-OUT) have been filled in to get you started.

ANSWER, PAGE 177

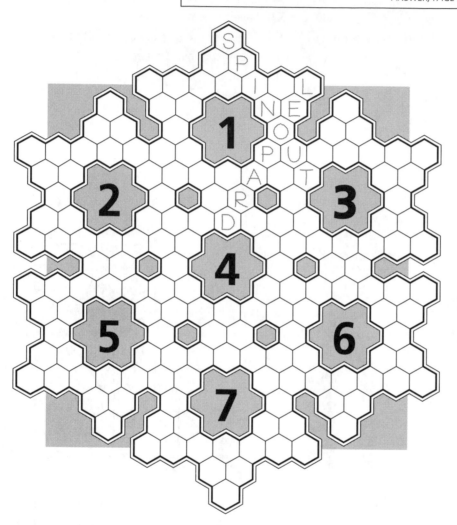

REGION 4
1 Sites of some cells
2 Quartet from Liverpool
3 Promising young actress
4 Highwaymen
5 Baseball league championship
6 Vivaldi quartet?

REGION 5
1 Sicily's capital
2 Printed matter in excess of the space allotted for it
3 Yelled "Go, team, go!"
4 Lowly farmer
5 Puddinglike dessert
6 Stupid person

REGION 6
1 Insurance payment
2 Charles Schulz's comic strip
3 Guinea pigs' cousins
4 Actors Short and Sheen
5 Taking a break
6 Mates of strutting birds

REGION 7
1 *Hans Brinker* setting
2 Salad dressing choice
3 Saved
4 Less blue
5 Squabble
6 Relief pitcher's warmup spot

REGION 1
1 It's spotted in Africa
2 Indy racer's worry on a turn
3 Scallops, clams, oysters, lobster, etc.
4 Droopy-eared dog
5 Cornered
6 Did a heavy-footed jazz dance

REGION 2
1 More impoverished
2 Carter's vice president
3 Chocolate-iced bakery treats
4 Sleep-inducing fellow
5 Club constituents
6 Common desk accessory

REGION 3
1 Edgar and Candice
2 Popular men's hat brand
3 Char, perhaps
4 What topographical maps show
5 *Boris Godunov* author
6 Roll call response

ROWED SIGNS

BY PATRICK BERRY

To solve each of the Rowed Signs below, you'll need to fill two consecutive words into each row of the grid. These "Row Words," with a total of ten letters for each pair, are indicated in order by the clues for each row. Then look for an "Inner Word" straddling the two Row Words. For example, a row might hold the words DRAGON and YEAR, with the Inner Word AGONY reading between them. The Inner Words are clued in random order for each puzzle; it's up to you to determine which clue goes with which row. As you solve each row, cross out the letters of the Inner Word. When you have completed the puzzle, the remaining letters (reading from left to right by rows) will spell out a sign that might be found at the location specified by the puzzle's heading. *ANSWERS, PAGE 177*

AT AN EXPLOSIVES FACTORY

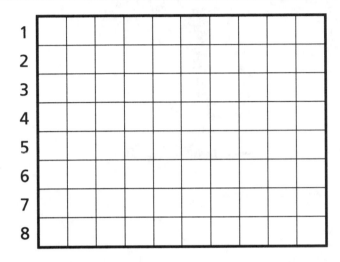

ROW WORDS

1 Becomes responsible for, as a debt
Killer whale of a 1977 film
2 Choose
Pudding choice
3 Type of lithographic printing
Garr of *Young Frankenstein*
4 Prepare leftovers
Parsley, sage, rosemary, or thyme
5 Brings in the wheat
Atlanta cagers
6 ___ duck (crispy-skinned dish)
Air freshener scent

7 Shortage
Harp's ancestor
8 Shaped like a dunce cap
Grazing groups

INNER WORDS

a Expression of disbelief
b Secular
c Hunting dog
d Like most rock guitars
e Top dog
f Blinking square on a computer terminal
g Place for a statue
h Flowering plant of the Highlands

IN THE WINDOW OF A BURGLAR ALARM STORE

ROW WORDS

1 Stole stuff?
Robocop star Peter
2 What must go above the bar in a proper pull-up
Turkish sovereign
3 Flying saucer?
Unabridged dictionary, for one
4 Notion
Deliberately loses
5 Suitable
Catching need
6 Corn unit
Made into law
7 Treat the turkey
Fraught with peril
8 File representation on a computer screen
Spoils

9 Issue forth, as light
Polar worker

INNER WORDS

a Paper for a hunter or a would-be driver
b "Your mother wears army boots," for example
c Normal practice
d Sea cow
e Star of the printing industry?
f The Coliseum or the Spectrum
g Where quills get dunked
h Waiting area for someone with conviction?: 2 wds.
i Hold

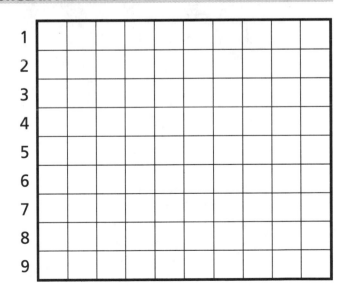

Sign a Song

BY OWEN O'DONNELL

Welcome to the Opt 40 Countdown, where all the songs have anagrams! This week we'll be spinning some hot new sounds—"The Sounds of License," you might say. Heading up the list are the 12 tunes we've illustrated below. Each is a familiar song title in which one of the words has been anagrammed to form a new word, with the resulting new version of the title pictured. For example, #1 below shows BOWLIN' IN THE WIND, our new version of "Blowin' in the Wind." The number of words and letters in each answer is indicated by the blanks beneath the drawing.

ANSWERS, PAGE 177

1. _ _ _ _ _ _ _ _ _ _ _ _
   _ _ _ _

2. _ _ _ _ _ _ _ _ _ _ _ _ _
   _ _ _ _

3. _ _ _ _ _ _ _ _ _ _ _ _

4. _ _ _ _ _ _ _ _ _
   _ _ _ _ _

5. _ _ _ _ _ _ _ _ _
   _ _ _ _ _

6. _ _ _ _ _ _ _ _
   _ _ _ _

7. _ _ _ _ _ _ _ _ _ _ _ _

8. _ _ _ _ _ _ _ _ _ _ _

9. _ _' _ _ _ _ _ _ _ _ _ _ _ _ _ _

10. _ _ _ _ _ _ _ _ _ _ _

11. _ _ _ _ _ _ _ _ _ _ _ _

12. _ _ _ _ _ _ _ _ _ _

CROSSHATCH

BY TRIP PAYNE

When completed, the grid for this do-it-yourself crisscross will contain the 41 art terms listed at the bottom of the page. These will interlock across and down as in a standard crisscross puzzle or Scrabble game. The only words that go in the puzzle are the ones in the list. Can you fill them in? To help you, all the A's, R's, and T's have been put in the grid for you. Thus ART is already spelled out (lower left), and some of the other words (such as PORTRAIT) will fit in only one place. Every word you enter will, in turn, restrict where the remaining words can go. The finished puzzle has a unique solution.

ANSWER, PAGE 177

ART	COLOR	CANVAS	CURATOR	ABSTRACT	MINIATURE
INK	FRAME	PASTEL	EXHIBIT	AESTHETE	PRIMITIVE
OIL	GENRE	PATRON	IMPASTO	CERAMICS	STILL LIFE
CAST	MODEL	POSTER	PAINTER	FIGURINE	ALTARPIECE
ETCH	PIETA	RELIEF	PALETTE	PORTRAIT	HANDICRAFT
TONE	PRINT	STATUE	STENCIL	SCULPTOR	PHOTOGRAPH
BRUSH	STYLE	COLLAGE	TEMPERA	CLASSICAL	

THE TROUBLE WITH TRIPLES

BY STEPHEN SNIDERMAN

Complete each sentence below by filling in the blanks with three words that differ by only one letter. The changed letter will be in the same position in all three words. For example, to complete the sentence, "____ they were at Sea World, the ____ class cheered the killer ____" you would add the words WHILE, WHOLE, and WHALE; in this case the third letter of each word was changed. Getting 12 or more right is very GOOD; if you GOAD yourself into getting 15 or more, you earn a GOLD star!

ANSWERS, PAGE 177

1. To avoid getting a _____, the _____ ate a bowl of hot _____.

2. With all _____ imaginative _____ parks, _____ must be someplace we can take the kids.

3. We have to be back on the bus at _____, which only gives us an _____ to _____ the ruins.

4. _____ of the travelers had ever _____ into another time _____.

5. Our first night on the ocean _____, we washed down the _____ pâté with a whole _____ of wine.

6. Around _____, anyone who can round up an entire _____ of stampeding cattle is considered a _____.

7. The cryptographer couldn't _____ if he should keep trying to _____ the message he'd been working on for nearly a _____.

8. When we're at the lake, _____ is the avid _____ of the family, whereas the rest of us would _____ go canoeing or just bask on the shore.

9. There's no _____ in opening up a new _____ store until you can _____ up plenty of advertising flyers showing the range of colors you stock.

10. Our treasurer is quite a _____ money manager, and she soon made a _____ in the group's _____.

11. Finding the perfect _____ to accompany a _____ is one of a composer's most difficult _____.

12. The _____ persuaded the city council to make a _____ contribution to the fund to renovate his _____ house.

13. A prudent florist orders extra daffodils and _____ as the need _____, thus averting _____.

14. To _____ up our spirits, we should keep ourselves _____ and try to _____ our woes.

15. The youngest son of the English country _____ is a little _____ who can _____ his way out of any trouble.

16. Although the _____ of the evening's _____ was quite original, it was marred by the conductor's haughtiness and _____.

17. The next time I spend extra money for a _____ umbrella, I won't _____ myself about its ability to survive a real _____.

18. The bootlegging Chicago _____ became a real _____ when he was served dry cake, and he demanded something _____ ...

19. ... unfortunately, there was only a _____ amount of fresh Danish _____ on the _____ shelf.

20. Any solver who _____ to tackle these word _____ will probably need to make several _____ through the puzzle.

LINEAR THOUGHT

BY ROBERT LEIGHTON

The average connect-the-dots puzzle doesn't require much analysis—you just have to be able to count. The puzzle below, though, requires a somewhat higher level of thought. To finish it, you'll use a sequence of word associations rather than numbers. Start by drawing a line from BLUE JEANS (near the upper left) to something else with BLUE in it, such as BLUEPRINT, just below it to the right. Then continue the line to something else with PRINT in it (either at the start or end of the word). Keep drawing lines from one item to the next, following the trail of connected words, finishing up with BLACK WIDOW. If you follow the right "string of consciousness," your lines will form an appropriate "mental" image.

WORD LIST, PAGE 179   ANSWER, PAGE 177

QUOTE BOXES

BY LESLIE BILLIG

To solve Quote Boxes, drop the letters from each vertical column—not necessarily in the order in which they appear—into the empty squares below them to spell a quotation reading from left to right, line by line. Black squares indicate ends of words. A word not stopped at the end of one line is continued on the next. The author of each quote is given above the grid.

ANSWERS, PAGE 177

1. IGOR STRAVINSKY

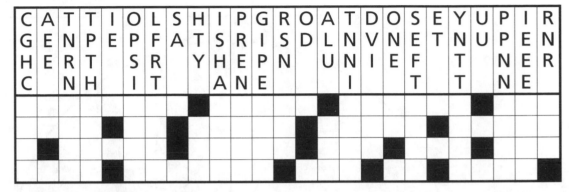

2. DAVID FROST

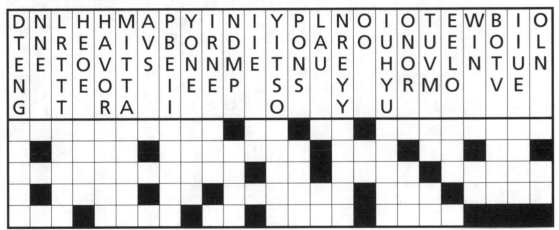

3. MISS MANNERS

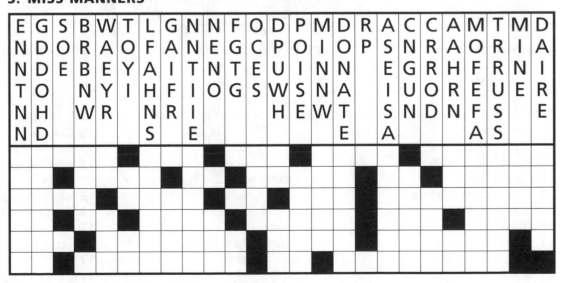

Stained Glass

BY PATRICK BERRY

Half of the answers in this puzzle (all of which are six letters long) read inward, and half read outward. Each Inward answer starts in the space of the outer ring next to the corresponding number and continues toward the center of the grid, ending in the space next to the same number. Each Outward answer does the reverse, starting in the inner ring and ending in the outer ring. In the example shown at right, the word TIEPIN reads inward, while NITWIT reads outward. It's up to you to determine whether a given word detours around the shaded diamond to the left or the right. In each case, the Inward answer will go to one side while the matching Outward answer will go to the other. Each space in the grid will be used in exactly two words.

ANSWER, PAGE 177

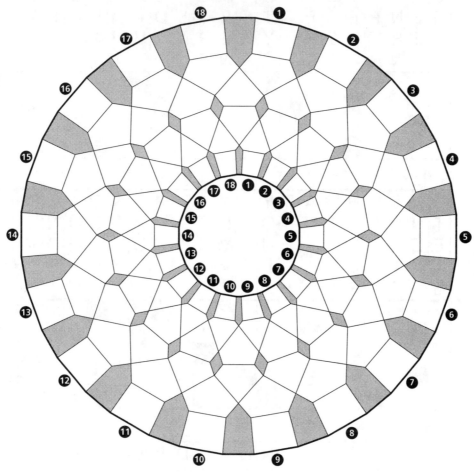

INWARD

1 Wound down
2 Men's store buy
3 High-quality
4 Puts into office
5 January birthstone
6 Rutabaga's cousin
7 Customary
8 Speech from the pulpit
9 Fundamentals
10 Whiskey bottles
11 Stole, as a wallet
12 One-celled organism
13 Wreckage
14 Once in a blue moon
15 Make oneself beloved
16 Natural, in craps
17 More frilly, as a negligee
18 Easily handled

OUTWARD

1 Stickers for model cars
2 Skeleton toppers
3 Go above and beyond
4 Unlikely to collapse
5 Brewing need: 2 wds.
6 Have an eating binge: 2 wds.
7 Swimming site on *Gilligan's Island*
8 Honks, clunks, and thuds, e.g.
9 Egyptian amulet symbol
10 Zhivago's portrayer
11 Specific military duty
12 Preoccupied with gruesome subjects
13 Moved like a crab
14 Universal output
15 Narrow canyon
16 Ridicule playfully
17 Uncover
18 Jimmy Stewart's *Harvey* role

WACKY WORDIES REVISITED

BY ERNEST COUTURE

Okay, but just this *one* time. We swore (several times, in fact) we'd never print another page of Wacky Wordies. Since we've received a number of letters from the Wacky Wordies fans out there begging for more, we've relented. Here are 24 more puzzles for you to solve.

As always, the object is to discern a familiar word, phrase, or saying from each arrangement of letters and symbols. For example, #1 below depicts "a house divided."

We hope this batch satisfies your craving for Wacky Wordies so we won't have to publish any more of them.

ANSWERS, PAGE 177

1 HO USE	**2** W I R E S / W I R E S	**3** MIND ↑	**4** CCCCC
5 AWAKE	**6** U___N △	**7** AT WINDMILLS	**8** JAIL
9 EVIL → evil	**10** SCISAB2	**11** en	**12** wad
13 itself (end)	**14** wh ey / we igh	**15** NIGHT ↑	**16** 1 1 the other / 1 1 the other / the other / 1 1 the other / the other / 1 1 the other
17 on the looking	**18** George Gilbert Geoffrey Gerald	**19** GRAND	**20** OHIOWA
21 CHEESE	**22** AMERICAN	**23** lickety	**24** HE AD

DIAL "M" FOR MIX-UP

BY AMY GOLDSTEIN

When literal-minded Larry got his new phone book and started to flip through the yellow pages, the first heading he saw was BRIDGE CLUBS. Poor Larry couldn't understand why on earth anyone would want a cudgel especially for beating on bridges, as shown in #1 below. He was perplexed by some of the other entries too. Can you figure out which of the remaining 14 headings on the phone book page at right confused Larry into having each of the mental images below?

ANSWERS, PAGE 177

▶ Antique Dealers	▶ Dating Services	▶ Private Investigators
▶ Boxing Instruction	▶ Diamond Setting	▶ Rubber Stamps
▶ Bridge Clubs	▶ Muffler Repair	▶ Squash Courts
▶ Computer Services	▶ Paging Services	▶ Stocks and Bonds
▶ Dancing Schools	▶ Paper Hangers	▶ Weight Loss Centers

9

10

11

12

13

14

15

R.I.P. I.B.M.

MP

STEVE MELLOR

DOUBLE CROSS

BY ANNE BROWN

Answer the clues for words to be entered on the numbered dashes. Then transfer the letters on the dashes to the correspondingly numbered squares in the puzzle grid to spell a quotation reading from left to right. Black squares separate words in the quotation. Work back and forth between grid and word list to complete the puzzle. When you're done, the initial letters of the words in the word list will spell the author's name and the source of the quotation.

ANSWER, PAGE 178

1Q	2J	3G	■	4L	5U	6H	■	7K	8R	9E	10W	11C	12G	13D	14F	■	15J	16U	17B	■	18H	19O	20V	21A	22M
23E	■	24N	25L	26Z	27P	28S	29Q	30X	31G	32K	■	33D	34H	■	35R	36C	37J	■	38A	39O	■	40F	41L	42N	43U
44I	■	45G	46V	47X	48Q	—	■	49E	50S	■	51R	52Y	53U	—	54M	55J	56O	57B	—	58D	59H	60K	61L	■	62U
63G	64Z	65E	66Q	67P	■	68V	69W	70A	■	71S	72D	73R	74C	■	75J	76N	77U	78X	79T	■	80A	81G	82I	83K	84L
85M	■	86Z	87Y	■	88F	89R	90Z	■	91Q	92K	93V	■	94J	95G	96Y	■	97B	98T	■	99N	100H	101I	■	102E	103U
104Y	105C	■	106K	107D	■	108R	109S	110L	111Z	■	112C	113W	114G	■	115U	116J	117M	118H	119P	■	120Q	121I	122K	123G	124Z
■	125L	126E	127T	128R	129O	■	130N	131X	132F	133D	134Q	135M	■	136G	137W	■	138L	■	139C	140B	141K	142J	■	143Q	144X
145D	146S	147A	148E	149M	150P	151V	■	152U	153L	154O	155V	156J	■	157F	158H	159U	■	160E	161P	162Q	163D	164U	■	165C	166B
167G	168R	169M	170J	■	171H	172N	■	173W	174B	175V	■	176L	177F	178K	179O	180D	181A	182N	■	183G	184Q	185V	■	186R	187K
■	188G	189T	190X	191C	—	■	192P	193H	194S	195R	196Q	197J	198L	■	199E	200B	201C	202Z	203O	■	204Q	205H	■		

A. King of the Old South
80 38 21 70 147 181

B. Pueblo-like housing built for Montreal's Expo '67
174 140 200 97 17 166 57

C. Sugar in large, hard crystals (2 wds.)
74 201 165 105 139 11 36 191 112

D. Harmful but enticing
33 163 145 13 58 133 72 180 107

E. Former British penal colony on the Australian coast (2 wds.)
160 49 65 9 148 102 126 199 23

F. On the move
88 14 40 157 132 177

G. Faulkner novel about the ill-fated Joe Christmas (3 wds.)
167 31 45 81 12 136 123 183 95 188 114 3 63

H. Canine cleaner?
205 171 59 6 118 18 193 34 158 100

I. Commander of the British forces during the Revolutionary War
121 82 101 44

J. Longtime home of the Brooklyn Dodgers (2 wds.)
197 15 94 37 2 156 75 116 55 142 170

K. Lustful
141 83 178 106 7 122 32 60 92 187

L. Texas governor elected in 1990 (2 wds.)
138 4 153 61 25 84 41 125 176 198 110

M. IRA, for example (2 wds.)
54 85 149 22 169 117 135

N. Notable street in London's Whitehall District
182 42 24 172 76 99 130

O. Dance created for the 1913 Ziegfeld Follies (2 wds.)
39 154 56 203 19 179 129

P. Entomology subject
150 192 67 161 27 119

Q. Film for which Peter O'Toole got his second Best Actor nomination as Henry II, with *The* (3 wds.)
48 1 91 134 162 29 143 204 184 120 66 196

R. Mournful and gloomy
168 73 51 195 108 8 186 35 128 89

S. Vehement protest
28 109 194 146 50 71

T. Iamb or anapest, in poetry
98 127 189 79

U. Composer of *Boris Godunov*
115 103 16 43 62 5 77 164 159 152 53

V. Interwoven
20 68 93 155 46 151 175 185

W. Alaska's is "North to the Future"
10 69 137 173 113

X. Egyptian god of the dead
190 30 131 47 144 78

Y. Shellacking
104 87 52 96

Z. Territory neighboring Siberia on a Risk board
111 64 90 202 86 26 124

4 A COLORFUL JOURNEY THROUGH THE PAGES OF GAMES

WATCH OUT!

BY MARGOT SEIDES

Of course you can tell time—but don't try it with *this* pocket watch. It contains 20 errors and other illogicalities, starting with the reversal/inversion of the 2 and the 5 on the dial. You have 15 minutes (measured on your watch, not ours) to find as many of the other mistakes as you can.

ANSWERS, PAGE 178

ILLUSTRATION BY RICK STARK

SYNCRONIZED

FISH STORY

WRITTEN AND ILLUSTRATED BY LEAH PALMER PREISS

Well, this is a fine kettle of fish. All the fishy goings-on here represent 24 familiar words and phrases containing the word FISH. For example, #1, the fish with the halo and wings, is an ANGELFISH. Only truly efficient solvers will catch all 24 fishing lines, but if you do, you're the Fisher King! If you're reelly floundering, though, we'll let you off the hook—just fish for the answers on page 178.

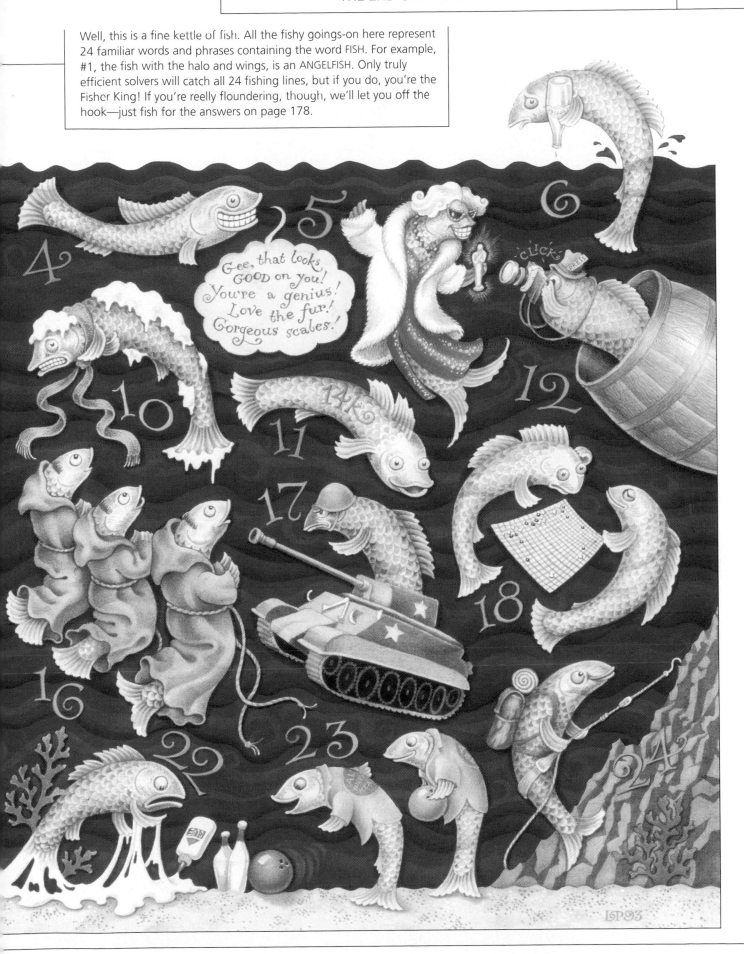

It's Oscar night, and the beautiful people are getting together for fabulous star-studded parties. Here's the most exclusive gathering of all, reserved not for celebrities but for their dolls--in particular, dolls that depict Hollywood's most successful actors in some of their most memorable roles. Although celebrity dolls can be hard to identify from their faces their costumes are carefully designed to evoke characters in specific films. How many of the real-life actors represented by these dols can you identify? And for extra credit, can you name the films (or film series) and the names of the movie characters?

ANSWERS, PAGE 178

ALL DOLLED UP

BY WILLIAM WHITEHURST

MILITARY VEHICLES

CARTOON CHARACTERS

BY MICHAEL AUBORN

TRIPLE PLAY

DINOSAUR CHARACTERS

PLAYING CARDS

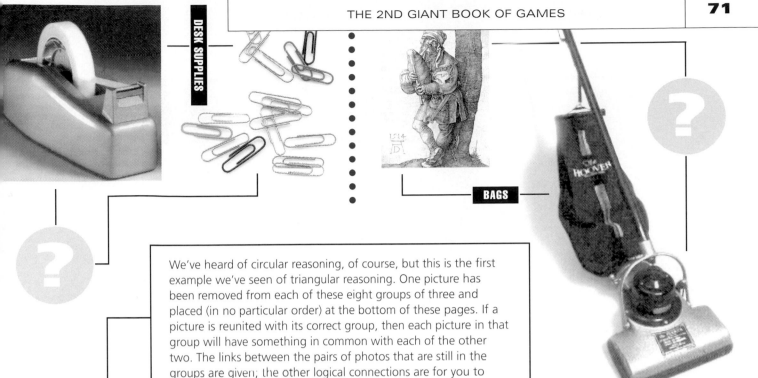

DESK SUPPLIES

?

BAGS

?

We've heard of circular reasoning, of course, but this is the first example we've seen of triangular reasoning. One picture has been removed from each of these eight groups of three and placed (in no particular order) at the bottom of these pages. If a picture is reunited with its correct group, then each picture in that group will have something in common with each of the other two. The links between the pairs of photos that are still in the groups are given; the other logical connections are for you to determine. For each group, all three links are different. Can you match each picture to its correct group?

ANSWERS, PAGE 179

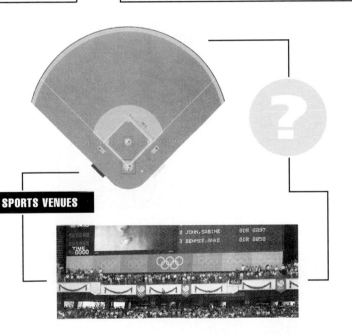

SPORTS VENUES

?

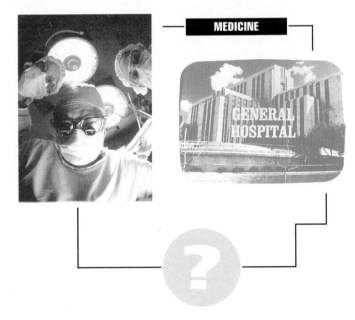

MEDICINE

?

1

2

3

6

7

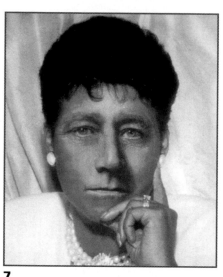

8

11

12

13

4

5

LAST NAME FIRST

*The last shall be first
and the first last.*

BY PETER GORDON

We've taken pairs of well-known people with overlapping names—such as Harry Truman Capote—and, in each pair, merged the facial features of one with the head of another. Can you put two names to each face?

ANSWERS, PAGE 178

9

10

14

15

PIXTURES BY DAVID RUDES

LIQUID ASSETS

1

2

3

4

9

10

11

When that burst pipe flooded Noah's Market, all the labels detached from these bottled products. By studying each bottle's distinctive shape and its contents, can you identify these common supermarket items and help Noah complete his insurance claim? (Brand names are worth extra credit.)

ANSWERS, PAGE 179

5

6

7

8

12

13

14

PLUMB LOCO

PRODUCED AND ILLUSTRATED BY DAVE TEICH

■ s this scene (a) the set of a new science fiction movie, (b) the basement of a long-abandoned nuclear facility, or (c) the lunchroom at GAMES? Take your pick, because determining the origin of these giant mutant insects isn't the puzzle here.

Nine of these colorful creatures are creeping about, each of them looking straight ahead in the direction it is crawling. Through observation and logic, can you match each of the insects (1-9) to its bug's-eye view (A-II)? Note that some of the things the insects see may not be visible from your point of view. *ANSWERS, PAGE 179*

A

B

C

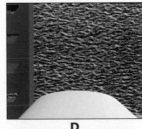

D

E

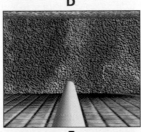

F

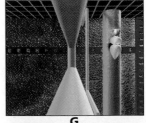

G

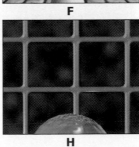

H

I

BASED ON AN IDEA BY TOM CUSHWA

SITE SEEKING

A MAPPIT WITH CLUES BY R. WAYNE SCHMITTBERGER

In 1830, eight years after the Spanish lost the Battle of Mt. Pichincha, this country seceded from Greater Colombia.

Olivia de Havilland was born there in 1916, as was her sister Joan Fontaine the following year.

Many Renaissance paintings were damaged by flying glass when a car bomb exploded at this country's Uffizi Gallery last May.

Northeastern residents of this country can ski locally in the Dolomites, of which the highest peak is Marmolada (10,964 feet).

Romans named this country's current capital Lutetia when it consisted only of an island in a river.

This monument, placed in 1735 by San de la Condamine, actually belongs a few hundred feet from where it stands.

Running through this country for more than 2,000 miles is the Tropic of Capricorn.

Rules of the board game senet, which was first played in this country more than 5,500 years ago, have been reconstructed in considerable detail by archaeologists.

So *Long at the Fair*, a 1950 British movie starring Dirk Bogarde and Jean Simmons, was set at this country's 1889 World's Fair.

Approximately 95 percent of this country's households subscribe to a newspaper, one of which, the daily *Yomiuri Shimbun*, has the largest circulation in the world.

Ancient inhabitants of this country fought the three Punic Wars against Carthage, which today would be located in Tunisia.

Population density in this country's six states and two territories averages only about six people per square mile.

Impassable to ground forces, this country's 7,000-square-mile Qattara Depression, which in places is 440 feet below sea level, was a strategic obstacle during World War II.

This is the only country south of the equator ever to have hosted the Olympics (1956).

Kanji, derived from Chinese, and kana, developed natively, are both used to write this country's language.

Places everyone! The 30 clues below refer to six different countries of the world. There are five clues for each country, no two of which will ever appear in the same row or column. Can you determine which clues go together, and then name all six countries? When all the clues are correctly grouped, the first letter of the clues for each country can be rearranged to spell the five-letter name of a city in that country.

ANSWERS, PAGE 179

Europeans first reached this country in 1606, when the Dutch—who later named the country New Holland—sailed into the Gulf of Carpentaria on the north coast.

After being known for more than a decade as the United Arab Republic—part of the time with Syria, and part of the time by itself—this country reverted to its older name in 1971.

Appointment as court painter brought Leonardo da Vinci to this country, where he died in 1519.

Chiang Kai-shek, Winston Churchill, and Franklin Roosevelt met in this country's capital, the largest city on its continent, in November 1943.

Stylized drawings of plants and animals identify the suits and point values in this country's Flower Card Game.

Here "sheila" means a young woman and a "matilda" is a knapsack.

At her marriage in June to this country's crown prince, the future empress, a 1985 Harvard graduate, wore a garment reportedly costing more than $300,000.

If the legend is true, twin brothers who founded this country's largest city were raised by wolves.

Over 2 million people live in Guayaquil, this country's largest city, which has seen an eightfold population growth since 1950.

Provençal, Breton, and other regional languages in this country are being taught again in schools after having been discouraged for many decades.

Quinine is obtained from the bark of the *quina roja*, this country's national tree.

Oases in this country's deserts include Bahariya, Dakhla, Farafra, Kharga, and Siwa.

Unusual species such as the world's largest tortoises inhabit this country's Galápagos Islands, which lie 600 miles west of the mainland.

In 1783 the treaty ending the American Revolution was signed here.

Lying completely within this country's borders are two small sovereign states.

SYMBOL LOGIC

BY WILLIAM WHITEHURST

It's the year 3000, and the Museum of Old Earth Languages has just opened a new interactive exhibit. In one of its displays, visitors are challenged to identify symbols used in the 20th century. How many of the symbols shown here (including those in the title) can you match to the list below?

ANSWERS, PAGE 179.

ALPHABETS & CODES
a. Morse code letter A
b. American Sign Language letter B
c. Semaphore letter C
d. Braille letter D
e. Marine flag letter E
f. Hebrew letter aleph
g. Sanskrit letter "kh"
h. Arabic letter "sh"
i. Russian letter "ya"
j. Greek letter omega

ASTRONOMY & ASTROLOGY
a. Comet
b. Neptune
c. New moon
d. Scorpio

CATTLE BRANDS
a. Flying 7 Ranch
b. Lazy H Ranch
c. Rocking R Ranch

FAMILY & MEDICINE
a. Divorce
b. First aid
c. Hospital
d. Pregnancy
e. Prescription
f. X-ray

GAME SYMBOLS
a. Bishop (chess)
b. Bomb (Stratego)
c. Club (French cards)
d. Club (Spanish cards)
e. Dot (mah-jongg)
f. Horse (Chinese chess)
g. Horseman (Risk)
h. Railroad (Monopoly)

HAZARDS
a. All power off
b. Bio-hazard
c. Do not touch
d. Thin ice
e. Warning

HOBO SIGNS
a. Kind woman lives here
b. Man with a gun lives here
c. Religious talk gets free meal

MANUFACTURING
a. Construction
b. Gram
c. Keep frozen
d. Laser radiation

e. Mix
f. Ounce
g. Radiation

MAPS
a. Battlefield
b. Electric fence
c. School
d. Well

MATHEMATICS
a. Empty set
b. Is an element of
c. Is not parallel to
d. Summation of

METEOROLOGY
a. Hurricane
b. Sandstorm
c. Thunderstorm

MONEY
a. American cent
b. British pound
c. Japanese yen

MUSIC
a. Bass clef
b. Flat
c. Quarter rest

TRAFFIC & CARS
a. Air conditioning
b. Merge
c. Parking lights
d. Two-way traffic

TRAVEL
a. Baggage claim
b. Elevator
c. Information
d. Observation deck

Sum-Buddy Special

BY MARK DANNA

Celebrity wannabes are always looking to make a name for themselves. But in this puzzle, the already famous are getting together to make an even *bigger* name for themselves. When properly paired, the last names of the celebrities shown here will combine to form a common new word, phrase, or name. For example, if Shelley Long and Gordon Jump were pictured, they could combine to produce LONG JUMP, while Sean Young and Cheryl Ladd would make YOUNG LAD (homophones are allowed). Pairs may be located on different pages. Some names may combine in more than one way, but to complete the puzzle, you'll need to use each celebrity exactly once. Getting 12 of the 23 pairs is sum-thing special, and with 18 or more, you've definitely reached the sum-mit.

NAME LIST, PAGE 180   ANSWERS, PAGE 176

SHIP-WRECKED

PUZZLE BY RON BARRETT   PRODUCED BY DAVE TEICH

Okay, so it wasn't such a good idea to store the unlabeled crate of fireworks next to the space heater last summer. But after all, no one was using the heater—*back then*.

Luckily, no one was around the warehouse when eight items were blown from their boxes, as captured on our security camera a split second after the explosion started. Three of the items had been packed with just one piece of foam insert, while the others used two pieces of foam each—which always matched in color.

Keeping in mind that some objects are farther away than others, and that foam inserts generally surround only certain parts of an object being shipped, can you match the eight items to their packaging?

ANSWERS, PAGE 179

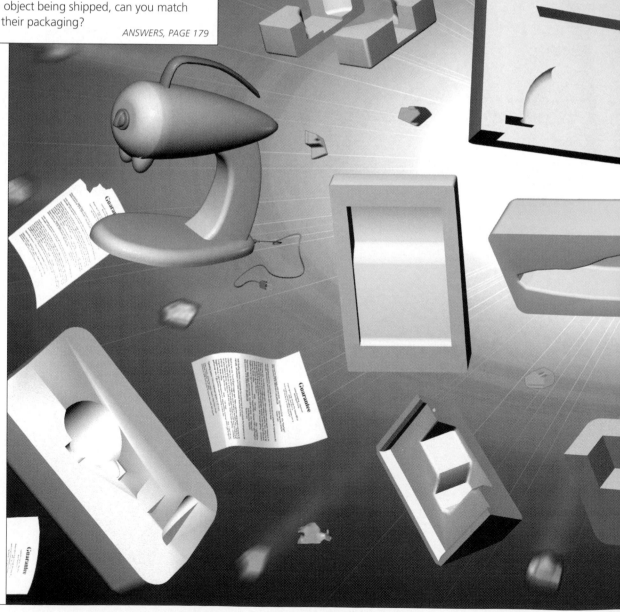

TIME AFTER TIME

A MAZE
BY R. WAYNE SCHMITTBERGER

PHOTOGRAPH BY
WILLIAM WHITEHURST

Justin Thyme has two passions: clock collecting and puzzles. So he was quite pleased with himself when he found a way to create a maze with the clock faces in his workshop. He arranged his clocks—including pictures of watches and other clocks—into 11 groups of 6 timepieces each, as shown. Groups include the six small pictures tacked to the wall, the six wall clocks on the right, the clocks on each shelf, and the other sets of six clocks that are placed next to one another.

The object is to advance in time from the clock showing 5:00 (in the photo of pocket watches

in the upper left) to the one showing 12:00 (in the open catalog at the bottom). You can move from clock to clock in two different ways: (i) Within any group of clocks, you can move to a clock showing a *later* time that is not more than one hour ahead of the clock you are on; and (ii) You can move to a clock in a different group that is showing the *same* time as the clock you are on. (Clocks showing times less than a minute apart should be considered the same.) From 5:00, therefore, you can move within the group to 5:30, 5:45, or 6:00; and after one of these moves, you can jump to any clock showing the same time. Have a good time!

ANSWER, PAGE 180

SNOWPLACE LIKE DOME

BY DAVID AND JAN PETERS

ILLUSTRATED BY DAVID PETERS

Oh, the weather *inside* is frightful—it's always winter in these souvenir snow domes. There are no snows of Kilimanjaro here, but see if you can identify 20 well-known places from the buildings, animals, and other clues shown in each dome. Those numbered in red represent 15 cities (12 dome-estic and 3 foreign), and those with black numbers come from 4 states and an island. If this snow job leaves you feeling flaky, 's no wonder— only real globe-trotters will get 15 or more.

ANSWERS, PAGE 179

PETERS

MAKE ROOM FOR DADDY

BY AMY GOLDSTEIN

When Father's Day arrives, you'll be ready with this pop quiz. Shown here are 16 actors (a–p) who have played 16 of TV's top pops, past and present. Can you reunite them with their families (1–16) and, for each, name the show, his character, and the actor too? If you can do all that for even 10 shows, dad's incredible! *ANSWERS, PAGE 180*

BASED ON AN IDEA BY EVIE EYSENBURG

PUT YOUR FEW CENTS IN

EYEBALL BENDERS

Are you penny-wise? Then you'll have the cents to identify these coin-operated machines. Get them all, and you're a quartermaster!

ANSWERS, PAGE 180

BY KEITH GLASGOW

3

1

2
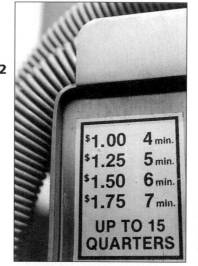

9

7

8

13

12

14

4

50¢
1. Place items inside
2. Close door
3. Insert only 2 quarters
4. Turn key

5

$3.00 QUARTERS ONLY !
INCLUDES ALL FEDERAL & STATE TAXES

INSE
COIN

6

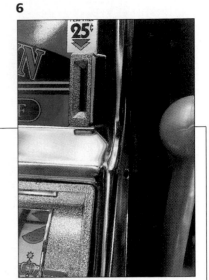

25¢

10

Down on Glass

15¢

F: The cons

11

SEGA

15

QUARTERS ONLY

25¢

TO OPERATE

16

5·10
U.S. COIN ONL

antic Company

17

35¢ DAILY
$1.25 SUNDAY
COIN ⬇ RETURN
DO

18

DRY ONLY WATER WASHED FABRIC
NO PLASTIC OR RUBBERIZED ITEM

INSERT QUART
TURN KNOB

25¢

19

INSERT C
TURN KNOB
25
QUARTERMASTER

SELF SE
COMPRES
DISPE

BY
AIR

SEW WHAT

BY WILLIAM
WHITEHURST

Button, button, have we ever got the buttons ...
and all but one of them have at least one identical mate somewhere in the
picture. Can you find the button that's unique? While you're at it, see if you
can also find the three sets of more than two matching
buttons. There are identical sets of three, four, and
five—and you'll have to push all the right buttons
to find them all.

ANSWERS, PAGE 180

AGE DISCRIMINATION

BY KEITH GLASGOW

Photographer Keith Glasgow doesn't kid around when it comes to girlwatching—if the girl is his daughter Alison, that is. First he took us through her infancy in "Bringing Up Baby" (Aug./Sept. 1987 GAMES), and now she's back in another time sequence challenge that's not just kid stuff. The 12 pictures below show Alison at six-month intervals from age 1½ through age 7—but the photos have been rearranged (since girls just want to have fun), and now all of them are in the wrong places. If you can get the chronology straight, you'll be all set for "Alison Goes to College," bound to appear in 2004 or so.

ANSWER, PAGE 180

1. AGE 1½
2. AGE 2
3. AGE 2½
4. AGE 3
5. AGE 3½
6. AGE 4
7. AGE 4½
8. AGE 5
9. AGE 5½
10. AGE 6
11. AGE 6½
12. AGE 7

MATH, LOGIC, AND A LITTLE MYSTERY

POOLING RANK

BY R. WAYNE SCHMITTBERGER

Because of new federal Clean Air Act regulations, employees of the XYZ Corporation will be required to form carpools whenever possible for each work day (Monday through Friday). In addition, employees will have to work at home one day a week. Five employees who live near each other—Vlady Vostok, Wendy Wonder, Xanny Xanthos, Yancy Yoko, and Ziggy Zaggy—have been asked to work out a schedule in which each of them works at home on a different day of the week and each of them drives once a week. What complicates the scheduling is that the employees have made a number of requests, listed below. Can you figure out a schedule that will meet all these conditions?

ANSWERS, PAGE 181

REQUESTS

1. Three people who like to play cards with each other twice a week want to be passengers together on Monday and Thursday.
2. Vlady Vostok wants to work at home the day before he drives.
3. Yancy Yoko wants to stay home the day after Xanny Xanthos does, but does not want to stay home on Friday.
4. Wendy Wonder refuses to be in a car if Xanny Xanthos is driving.

	MON	TUE	WED	THU	FRI
DRIVER					
PASSENGER					
PASSENGER					
PASSENGER					
WORK AT HOME					

CROSS MATH

BY CHARLES WEAVER

To solve a Cross Math puzzle, place all of the digits 1 through 9 into the empty squares of the grid so that the three rows across and three columns down form correct arithmetic sequences. All calculations (which involve only positive whole numbers) should be performed in order from left to right and top to bottom.

ANSWERS, PAGE 181

PUZZLE 1

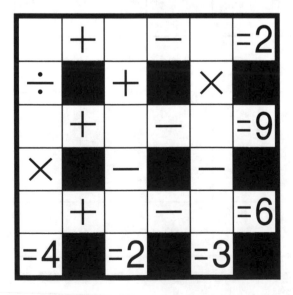

PUZZLE 2

GEOGRAPHY SQUARES

BY RAYMOND YOUNG

We've replaced the digits 0 to 9 in each of the multiplications below with letters. The digit-letter substitutions are constant throughout each problem, but change from one problem to the next. Can you reconstruct the original multiplications?

ANSWERS, PAGE 181

1.

```
        T E A
    x   T E A
   _____
        S E A
      T N A
      T E A
   _____
      C H I N A
```

2.

```
        F U R
    x   F U R
   _____
      U N T A
      C U C C
    C R F G
   _____
    C A N A D A
```

3.

```
        F E Z
    x   F E Z
   _____
      A W A Y
    Z Z T A
    K T E E
   _____
    T U R K E Y
```

THE ANTIQUES THIEF

BY ROBERT LEIGHTON

The antique show was in town for a week and, although turnout was great, one hitch marred the event: Every night, three items were stolen from the show. Looking for a pattern to the thefts, the chief of police cut out pictures of the stolen items from the catalog and pinned them to his bulletin board. The first three items stolen were desk supplies, which seemed to provide a clue, but by the next day the thief had changed his course. With apparently no pattern to the thefts, the chief was stumped.

That is, until Sunday night, when a rookie cop walked in, examined the items, and said, "Not only is there a pattern, Chief, but I can tell you the name of the crook."

Who stole the antiques and how did the rookie figure out his name?

ANSWER, PAGE 181

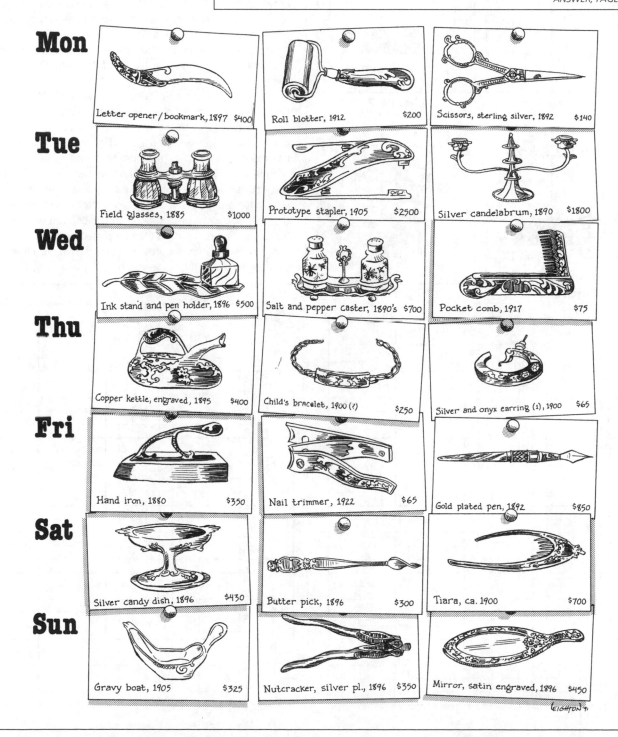

Mon Letter opener / bookmark, 1897 $400	Roll blotter, 1912 $200	Scissors, sterling silver, 1892 $140
Tue Field glasses, 1885 $1000	Prototype stapler, 1905 $2500	Silver candelabrum, 1890 $1800
Wed Ink stand and pen holder, 1896 $500	Salt and pepper caster, 1890's $700	Pocket comb, 1917 $75
Thu Copper kettle, engraved, 1895 $400	Child's bracelet, 1900 (?) $250	Silver and onyx earring (1), 1900 $65
Fri Hand iron, 1880 $350	Nail trimmer, 1922 $65	Gold plated pen, 1892 $850
Sat Silver candy dish, 1896 $430	Butter pick, 1896 $300	Tiara, ca. 1900 $700
Sun Gravy boat, 1905 $325	Nutcracker, silver pl., 1896 $350	Mirror, satin engraved, 1896 $450

LEIGHTON '91

PAINT BY NUMBERS

BY NON ISHIDA

The six puzzles on these pages, created by Non Ishida for London's *Sunday Telegraph*, feature a unique blend of logic and art. The numbers at the left and top of each grid are all you need to determine which squares should be filled in to form a miniature picture. Here's how it's done:

The numbers on the left of each row and the top of each column tell you how many groups of black squares there are in that line and, in order, how many consecutive black squares there are in each group. For example, 4 5 9 2 tells you that there will be four groups that will contain, in order, 4, 5, 9, and 2 consecutive black squares. The fact that the numbers are separated tells you that there is *at least* one empty square between them. (There may also be empty squares at the ends of lines.) The trick is to figure out how many empty squares come between the black ones.

Here's a starting hint: When there's a single number in a row and that number is greater than half the number of squares in the line, you can fill in one or more center squares. For example, in the sample puzzle at left (Figure 1), which is 10 squares wide, the sixth and seventh rows each have the number 8. No matter how you place eight consecutive black squares in a row, the middle six squares will be filled in (Figure 2). Similar logic can be used to start a line that has more than one number in it. In the sample, the third column contains the numbers 1 6. The single black square and the following empty square must take up at least two squares above the 6. No matter how they get placed, the fifth through eighth squares of the column will be black (Figure 3). Figure 4 shows the completed picture.

Now try the other six puzzles on your own. You'll discover other solving techniques as you go.

ANSWERS, PAGE 181

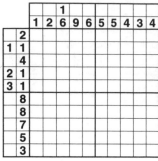

Figure 1

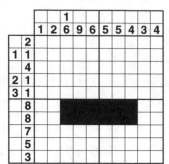

Figure 2

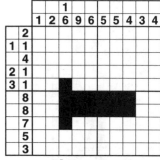

Figure 3

Figure 4

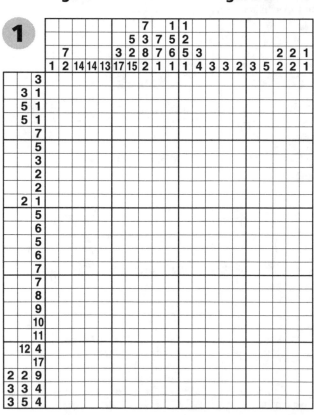

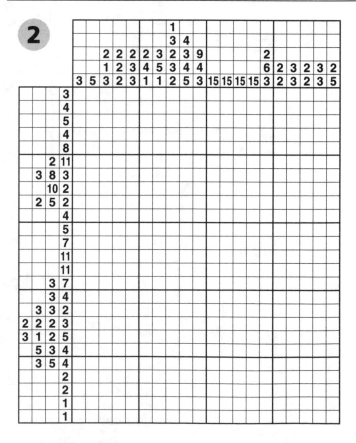

3

4

5

6

DIGITITIS

BY PETER GORDON

We've removed most of the digits from the four long-division problems below. Can you replace the numbers, one digit per dash, so that each completed division is mathematically correct? Each puzzle has a unique solution. If you've never tried a Digititis puzzle before, it may look baffling at first. But don't panic—the solution requires nothing more than logic and basic arithmetic.

ANSWERS, PAGE 181

PUZZLE 1

PUZZLE 2

PUZZLE 3

PUZZLE 4

PUZZLE PALACE

BY JIM WINSLOW

Shown below are plans to the four main floors and basement of the Puzzle Palace, a modern office building catering to the needs of today's mathematical puzzle creator. Each of the five floors is divided into a number of office suites, each consisting of two or more basic square offices. Since their potential tenants rarely do anything the easy way, the building's owners haven't bothered to indicate the internal walls separating the suites. Instead, they've put a number in each office indicating how many other offices a person standing in the middle of that office could see through open doorways. For example, in the floor plan below with suite walls already indicated, a tenant in the first office could see into two other offices to the east (assuming north is up in the diagrams); in the second office, one could see three other offices, one to the west, one to the east, and one to the south. Can you complete the plans for the Puzzle Palace's five floors?

ANSWERS, PAGE 181

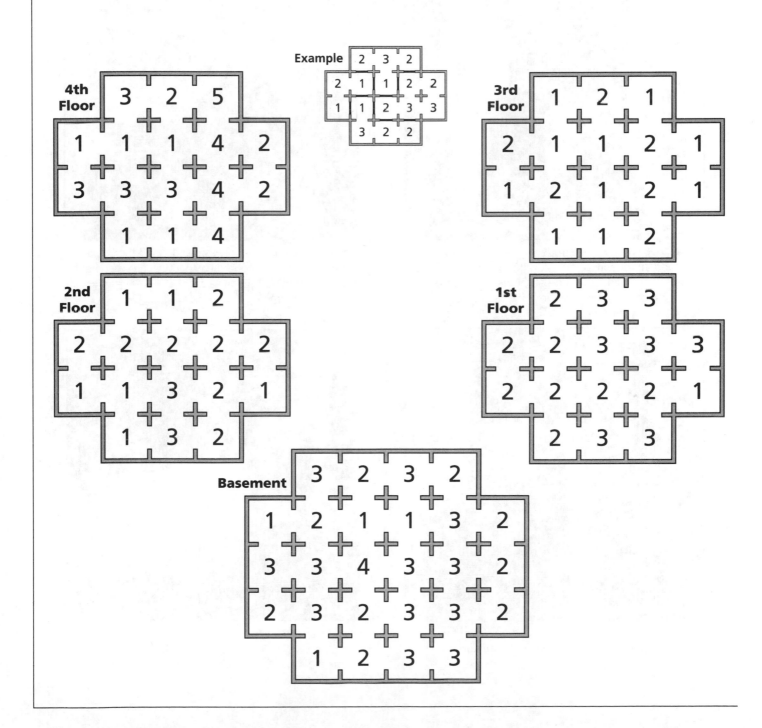

THE CAPE DIAMOND THEFT

BY MARVIN MILLER

PHOTOCRIME

The harsh jangle of the phone brought Detective Simon Hawk unwillingly awake. His bedside clock, he noticed with a groan, read 8:30 A.M. Having spent most of the night working on a major case, he had had only a few hours' sleep.

"Yeah?" he grumbled into the receiver.

"Good morning, Detective. This is Sergeant Norton. Empire Diamond Imports was hit last night ..."

"Why are you bothering me with a routine burglary, Norton?"

"This is hardly routine, Detective. The Cape Diamond was stolen."

Hawk, now wide-awake, jumped out of bed and got dressed.

1 It was 9:00 when Hawk strode into the offices of Empire Diamond Imports, two rooms on the ground floor of the Trade Center. Carl Tyson, one of the partners, introduced himself and led Hawk into the rear office. Tyson was obviously distraught.

2 Hawk inspected the empty safe and noted the open window nearby. "I found the window open when I got here this morning," Tyson said. "The alarm system must have been disarmed."

3 Tyson pointed to a portable typewriter next to the empty jewelry tray. The thief had left an extortion note.

4 Hawk started to remove the note. "The thief must know there's no way he can sell the Cape Diamond without attracting attention," Tyson said. "So he's probably going to ask a huge sum for its return."

5

After carefully reading the note, Hawk asked Tyson, "When did you last see the diamond?"

6

"I watched my partner, Oliver Pratt, lock it in the safe around 6:00 last night, just before I left the office for a meeting with a client. We finished around midnight."

7

Pratt arrived as they were speaking. When Tyson told him about the theft, Pratt slumped in a chair. He said he had stayed in the office to close out the month's books and left about two hours after Tyson.

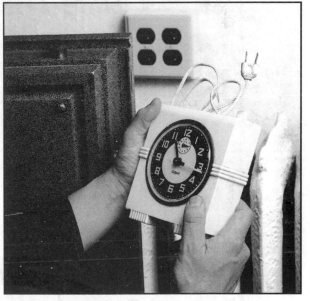

8

Hawk discovered a clock lying face down on the floor next to the desk. The thief had apparently tripped on the cord and pulled it out when he climbed through the window. The clock indicated the time of the break-in was 11:16 last night.

PHOTOGRAPHS BY CARL WALTZER

Detective Hawk glanced at the window and then spun around to face the two partners. "This break-in is a phony," he said. "The thief is right here in this room!"

WHO STOLE THE CAPE DIAMOND AND HOW DID DETECTIVE HAWK KNOW?

ANSWER, PAGE 181

ACROSS TOWN

BY PETER MAY

The new city planner decided traffic routing in town could be improved, so she's strictly controlled every intersection, as the symbols indicate. The mayor, besieged by irate citizens, is holding a hearing on the changes. Make your way from the north of town to the municipal center, at the bottom, if you want to testify that the new system is driving you to distraction ... and, to be a credible witness, don't arrive with a ticket because you made a wrong turn! (All turns should be made relative to your current direction of travel; for example, if you're heading east and come to a right-turn-only symbol, you must turn south at the intersection.) To save gas, find the shortest route by avoiding any unnecessary loops.

ANSWER, PAGE 182

◆ Right turn only   ▲ Right or left turn only
● Left turn only   ■ Straight ahead or U-turn only

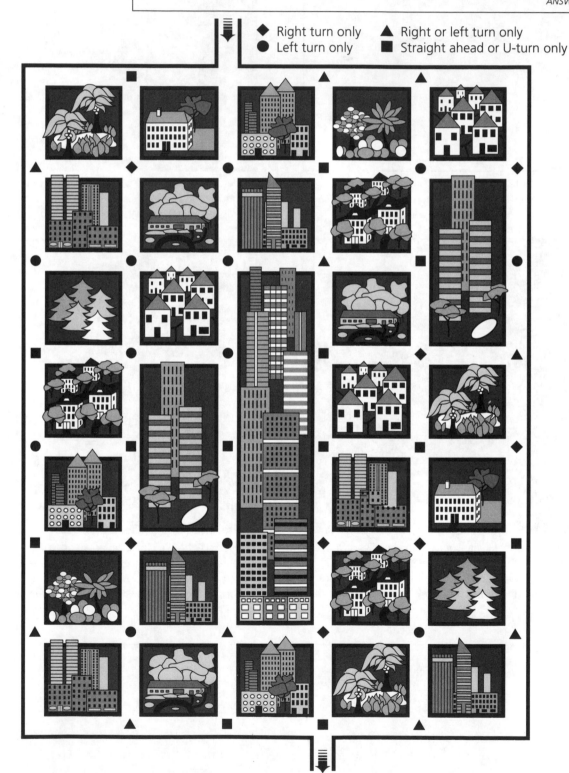

BALANCING ACT

BY PETER GORDON

The object of each puzzle below is to determine which of the given weights goes in each place on the bars to make the structure balance. Here's how it works: For each weight that hangs off a balanced bar, take its weight and multiply it by its distance (in unit spaces) from the balancing cord. The sum of these numbers for the portion of the bar on each side of the cord must be the same to make it balance. (Assume the weights of the bars and cords are negligible.) For example, the lower bar in the example at left balances because the left side has a weight of 3 that is 2 units away from the cord (a total of 3 x 2 = 6), while the right side has a weight of 2 that is 1 unit away and a weight of 1 that is 4 units away, for a sum of (2 x 1) + (1 x 4) = 6, the same total as the left side. The upper bar also balances because on the left side there is a weight of 6 (the 3, 2, and 1 all added together) at a distance of 2 units (the weight pulls from where the balancing string is), to make a total of 6 x 2 = 12, while the right side has a weight of 4 that is 3 units away, for a total of 4 x 3 = 12, the same total as the left side. (The lengths of the cords holding the weights are irrelevant.)

Below are three puzzles for you to try. They get progressively harder, the last one for heavy-duty solvers only.

ANSWERS, PAGE 182

EXAMPLE

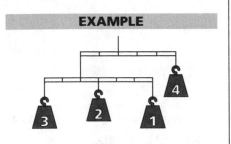

PUZZLE 1

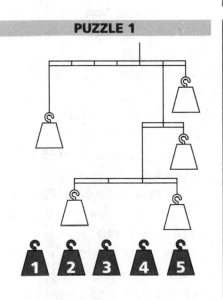

PUZZLE 2

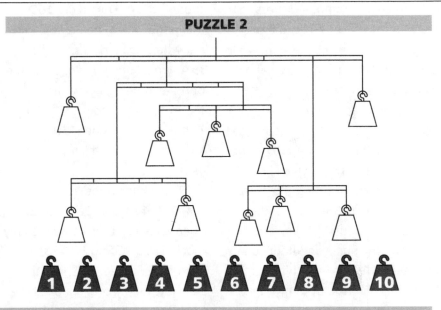

PUZZLE 3

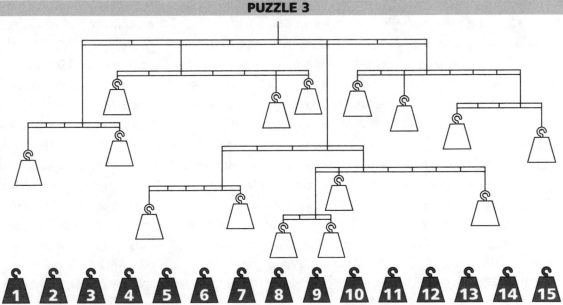

My first Case

The missing words in this story will solve the puzzle, and vice versa—solving the puzzle will decipher the story. (A=Across; D=Down)

ANSWER, PAGE 182

BY EMILY COX AND HENRY RATHVON

It's funny—**42A** Harbor always **15D** me of my first case, that **13D** day in the last **31A** of 1986 when, on a snowy morning, a distress call reached my office. When the phone rang, I could hardly believe my **43A**: an actual client, telling me that a **27A** had been stolen!

My mind aswirl with visions of riches by the sackful, I roused myself from the **10D** daze, the **25D** torpor (practically a **47D**) in which I'd languished since renting the office from my greedy **26D**, our family slumlord. I grabbed my keys, my coat, and my purse and hopped into my little **36A** (the only thing I'd kept after my **20A** from my husband), and headed out Grove St. to Maple and Oak **12A**, and then to **33A** 80, toward an out-of-town address. The snow was heavy, and the heater in my **36A** wasn't working. What was true in the beginning remains true: Nobody ever **35A** a shamus on a nice day.

As I struggled along at about 20 miles **7D** hour, thinking about the **27A**, I pictured a rich widower or a wealthy **35D** who would gladly **1A** a **51A** young gumshoe like me **42D** of dough to recover the goods. But when I arrived, the building didn't

look **29D** (2wds.) swanky nor the grounds especially **9D**, with their unkempt thorny **28D** bushes (though the **44D** yard did **36D** a little pond with a man-made **19A** in it where some ducks, possibly **39A**, were huddled). Inside, in the lobby, a crude sign gave the abbreviated message: "**45D** for rent. Call Jack Lambert, **59A**." Another lawyer slumlord, I noted sourly.

The name on the door of the first-floor **44A** was Delgado, so when a teenaged boy answered my knock, I said "*Cómo* **50D** *usted?*" The kid just stared. Maybe with all the snow on my coat, I looked like a wild **3D** of Tibet. Certainly I was shivering like an **6D** sufferer.

"Who's the client here, **1D**?" I asked. (Calling people "**1D**" was, I figured, part of the **8A** private-eye patter I had to learn.) "My **27A** is missing!" answered the kid.

So *he* was my client. I looked him over: a pretty nerdy specimen, I thought, with acne **27D** on his puffy face and a nasal voice probably due to a bad case of **40A**.

"Just what valuables," I asked him, "did this **27A** of yours contain?"

"Well," he said, "there's a **42A** inside that's very **8D**."

I didn't mean to be **16A**, but I felt my eyebrow **34A**. Why would this kid have a **42A**? And why was it **8D**?

"Where did you last see it?" I asked.

He pointed to a door.

"**58A** here," I said.

"Looking through my **55A**," said the kid, "will be rough."

His **55A**? What kind of a **56A** was he trying to pull? Was this kid a kidder, a mere **39D**? I had to wonder. But I was so **14A** to start my **4D** that I stepped into his bedroom. What I confronted was a scene of typical adolescent disarray, certainly not bad enough to bury anyone in. I spied heaps of clothes, the gear of an **2D** sports nut (including a baseball **49D** with the price **60A** still attached), a **25A** of records (mostly by rock **32A**, though in addition to Van Halen and **38D** Jett I did see **57A** James and **37A** Torme, so maybe the **38A** kid wasn't a completely twerpy low-brow), plus some scattered food-stuffs (old pizza slices, a bottle of A&W **46D** **11D** with some insect, probably a **18D**, crawling **41D**)—but not the slightest **24A** of the **27A**.

Just then the kid gave a cry, and I darted into the hallway in time to see a woman standing there. She looked prim, the sort of lady you'd expect to find at church and **53D** meetings at school, yet she was holding, unfolded, a sample of periodical **17A** not usually associated with her type.

"**31D**," the boy was whining, his face in a sullen **48D**, "how could you rake that from my **55A**?"

What was going on? "That's no **27A**!" I cried, a bit stupidly.

"No, I'm sorry," said the boy's smiling **21A**, "but you see, in this family, we tend to **5D** our **32D**."

5D 32D? What did the class **12A** have to do with anything? Then it hit me. **23A** time the kid and his **21A** spoke, they'd uttered a **52A**! (I **48A** you know that this involves a **4A** of sounds.)

So it all made sense, as I gazed at the periodical **17A**, the **54D** with the telltale **43A** on the **44D**.

Case solved, then. And I'll tell you, no matter how cryptically **45A** any case **30D** (and I've had some obscure **22D** over the years), none matches that first caper for quirky humor. I didn't even mind that they couldn't **1A** me. As I said to them in parting, "**37A**, **24D** isn't everything."

CONCENTRATED CHALLENGES

BY STEVE RYAN

Ever wonder who's behind those rebuses on TV's *Concentration*? It's Steve Ryan, a graphic artist from Beverly Hills, California, who is also one of the most widely syndicated puzzlemakers in America. Besides creating all the rebuses for *Classic Concentration*, as the program has been known since 1987, he makes pencil-and-paper puzzles that Copley News Service syndicates to more than 150 newspapers across the U.S. and Canada.

For his syndicated puzzles, Ryan's particular talent is to think of a genuinely original idea and present it in an appealingly visual manner. His goal is both to capture the eye and to pique the curiosity. Ryan gets his ideas from looking at what's around him and "dissecting things in an unusual way." When he sees something that suggests puzzle possibilities, he plays with it on paper, doing all the artwork himself.

"I have a small sculpture of a prospector that sits in my office," Ryan says. "It symbolizes that I'm always searching for that *nugget* of an idea that will lead to a new and exciting puzzle or game." Ryan makes sure that pencil and paper are always handy, even by his bed, since ideas can come at any time.

Ryan, 44, has been captivated by puzzles since childhood. He started a collection of mechanical puzzles in the third grade—now numbering over 1,000—and began creating brainteasers for himself and his friends in the fifth grade. He later earned a bachelor's degree in art from Long Beach State. That artistic bent, Ryan feels, is a key to his success; the ability to translate a concept onto paper and work out the puzzle while drawing it is critical to the process for him. Ryan cites the playful M.C. Escher as his favorite artist and a major influence.

Creating thousands of newspaper puzzles—for 20 years to date—might seem like a full-time job, but that's only the half of it. Since 1978 Ryan has worked for Mark Goodson Productions, the TV game show packager, as creator, writer, and producer of a variety of shows. He also wrote the book *Classic Concentration* and co-authored *The Encyclopedia of TV Game Shows*. His syndicated puzzles have been collected in six books.

We present here a sampling of Steve Ryan's amazingly diverse output.

—Amy Goldstein

ANSWERS, PAGE 182

1. THE OLYMPI-ADD

Place the numbers 1 through 9 into the nine divided areas that make up these Olympic rings so that the sum of the numbers in each ring is 11.

2. MATCH WITS

The matches in this puzzle will only burn in one direction, from the head to the other end. Which match will burn last if the two top matches start to burn simultaneously? All matches burn at the same rate. When a match burns down to an intersection, all match heads in that intersection will ignite simultaneously.

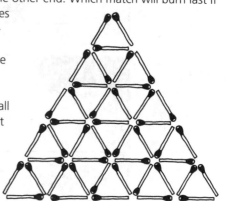

3. BEHIND CLOSED DOORS

Opening one of the numbered doors shown cancels out two numbers, the number on the door itself and the door covered by the opened door. For example, opening the first door cancels both the 2 on the door itself and the 6 on the door it covers. In compensation, behind each door is a number half the value on the door, revealed when the door is opened. For example, opening the first door reveals a 1 (half of 2) behind it. Can you open four doors so that all the horizontal and vertical rows add up to the same total?

4. BUTTONS AND BOWS

Travel through this maze starting at one of the dark buttons, connecting all the buttons and bows without passing over any button, bow, or thread more than once, and finish at the other dark button.

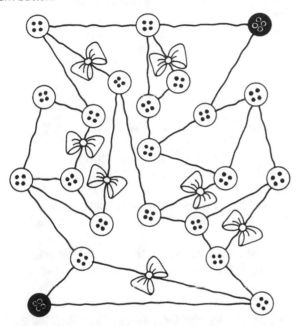

5. LOOKOUTS FOR NO. 1

Position two lookouts in vacant intersections of this grid so they can observe all the number 1 figures. No single 1 may be seen by both lookouts.

6. PERFECT PERFECT VISION

Draw four straight lines dividing this box into nine pieces so that if you add the numbers in each piece you get the same total.

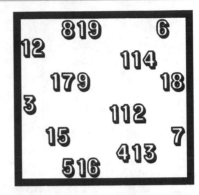

7. TRIP-WIRE

The object of the strategic two-player game of Trip-Wire is to lay the final wire, preventing an opponent from making any additional moves. Players alternately string a single wire between unused posts on two different sides of the board, keeping in mind the rule that a new wire may not cross more than one previously laid wire. In this game in progress, can you place the next wire to win the game?

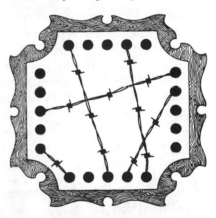

8. WORD WRESTLE

Solve this crossword by using each of the 26 letters of the alphabet exactly once. Five letters have been placed to get you started. To fill in the rest of the letters, form the proper word associations from the seven clue words below and insert them into the grid. For example, the clue word YELLOW might bring to mind LEMON, COWARD, or MUSTARD. The clue words are: CHECKERS, CHESS, LINGERIE, SHIP, HORN, CRYSTAL, FINGERS.

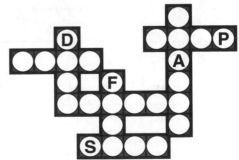

Role Models

BY VIRGINIA MCCARTHY

The Plotline Players launched their new season of theatrical productions with a performance or *Draft in the Drawing Room*—a play in three two-scene acts. The six successful auctioneers were cast (appropriately as to sex) in the roles of Angela Lone (a widow), Fragilica Lone (the widow's daughter), Titus Stint (the widow's uncle), Senta Pokenose (the widow's neighbor), Mr. Vested (a banker), and Mr. Pounce (a lone shark). The understudies hovered hopefully, but to no avail, while the starring cast—whose first names were Charlie, Dana, Georgie, Kelly, Robin, and Terri; and whose last names were Curtin, Hamm, Moodie, Spouter, Stagey, and Stentor—worked devotedly though rehearsal. At the long-awaited performance, the nervous strain was such that each player sullied a different scene by conspicuously muffing a line. Given the following observations on the opening performance, can you assign the thespians, by full names, to the roles they played, and determine who blundered in which scene?

ANSWER, PAGE 183

CLUES

1. Terry came on stage in Act I and performed flawlessly through the end of Act II.
2. Curtin's mess-up came after Charlie's and before Robin's.
3. Mr. Spouter's boner, not the evening's first, was made before Senta Pokenose had even made her entry.
4. When Fragilica burst handwringingly onto the stage in Act I to join the three characters already there, she blanked out on her heartrending entry line and could only stammer inanities.
5. Stagey was not the first one to muff a line, and the thespian who played the neighbor was not the last.
6. The Act III blunders were made by Dana and Hamm; the latter did not play the role of the widow.
7. The first onstage botch was made by the actor named Georgie—though he was not in the role of Mr. Vested.
8. Neither Uncle Titus nor another character (who was played by Moodie) appeared on the stage until Act II.

ORDER OF BLUNDER	THESPIAN'S FIRST NAME	THESPIAN'S LAST NAME	CHARACTER IN PLAY
I, 1			
I, 2			
II, 1			
II, 2			
III, 1			
III, 2			

BATTLESHIPS

BY PETER GORDON & MIKE SHENK

The six puzzles on this page are solitaire versions of the classic paper-and-pencil game of Battleships. Each grid represents a section of ocean in which the entire fleet is hiding. This fleet consists of one battleship (four grid squares in length), two cruisers (each three squares long), three destroyers (each two squares long), and four submarines (one square each). The ships may be oriented either horizontally or vertically, and no two ships will occupy adjacent grid squares, *even diagonally*. The digits along the right side of and below the grid indicate the number of grid squares in the corresponding rows and columns that are occupied by vessels.

In each of the puzzles below, one or more shots have been taken to start you off. These may show water (indicated by wavy lines), a complete submarine (a circle), or the middle (a square) or the end (a rounded-off square) of a longer vessel. The puzzles get harder as you go. Only Battleships geniuses will reach the rank of admiral by finding all the fleets.

ANSWERS, PAGE 183

- Water
- Middle of a ship (will continue either left and right or up and down)
- Submarine
- End of a ship (will continue in the direction of the flat side)

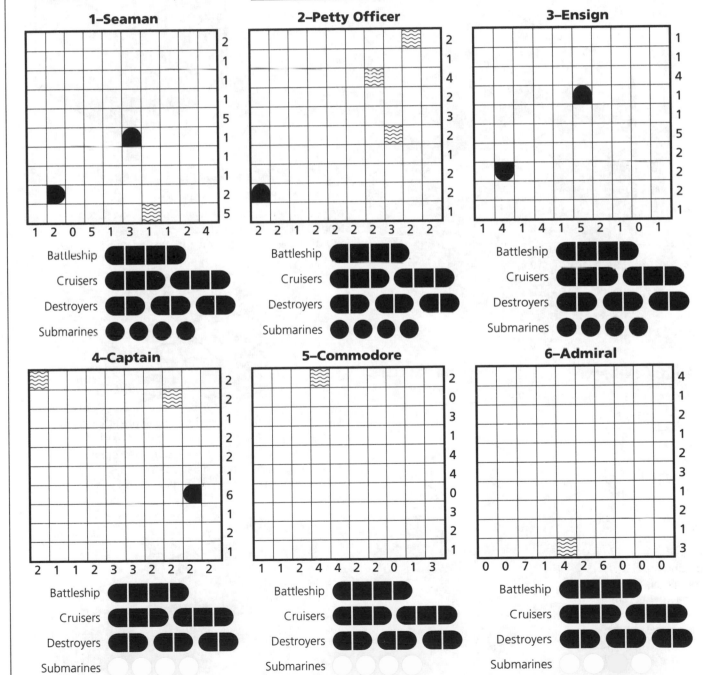

BOXED IN

The four brainteasers on this page all involve boxes. Don't be surprised if you encounter some mental blocks while trying them.

ANSWERS, PAGE 183

FROM THE GAMES LIBRARY

1. STACKING BOXES

BY KEN H. MACLEISH

We started with a six-by-six-by-six stack of boxes and removed a number of them, as shown below. If every box has another box beneath it (except for the ones in the bottom layer), what's the largest number of boxes the stack could contain?

2. CUTTING BOXES

BY P. M. H. KENDALL AND G. M. THOMAS

A solid cube measuring three inches on each side may be cut into 27 one-inch cubes by cutting the large cube only six times (along the lines shown) without moving any pieces. By making one cut and placing the slice formed on top of the remainder before cutting again, what's the smallest number of cuts necessary to produce 27 cubes?

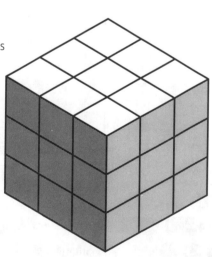

3. CROSSING BOXES

BY HENRY ERNEST DUDENEY

A fly, starting from point A of the box below, can crawl around the four sides of the base in four minutes. What's the minimum amount of time it would take the fly to crawl from point A to point B at the opposite corner?

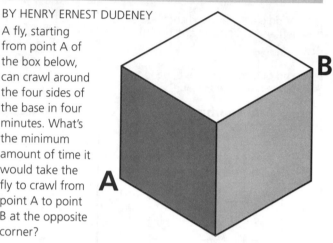

4. TIPPING BOXES

BY ROLAND SPRAGUE

Five cubical boxes, each with an A painted on its top side, stand together in a cross-shaped arrangement as shown below. The boxes are to be brought into line, but they're so

heavy that they can be moved only by tipping them over about an edge. With these conditions, it proves to be impossible to line them up with all the A's oriented upright, and the arrangement finally achieved has one sideways A as shown. Which of the boxes in this row of five was originally in the middle of the cross?

POLISH YOUR WITS

BY MAREK PENSZKO

Since the recent rebirth of democracy and private enterprise in Poland, our Polish correspondent has launched his own successful puzzle magazine. Meanwhile, he continues to devise novel ways to twist our gray matter. Herewith, his three latest examples.   *ANSWERS, PAGE 183*

1. ABSOLUTELY AMAZING

Start at the A in the upper left corner of the maze at right and trace a path to the Z at the lower right, visiting each of the 26 letters of the alphabet exactly once. Your path must not cross itself.

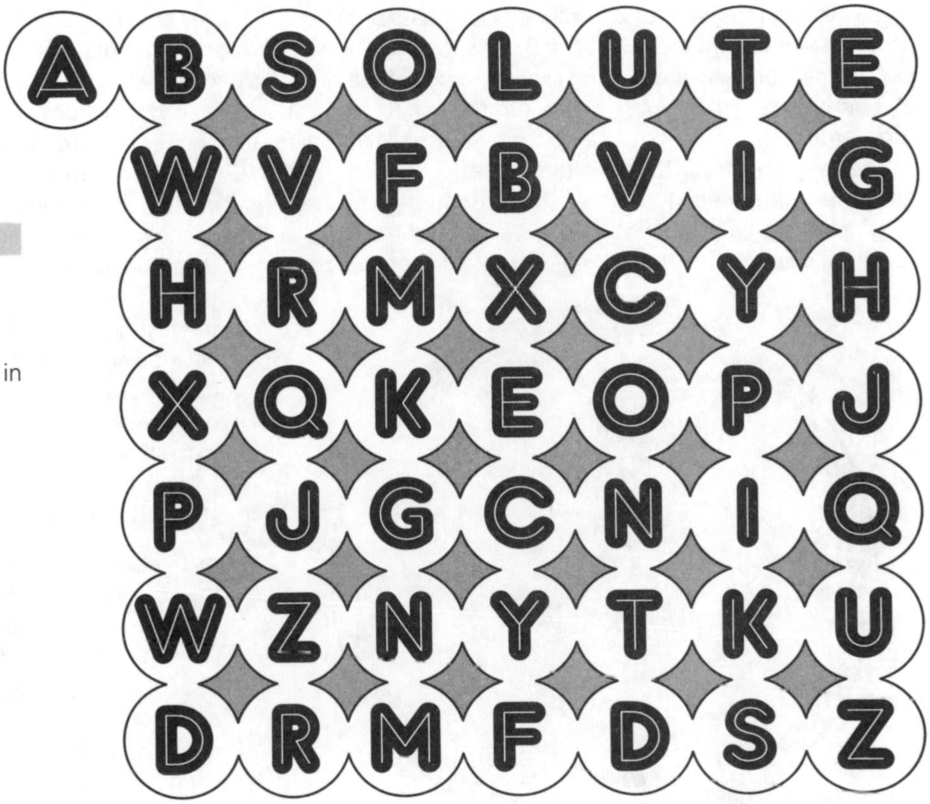

2. ORDERLY ADDITION

We've replaced all the digits of a simple addition problem with dashes. We did notice, though, that each digit was one more than the digit immediately below it in the same column. What was the original addition problem?

```
        — — —
        — —
      — — — —
  +   — — — —
      — — — —
```

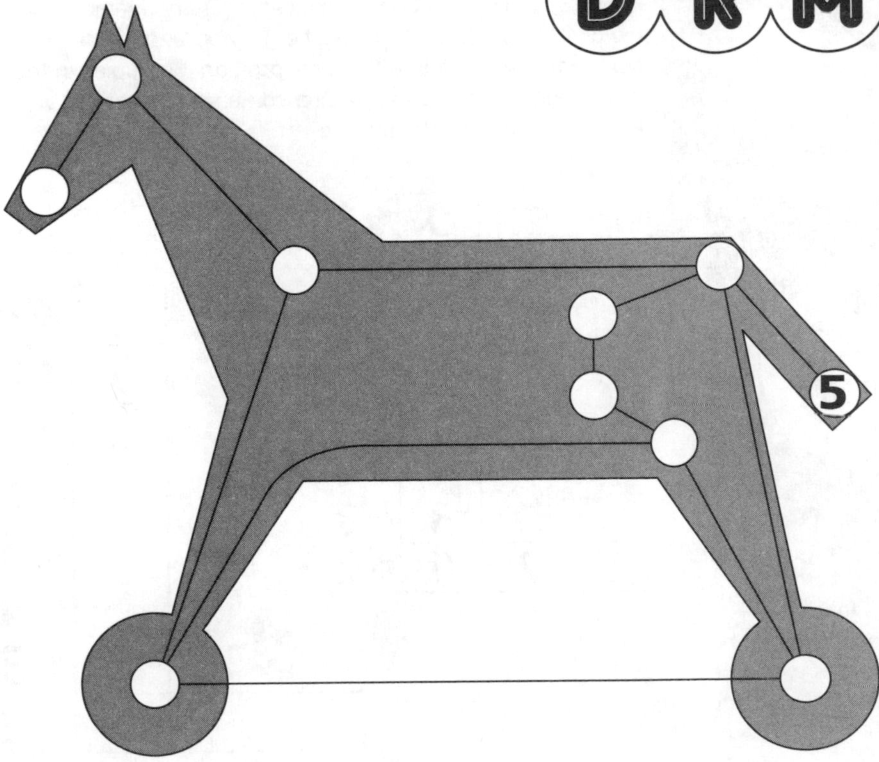

3. THE TROJAN HORSE

Place the digits 0 to 9 in the nine circles of the Trojan Horse pictured at left according to the following rule: Each pair of digits connected by a line, in one order or the other, must make a two-digit number that is evenly divisible by either 7 or 13. The digit 5 has been placed at the tail as a start.

JUEGOS ARGENTINOS

BY JAIME PONIACHIK

The five puzzles on this page were created by Buenos Aires's Jaime Poniachik, editor and co-owner of Juegos & Co., a publisher of quality puzzle magazines popular in Argentina and elsewhere in South America. Solving three or four of the puzzles is *muy bueno*, and getting all five is *excelente*.

SOLUCIONES, PÁGINA 184

1. THE CLOCKWISE ANT

Just as the minute hand of an accurate clock passes the 12, an ant crawls onto the clock at the 6 mark, and begins walking counterclockwise around the circumference of the clock at a uniform speed. When she runs into the minute hand, she turns around and proceeds in a clockwise path, still maintaining her original speed. Then, 45 minutes after her first encounter with the minute hand, she runs into the minute hand a second time. Frustrated, she crawls off the clock in search of safer ground. How long did the ant spend on the clock?

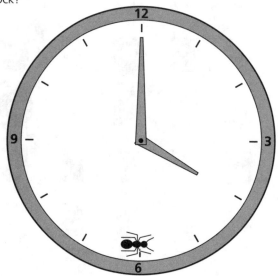

2. DIE PEEKING

Looking through a very small peephole, we can see one corner of an ordinary die from a game. It's impossible to say what numbers are on the three sides we can see, but we *can* be sure that one of these three sides is a ... *what*?

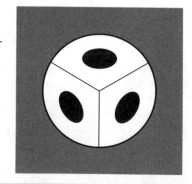

3. ASTROLOGICAL AGE

When asked her zodiac sign, the mathematics teacher answered, "Today's date—that is, the day of the month—is the same as my present age, but before the end of this week, there will be a date that will be only one fifth of my new age on that day." What is her zodiac sign?

4. MYSTERY MENU

At the Nine Meals Inn in the city of Nonsensica, the menu always contains just nine items: abberflooies, bommeljips, curwinkles, dinquapods, ecka-eckas, flophummers, grob-volleys, hinkboos, and ibbergats. Five travelers, strangers to Nonsensica, stop by the Inn, and each orders one item from the menu without the slightest idea of what it might be. The waiter returns with the five plates, placing them in the middle of the table so the guests may divide them as they see fit. The diners enjoy themselves tremendously, so they return the next two nights, and both times each guest orders one item, as on the first night. On the fourth night, the guests return, but by now, being logical diners, they are able to determine which name goes with each of the Inn's dishes. Can you determine what each of the three nights' five orders could have been to make this possible?

5. MULTIPLE TOWERS

As the two-cell elevator below rises along the eight-floor tower, it forms a series of three-digit numbers, by combining the 7 and 2 in the elevator with each successive digit in the tower. What's more, these three-digit numbers are multiples of 2, 3, 4, etc., up to 9. (That is, on the lowest level, 726 is evenly divisible by 2; on the second level, 723 is evenly divisible by 3; and so on.) Can you find another arrangement for the digits 0 to 9 (using each digit exactly once, one digit per box) so that no digit is in the same position it occupied in the first arrangement and the elevator combines with each level to form an appropriate multiple?

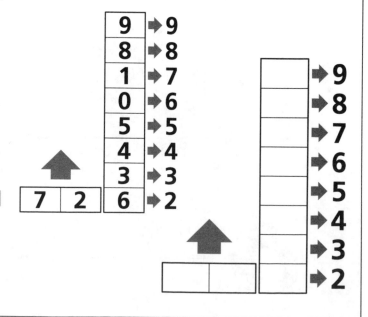

6 WHAT DO YOU KNOW? A QUIZ FOR (ALMOST) EVERY OCCASION

CAPITAL STATE 20 QUESTIONS

BY GAYLE BLAIR URBAN

The answers to the trivia questions below are the names of U.S. state capitals. Each question has multiple answers, the number in parentheses indicating how many. Each capital will be used exactly once in the quiz. To keep track, and to help jog your memory, the 50 post office abbreviations of the states are listed below the questions. Only true capitalists will get them all. *ANSWERS, PAGE 184*

Which state …

1. …makes a common uncapitalized word when its first and last letters are switched? (2)
2. …starts with the name of a month? (2)
3. …contains the letter sequence ENTO? (2)
4. …rhymes with another state capital of the same number of syllables? (2)
5. …when combined with its state consists of four words? (2)
6. …starts with the same six letters as another state capital? (2)
7. …ends with the same eight letters as another state capital? (2)
8. …contains the letter sequence DEN? (2)
9. …has seven letters, with the last four making a common uncapitalized word? (2)
10. …contains a K and is in a state that contains a K? (5)
11. …is over nine letters long but has only two syllables? (2)
12. …consists of one word that has within it a four-letter palindromic sequence (a sequence that reads the same forward and backward)? (4)
13. …consists entirely of a last name of a U.S. president? (3)
14. …contains the letter sequence MON? (3)
15. …has its first letter used twice more in its name? (2)
16. …consists of two words, and with its state contains each of the five vowels at least once? (2)
17. …starts with an H? (4)
18. …when printed in uppercase letters has all straight letters except for the third? (2)
19. …contains the letter sequence OI? (2)
20. …has seven letters, none of which are repeated, and doesn't end with an N? (3)

AK AL AR AZ CA CO CT DE FL GA HI IA ID IL
IN KS KY LA MA MD ME MI MN MO MS MT NC
ND NE NH NJ NM NV NY OH OK OR PA RI SC
SD TN TX UT VA VT WA WI WV WY

HIGH-LOW QUIZ

BY MARK DANNA

One of the most popular features on the TV game show *The Price Is Right* is "High/Low," where the contestant is given a price for an object and must guess if it is too high or too low. This illustrated trivia quiz works on the same principle. Just read the 15 statements below and guess whether the highlighted number in each one is too high or too low. A score of 9 correct answers is fair; 11 is good; 13 is excellent. Only trivia masters (or lucky guessers) will get all 15.

ANSWERS, PAGE 184

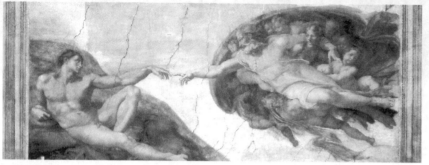

1. This Sistine Chapel painting resides in the least populous independent country in the world. It has just **1,400** people.
High ___ Low ___

2. After performing in a Donizetti opera, this singer once received curtain calls lasting **2 hours and 15 minutes**.
High ___ Low ___

3. This type of vision aid was invented **51** years ago.
High ___ Low ___

4. The earliest dated puzzle of this sort was created **188** years ago.
High ___ Low ___

5. The number of units in a one-pound bag of these plain candies is **425**.
High ___ Low ___

6. This Paris landmark (at left) is taller than this Washington landmark (at right) by **300** feet.
High ___ Low ___

7. For this game, every year Parker Brothers, its manufacturer, produces **5** times as much money as the U.S. Bureau of Engraving and Printing does actual money.
High ___ Low ___

8. On its first day of business in 1858, in its original building on Sixth Avenue near 14th Street in Manhattan, this store took in **$42** in sales.

High ___   Low ___

9. The tallest vehicle of this kind ever mastered was **46** feet high.

High ___   Low ___

10. Over the course of his lifetime, the real-life king portrayed by this actor had **6,500** wives and concubines.

High ___   Low ___

11. This founding father's last name is the name of counties in **38** states.

High ___   Low ___

12. In Japan, women were first allowed to watch this kind of match **16** years ago.

High ___   Low ___

13. The longest recorded life span for a queen of this insect species is **7** years.

High ___   Low ___

14. It takes **32** muscles to make this facial expression.

High ___   Low ___

15. Though slow-moving, the "box" version of this animal migrates **100** miles during a single year.

High ___   Low ___

IT'S SATURDAY NIGHT!

BY LOU KESTEN

On Saturday October 11, 1975, anyone who stayed up late enough while tuned to NBC heard for the first time the now-familiar refrain "Live from New York, it's *Saturday Night*!" The outlaw *Saturday Night Live* immediately revolutionized the world of comedy and went on to become an amazingly long-lived institution. In honor of 20 years of *SNL*, we offer this through-the-years quiz. There are 65 points in all. If you score under 35, you probably stopped watching years ago— or just started recently. A score of 35-50 is good—you're a fan. And if you get over 50, you've been staying up late for almost 20 years—get some sleep!

ANSWERS, PAGE 185

Who's Who

1. *Saturday Night Live* was originally called *NBC's Saturday Night*, to avoid conflict with a short-lived ABC variety program that featured "The Prime Time Players" (from which came the *SNL* troupe's title, "The Not Ready for Prime Time Players"). The ABC show was *Saturday Night Live With ...* whom?

2. Who hosted *SNL*'s first show?
   a. Albert Brooks
   b. George Carlin
   c. Robert Klein
   d. Lily Tomlin

3. Chevy Chase, actually hired as a writer rather than a performer, quickly became a star on the show. How many full seasons was he on?

4. Twice in its history, *SNL* was broadcast with a several-second delay. Who were the controversial hosts of those shows? *(1 point each)*

5. Which of these two cast members later married each other?
   a. Robin Duke and Tony Rosato
   b. Nora Dunn and Jon Lovitz
   c. Mary Gross and Tim Kazurinsky
   d. Julia Louis-Dreyfus and Brad Hall

6. An unusual comedian appeared on *SNL*'s premiere, lip-synching Mighty Mouse's "Here I come to save the day!" He later wrestled women on the show and finally staged an off-air fight with producer Dick Ebersol, followed by Ebersol's on-air announcement that viewers could call in and vote whether the comedian should be banned from the show. Who was he?

7. What performer, now best known for his numerous voices on *The Simpsons*, twice quit the show in midseason?

8. Which one of these politicians has *not* hosted the show?
   a. Jesse Jackson
   b. Ed Koch
   c. George McGovern
   d. Ross Perot

9. Three cast members had brothers who followed in their footsteps on *SNL*. Give yourself a point for each of the three later brothers you can name.

10. Why did unknown 80-year-old grandmother Miskel Spillman host the show once in its third season?

11. Two of the following were never regular cast members or featured players on the show. Which? *(1 point each)*
   a. Tim Allen
   b. Brett Butler
   c. Joan Cusack
   d. Denny Dillon
   e. Robert Downey Jr.
   f. Anthony Michael Hall
   g. Michael McKean
   h. Laurie Metcalf
   i. The Muppets
   j. Randy Quaid
   k. Damon Wayans

12. In *SNL*'s early years, what frequent host (who once received a bad cut on the forehead during a Samurai sketch) traditionally hosted the last show of the season, cheerfully performing the tasteless sketches that other hosts wouldn't touch?

On a Role

1. John Belushi reportedly found these insects, the show's first recurring characters, "loathsome." Who were they?

2. What namesake character was created by filmmaker Walter Williams?

3. Name the cable program—later a movie— that came to you on Community Access Channel 10 in Aurora, Illinois.

4. Who is the androgynous character at upper left?

5. Preteen Jeff Renaudo played what political figure in numerous sketches?

6. Match the characters with their catchphrases. *(1 point each)*
   a. Buckwheat
   b. The Church Lady
   c. Dieter, host of *Sprockets*
   d. Fernando
   e. Yortuk and Jorge Festrunk
   f. Tommy Flanagan, the pathological liar
   g. Hans and Franz
   h. Richard Laymer, the Richmeister
   i. Emily Litella
   j. Stuart Smalley
   k. The Superfans
   l. Doug and Wendy Whiner

   1. "You look *mahvelous*!"
   2. "Never mind."
   3. "How conveeenient."
   4. "But we've got diverticulitis!"
   5. "Makin' copies."
   6. "Yeah, that's the ticket."
   7. "I'm good enough, I'm smart enough, and doggone it, people like me."
   8. "Oh-tay!"
   9. "Hear me now and believe me later."
   10. "Touch my monkey."
   11. "Foxes!"
   12. "Da Bears."

7. Who are the lounge singers at left?

8. What bizarre medical anomaly was Lisa Loopner's father (God rest his soul) a victim of?

9. Two cast members regularly impersonated Frank Sinatra. Which two? *(1 point each)*

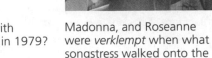

SATURDAY NIGHT LIVE

10. Billy Crystal, who was scheduled to do stand-up on the premiere but didn't make it on, later became a regular with several recurring characters. Most amazing, perhaps, was the transformation he made into what black singer?

11. What characters were inspired by a trip taken by Dan Aykroyd and Tom Davis to Easter Island?

12. Who is the cigar-chomping character at upper right?

13. "I wish outer-space guys would conquer Earth and make people their pets, because I'd like to have one of those little basket-beds with my name on it." From what continuing series does this come?

14. Name the vehicular menace with a driver's license from Texas.

15. What game show host was hyper-cowlicked Ed Grimley obsessed with?

16. What is the significance of this list?
- Dan Aykroyd
- Chevy Chase
- Dan Aykroyd, Dana Carvey
- Phil Hartman, Joe Piscopo, Charles Rocket, Harry Shearer, Robin Williams
- Dana Carvey, Jim Downey
- Phil Hartman

17. What can you get to drink at the diner above?

Musical Interlude

1. To what band did Lorne Michaels offer $3,000 in April 1976 to reunite on *SNL*?

2. Which band member later took him up on the offer, demanding his $750 share?

3. What rocker, who once on the show stopped his scheduled song after a few bars and proceeded to perform a different song, was the inspiration for nerds Lisa Loopner and Todd DiLaMuca?

A

4. One comedian and frequent host, whose response to *SNL*'s premiere had been, "They did the show everyone should have been doing," had a gold record in 1978 with a song he performed on the show in response to a blockbuster museum exhibit. Name him.

5. What musical guest boycotted the show when she learned that Andrew "Dice" Clay was hosting?

6. The same singer later created controversy when she tore up a picture following her performance, exhorting, "Fight the real enemy." Who was shown in the picture?

7. What rock belter, often parodied by John Belushi,

ultimately duetted with Belushi on the show in 1979?

8. Canadian producer Lorne Michaels originally resisted hiring the *SNL* band's first piano player, a Canadian, because he was having trouble getting so many green cards for the show. This musician went on to become a featured performer who did a wicked impersonation of rock promoter Don Kirshner. Who is he?

9. In one "Coffee Talk" sketch, Mike Myers,

B

C

News Cast

1. During Chevy Chase's stint as anchor of "Weekend Update," he regularly announced that who "is still dead"?

2. Following Chevy Chase's departure, Jane Curtin took over his "Update" anchor spot. Responding one night to supposed complaints about her staid journalistic demeanor, she cried, "Try these on for size, Connie Chung!" and did what?

Madonna, and Roseanne were *verklempt* when what songstress walked onto the set?

10. What successful musical act led to the departure of Dan Aykroyd and John Belushi from the show?

E

D

F

3. One smirking anchor had such a distinctive style that he was eventually impersonated by Dana Carvey during "Update." After leaving *SNL*, he went on to host his own talk show. Who is he?

4. What segment is cast member David Spade known for?

5. Give yourself a point for each of the six "Update" correspondents shown above that you can name.

REFERENCES ON REQUEST

BY MARGOT SEIDES

Whether you look things up in books every day or haven't taken a volume off the library's reference shelf in years, you should check out the clippings on this page. Through careful perusal and creative thinking, can you identify the kind of reference book in which you'd find the information in each excerpt? Getting 14 or more correct answers qualifies you to have your name appear under the listing "Expert" in our *Book of Puzzle Solvers*.

ANSWERS, PAGE 184

1

You won't miss too much if you skip the important commercial port of Leghorn (Livorno), but we heartily recommend a visit to Elba if you

2

adinerado *adj.* wealthy.
¡adiós! *interj.* good-bye!; farewell!; hello!; *Am.* you don't say!
aditamento *m.* addition; annex.
adivinación *f.* divination, prediction; guess.
adivinanza *f.* conundrum, riddle.
adivinar *v.* to guess.

3

Equinunk	18417
ERIE (1st) Main PO	16514
(Also See Appendix)	
Ernest	15739
Erwinna	18920

4

confuse 5 addle, befog, m... ...p, stump **6** baffle, muddle, ...zle, rattle **7** fluster, mis- ...mystify, nonplus, per- ...fuddle, bewilder,

5

.95 (*0-671-64885-3*, Fireside) S&S Trade.
...ok, Henry, ed. Simon & Schuster's Hooked O...
No. 5. 1992. pap. 8.99 (*0-671-70936-4*, Fir...
Trade.
Hook, Hilary. Home from the Hill. large ty...
496p. 1988. 15.95 (*0-7089-1899-9*) Ul...
Hook, J. Appropriate Word. 1990. 18.2...
Addison-Wesley.
Hook, J. B. & Poste, G., eds. Protein...
Development of New Therapeu...

6

8	M.	St. Dominic	Great Train Robbery, $7 million stolen, England, 1963	10:2	— for	liant orange color with ruby spots.
9	Tu.	on Eq. F stat.	President Nixon resigned, 1974 • Tides	11.0 10.5	Caesar.	The eft lives in the moist woods and thickets. It feeds on insects, earthworms. Not a bad life, proba-
10	W.	St. Laurence	Smithsonian Institution est., 1846		(Who's	
11	Th	St. Clare • Dog Days Good humor makes				

7

...rm protuberances, bosses, ...*v.i.* **17.** to become tied or ...rm knots or joints. [bef. ...tta; c. D *knot,* G *knoten* to ...e n.] —**knot/less,** *adj.*
...ew, gang, crowd. **7.** lump, ...zle, conundrum.

8

...d structure of nucleus, e... ...ergy scattering, gamma ... ...ator design. Home: 16 R... ...hysics Northeastern U Bo...
...KA, **EUGENE T.,** retired ...word puzzle constructor; b. ...tetto (dec. 1983); children: ...iv. 1988). A.B., Montclair ... U., 1955; LL.D. (hon.), M...

9

— **2.** buzzing, fuzzing, ...
2. buzzle, guzzle, muz...

10

The Saar.

changed hands between Fre... times. Some of its histor... stroyed in World War II... by the United States troop... (1955) 119,388.

SAARINEN, sä'ri-ně... Finnish architect: b. Helsin... Finland, Aug. 20, 1873;... Mich., July 1, 1950. Edu... Polytechnic in Helsinki,... prizes for his city plans ar...

11

Hackett, Raquel Welch, Richard Benja-min. Super murder-puzzler about jet-set gamester who devises what turns into a deadly game of whodunit. Many red her-rings make it all the more fun. Script by Anthony Perkins and Stephen Sondheim, real-life puzzle fans. [PG]▼

12

...t is humanly impossible to under- ...word of it; without these, one is wan- ...ut in a dark labyrinth.[2]

Il Saggiatore [162...

But it does move![4]
Attributed. From ABBÉ IRAILH, *Querelle...*

13

American Cryptogram As-sociation; American Crystal-lographic Association; Arts Council of America; Arts Council of Australia; Assem-bly Constitutional Amend-ment; Associated Chiropo-dists of America; Association of Correctional Administra-tors
A.C.A.: Associate of the Insti-tute of Chartered Accoun-tants (of England and Wales)
ACAA: Agricultural Conserva-

14

...y 1982 Robert Turcot of Québe... ...zle comprising 82,951 squares. ...,125 down and covered 38.28 ft.[2]
...most prolific compiler is Roger F... who compiles 42 published puzzl...

15

Irish), **Bjorn** (Swedish).
BERT—Old English: **Beorht.** "Shining, glorious one." See also **Albert, Herbert.** Bert Parks, entertainer; Bert Lahr, comedian; Burt Lancaster, actor.

BEVIS—Old French: **Beaveis.** "Fair view."
Foreign variation: **Beauvais** (French).

BICKFORD—Old English: **Bieca-ford.** "Hewer's ford." Charles Bickford, American

16

Eboli, *Italy*		41 B8	40	39N	15	2
Ebolowa, *Cameroon*		101 E7	2	55N	11	10
Ebrach, *Germany*		27 F6	49	50N	10	30
Ébrié, Lagune, *Ivory C.*		100 D4	5	12N	4	26
Ebro →, *Spain*		34 E5	40	43N	0	54

17

...d game; jigsaw pu... ...stery, riddle, con... ...roblem, dilemma, ...labyrinth, tangle, ...d book; oracle, da... ...meaning, riddle o... ...ut to crack, *Inf.* ... ...stumper, *Inf.* floo... ...confoundment, b... ...uncertainty, inc...

18

See NINE-TO-FIVER
fives *See* BUNCH OF FIVES
five-sided puzzle palace *n phr* Army The Pen-tagon
five-spot 1 *n* A five-dollar bill **2** *n underworld* A five-year prison sentence **3** *n* A five of playing cards
five square (or **five**) **1** *adj phr radio operators* Of a radio signal, strong and easy to understand;

PLACES OF NOTE

BY SANDY FEIN

We'll bet you could find Baltimore on a U.S. map—but would you know that's the city that completes the song title "The Lady Came From _____"? And you may know the song "Streets of Laredo," but could you locate Laredo on the map? Both kinds of knowledge will come in handy for this puzzle. On the map of the continental United States below, we've indicated 25 cities (labeled 1–25) and 10 states (shaded and labeled A–J). We've also listed 35 song titles, but the city or state is left out of each. Can you fill in the missing places *and* match them up with their locations on the map? If you get 25 or more, we'll certainly sing your praises—no matter where you live!

ANSWERS, PAGE 184

"By the Time I Get to _____"

"_____ Choo Choo"

"Deep in the Heart of _____"

"Do You Know the Way to _____?"

"_____ Freedom"

"_____ Honey"

"Hotel _____"

"I Left My Heart in _____"

"I Lost My Sugar in _____"

"I've Got a Gal in _____"

"_____ Lassie"

"_____ Lineman"

"Little Old Lady From _____"

"Meet Me in _____, Louis"

"Moonlight in _____"

"Moon Over _____"

"My Old _____ Home"

"Okie From _____"

"_____ on My Mind"

"On the Atchison, Topeka, and the _____"

"On the Boardwalk in _____"

"Please Come to _____"

"_____ Reel"

"Shuffle Off to _____"

"Sidewalks of _____"

"Sink the _____"

"_____ 6-5000"

"Stars Fell on _____"

"_____ Sue"

"The City of _____"

"The Night _____ Died"

"The _____ Traveler"

"Twenty Four Hours From _____"

"Viva _____"

"_____ Wants Me"

GOING THROUGH THE MOTIONS

BY MARK DANNA

"Anthropologists say 60% of communication is non-verbal, and it's particularly true when you cross cultural boundaries." So says Roger E. Axtell, author of *Gestures: The Do's and Taboos of Body Language Around the World*. What's especially tricky is that a gesture used one place may signify something very different—and perhaps totally *opposite*—somewhere else. So when you travel abroad or deal with foreigners at home, being oblivious to these differences can lead to embarrassment—or even a punch in the nose. As a public service, then, we offer 13 trivia questions based on international gestures described in Mr. Axtell's book.

For most readers, this quiz will be more a test of intuition than knowledge, so if it leaves you scratching your head (a nearly universal gesture meaning "I'm confused"), don't throw up your hands in despair. Since we expect only seasoned world travelers—and good guessers—to get most of the right answers, you deserve a pat on the back if you can get six or more of them. As a gesture of good faith, we've included all the answers on page 185.

1. Tribespeople in many places have remarkably different ways of indicating the same thing: In Tibet, they stick their tongues out at each other; in parts of East Africa, they spit at each other's feet; Maoris in New Zealand may rub noses together; and Eskimos bang a hand on each other's head or shoulders. What one thing do all these gestures mean?

2. The nose twist is apparently unique to France. It signifies:
   a. "He's henpecked"
   b. "You're a weakling"
   c. "He's drunk"
   d. "Let's have a beer"

3. Tapping the side of the nose means (circle two):
   a. "Watch out" in Italy
   b. "This wine has a beautiful bouquet" in France
   c. "Let's keep this a secret between us" in England
   d. "A pox on your house" in Portugal

4. In the U.S., rotating the forefinger around in front of the ear usually indicates that somebody is crazy. But in Argentina, it means:
   a. "You have a phone call"
   b. "Get to the point!"
   c. "Your ears could use a cleaning"
   d. "He's very smart"

5. These gestures from Greece (face stroking), Brazil (pretending to look through a telescope), Italy in the old days (the mustache twist), and Italy today (the cheek screw) all signify the same thing. What?

6. For most of Europe, waving has a meaning that is the opposite of what shaking the head means in Bulgaria. In the correct order, what is this pair of opposites?
   a. Hello and good-bye
   b. Good-bye and hello
   c. Yes and no
   d. No and yes

7. Circle all that are true. The thumbs-up gesture means:
   a. "Right on!" in the U.S.
   b. The number "one" in Germany
   c. The number "five" in Japan
   d. Something very rude in Australia

8. The flat hand flick is an almost universal gesture meaning "get lost" or "go away." Yet to an Ethiopian it signifies:
   a. "I love you"
   b. "Hello"
   c. "Want to eat?"
   d. "Deal the cards"

9. Be careful! Vertical horns, or "hook 'em horns," carry vastly different connotations. Depending on where you are, the gesture may bring you a smile or a smack in the face. It signifies (circle all that apply):
   a. "Your spouse is being unfaithful" in Italy
   b. A rally gesture for the University of Texas football team
   c. Two outs, in American baseball
   d. Cattle, to a Hindu dancer
   e. The horns of the devil, to Satanic cults
   f. Good luck, in Venezuela and Brazil
   g. A curse, or the "evil eye" (when pointed at someone), in parts of Africa
   h. The letter H, in American Sign Language

10. In the United States and most of Europe, the hand wag—rotating an extended flat hand over and back repeatedly—is used to answer "Just so-so" in response to a "How are you?" In Holland, this motion can also mean:
   a. "The sea is very rough"
   b. "Oh, it's very tricky"
   c. "I'm feeling pretty shaky"
   d. "I think it's a cover-up"

11. The hand flap, performed by stiffening the four fingers and flapping them down against the thumb, as if imitating the bill of a duck, means what in South Africa?
   a. "Time to eat?"
   b. "I know the answer"
   c. "Your car's turn signal is on"
   d. "It's an open-and-shut case"

12. In the U.S., pointing toward yourself means "me." In Japan, it means:
   a. "Me"
   b. "I sympathize with you"
   c. "I feel lonely"
   d. "I have to go to the bathroom"

13. Kissing someone's feet is not a universal sign of subservience or abasement. In fact, this beautiful gesture in Bangladesh means—appropriately enough, as this quiz comes to a close—what?

MONKEY BUSINESS

BY SUZIE ELLIOTT

What we have here is monkey bars for the mind. Follow the directions for each of the four quiz sections below, and have more fun than a barrel of monkeys—but watch out for monkeyshines! If your score is 10–15, you're very good at monkey business; if it's 16–20, go ape! And if it's 21 or more, you're obviously a 600-pound gorilla when it comes to primates.

ANSWERS, PAGE 185

PRIME-TIME PRIMATES

We guarantee the TV series described below actually aired. Can you identify them?

1. A handsome young trucker travels the country with his chimp companion, then settles down to run a trucking company staffed—naturally!—by seven beautiful young female truckers. *1 point*

2. An orangutan drinks an experimental mixture that gives him an IQ of 256 and the ability to speak; he moves to Washington to act as a government consultant on nuclear energy and missiles. *1 point*

3. A rock-and-roll band—NBC's answer to the Beatles—gets into zany situations. *1 point to name the band and show, and 1 point for each band member you can name*

4. A real estate agent and his wife, played by Jack Weston and Peggy Cass, take in three performing chimps. The wife treats them like human children, dressing them in kids' clothes, having them sit down to dinner, etc., to her husband's—and the neighbors'—chagrin. *1 point*

5. A group of simians with dubbed-in human voices act as secret agents, among them Mata Hairi, Dr. Strangemind, and Darwin, the head of the Agency to Prevent Evil (A.P.E.). *1 point*

CALL OUR BLUFF

Of the six expressions below incorporating references to primates, five are genuine, historical phrases. The other one, however, appears to be the by-product of that monkey who's typing away somewhere, trying to complete *Hamlet*. Can you pick the fake? *1 point*

1. To pay in monkey's money—to compensate in goods or personal services. When a monkey crossed a toll bridge in Paris, its owner had to pay a toll if the monkey was for sale; but if it was a performing monkey and not for sale, the monkey simply went through his tricks to pay the toll: *"... being an original [painting], paid for in court fashion with monkey's money."* (Rabelais, *IV, iii*)

2. To get one's monkey up—to be riled or enraged. Easily provoked, monkeys are often irritable.

3. To eat the monkey's dinner—to be left in the lurch by one's comrades; to be left holding the bag: *"By Cheshu, he is an ass, as in the world!... He'll leave us all to eat the monkey's dinner."* (Henry V, *III, ii*)

4. Monkey puzzle—a South American coniferous timber tree, so called because its branches are so twisted it would be perplexing for even a monkey to climb.

5. To suck the monkey—the Dutch call drinking "sucking the monkey" because the early morning, hair-of-the-dog rum was sipped with a "monkey spoon," a spoon with a handle decorated by a monkey sitting on a heart.

6. To lead apes in hell—the supposed fate of old maids; an *ape-leader*, to the Elizabethans, was an old maid: *"I will even take sixpence in earnest of the bearward, and lead his apes into hell."* (Much Ado About Nothing, *II, i*)

RHESUS PIECES

Match each factual or fictional monkey (or chimp) named at left with his or her claim to fame, listed at right and center. *1 point each*

1. Abu
2. Bubbles
3. Ham
4. Ignatz
5. J. Fred Muggs
6. Judy
7. Washoe
8. Zippie

a. the monkey aboard the *Venture*, the ship in the original *King Kong*
b. the first monkey to orbit the earth for the U.S. (1/31/61)
c. the first chimp trained to communicate with humans through sign language

d. Michael Jackson's pet chimp
e. the chimp on Dave Garroway's *Today* show
f. the chimp on the TV series *Daktari*
g. the chimp famous in the '50s for roller skating on TV
h. the monkey in Disney's *Aladdin*

SIMIAN CINEMA

Identify the movie (or series of movies) from which each of these scenes was taken. Correctly naming the movie or series is worth one point per picture, but just for fun, see how many of the actors and furry costars you can name. *1 point for each movie or series*

THROUGH THE YEARS

BY STEPHANIE SPADACCINI

Each of the 20 sets of clues below (lettered A through T) lists three events that took place during one of the past 20 centuries. There is one clue for each century from the 1st century A.D. through the 20th. Using your knowledge of history and a little logic, can you put the sets of clues in order?

ANSWERS, PAGE 185

CENTURIES

1st	2nd	3rd	4th	5th	6th	7th	8th	9th	10th	11th	12th	13th	14th	15th	16th	17th	18th	19th	20th
1	100	200	300	400	500	600	700	800	900	1000	1100	1200	1300	1400	1500	1600	1700	1800	1900	2000

A. Madame Tussaud leaves Paris and opens her wax museum in London.
The Siamese twins Chang and Eng marry sisters Sarah and Adelaide Yates.
Baseball clubs first play under Alexander Cartwright's standardized rules in Hoboken, New Jersey.

B. Macbeth is defeated by Malcolm, son of Duncan, at Dunsinane.
Westminster Abbey is built, and William the Conqueror begins construction of the Tower of London.
A supernova is visible in the daylight for 23 days, creating the Crab Nebula.

C. Shakespeare writes *Macbeth* based on events that took place more than five centuries earlier.
The dodo becomes extinct.
Santa Fe is founded in the first decade of the century.

D. Christopher Columbus dies in poverty and neglect in Spain.
Henry VIII is king of England.
Foods such as potatoes, peanuts, and chocolate are first brought to Europe from the Americas.

E. The Huns invade Europe and Russia.
Constantine the Great, the first Christian Roman emperor, prohibits work on Sundays.
Roman legions abandon Hadrian's Wall after maintaining it for more than 200 years.

F. The first crossword puzzle appears in the *New York World* newspaper.
Norwegian Roald Amundsen becomes the first person to reach the South Pole.
China abolishes slavery.

G. Mount Vesuvius erupts, burying Pompeii in lava, mud, and ashes.
Roman emperor Claudius is poisoned by Agrippina and is succeeded by her son, Nero.
Ovid is banished from Rome because of his poem *The Art of Love*.

H. Ferdinand and Isabella establish the Spanish Inquisition.
Leonardo da Vinci paints *The Last Supper* and Michelangelo begins his apprenticeship in Florence.
Six centuries after its discovery, coffee is introduced to Constantinople by the Turks

I. King John I is forced to sign the Magna Carta.
Genghis Khan dies at 65 after building an empire that stretches from the Pacific to Europe.
The moa, a giant bird of New Zealand, becomes extinct.

J. Roman emperor Hadrian orders construction of a 72-mile defensive wall in Britain.
The Greek physician Galen proves that blood, not air, flows through veins.
Emperor Commodus is murdered and succeeded by Septimius Severus.

K. Edmund Hoyle's *A Short Treatise on the Game of Whist* is published.
Madame Tussaud is imprisoned during the Reign of Terror.
Captain Cook rediscovers Hawaii 13 centuries after Hawaii-Loa sailed there.

L. Charlemagne becomes king of all the Franks.
The Moors invade Iberia and cross the Pyrenees, but are defeated at the Battle of Tours.
The world's first printed newspaper appears in China.

M. Construction begins in Paris on Notre Dame cathedral.
King Richard the Lion-Hearted is succeeded by King John I.
Thomas à Becket is murdered at Canterbury.

N. Pope Leo I persuades Attila to spare Rome, and the Huns eventually withdraw from Europe.
The Western Roman Empire falls, ushering in the Middle Ages.
Polynesian chief Hawaii-Loa sails 2,400 miles and discovers the Hawaiian Islands.

O. Notre Dame cathedral is completed after 182 years of construction.
Modern playing cards are developed in Europe.
Marco Polo dies in Venice, half a century after meeting Genghis Khan's grandson Kublai Khan.

P. Emperor Septimius Severus makes a royal visit to Britain.
Greek mathematician Diophantus writes the first book on algebra.
Gunpowder is invented by Chinese alchemists of the Wu dynasty.

Q. Vesuvius buries Pompeii again, 434 years after the initial eruption.
The emperor of China converts to Buddhism.
Mohammed is born in Mecca.

R. A 1000-volume encyclopedia is printed in China.
Leif Ericson arrives in North America around the last year of the century, nearly 500 years before Columbus's voyages.
Kyoto's five-story-high Daigo Pagoda is built over 29 years.

S. Mohammed dictates the Koran and begins to preach a new religion, Islam.
Pope Leo II heals the schism between Rome and Ravenna.
The Old English epic poem *Beowulf* is completed around the end of the century.

T. Charlemagne is succeeded as Holy Roman Emperor by his son Louis the Pious.
The Cyrillic alphabet is invented by two brothers, Cyril and Methodius.
Coffee is discovered in East Africa.

NEWS REELS

BY JEFF MORAN

Extra, extra! Watch all about it! The 12 newspaper headlines shown on these pages come straight off the screen from a dozen different movies. If you can identify nine or more of the films, you're an ace reporter!

ANSWERS, PAGE 185

1

2

3

4

5

6

7

8

9

10

11

12

BULL'S-EYE 20 QUESTIONS

BY WILL SHORTZ

Here's a test of your word "marksmanship." The answer to each of the 20 questions in the puzzle is one of the words in the bull's-eye target. Each answer scores a "hit," which you may cross off in the target since no answer word is used more than once. When all the clues have been answered, the unused words will form a comment by singer Sophie Tucker, when asked for some advice to live by. *ANSWER, PAGE 185*

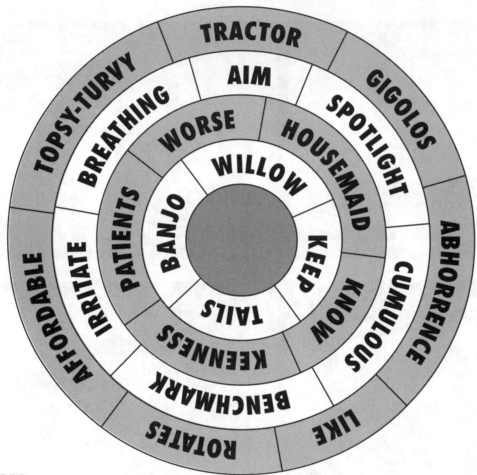

WHICH WORD ...

1. is pronounced the same as (but differs in spelling from) one of the words in the instructions above?
2. contains all five vowels?
3. would become a new word if you switched its second and fourth letters?
4. contains the name of a U.S. President hidden in consecutive letters?
5. would become a new word if prefixed with either "pro" or "con"?
6. contains the name of an article of apparel inside the name of another article of apparel?
7. is a noun, verb, adjective, and preposition?
8. sounds like a phrase meaning "won't pay up"?
9. contains three pairs of doubled letters?
10. would become a new word if you changed any of its individual letters to an R?
11. could be represented in a cryptogram by the word OPPONENT?

12. would, when spelled backward, become a phrase meaning "a musical performance for one person"?
13. is composed exclusively of letters in the second half of the alphabet?
14. would sound like a well-known "fort" if pronounced with a lisp?
15. would name a familiar kitchen appliance if its letters were properly rearranged?
16. starts and ends in a common man's name?
17. would, if you shifted each of its letters four letters later in the alphabet, become a word meaning "forest plants"?
18. would spell a word meaning "carried" if you removed all the letters in the odd-numbered positions?
19. could be either preceded or followed by "pin" to complete a new word?
20. has no letters in common with either of the two other remaining words?

ACROSS, DOWN, AND ALL AROUND: CROSSWORDS WITH A TWIST

HOPSCOTCH

BY TODD MCCLARY

This puzzle should keep you hopping. To solve it, you'll need to enter words into the grid in two ways. Answers to the Row clues are entered left to right in the correspondingly lettered row, one word after another in the order that they're clued. The answer to each of the remaining clues is "hopscotched" in the seven squares of the correspondingly numbered shaded or unshaded grid section. Each of these answers begins in the uppermost box of the section, moves down to the left, then right, down left, down left, right, and down left, as shown in the example. When the grid is filled in, the letters in the 14 boxes that stick out at the top and bottom of the grid will spell an occupation appropriate to plenty of "hopscotch."

ANSWERS, PAGE 186

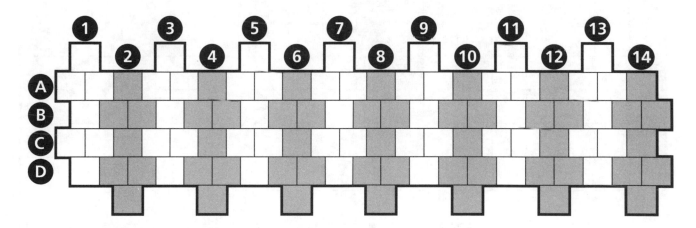

ROWS

A a Get out of bed
 b Australia's Great Barrier ___
 c Home of the Buccaneers
 d Video store rental
 e Voice one's weariness
B a Fit for some noblemen
 b Yoga instructor
 c Big event in high school

 d Entered the race
 e Stocking shades
C a Lesson reader, in church
 b Alternative to a convertible
 c Lions or Tigers or Bears
 d Wandering
D a Total
 b Indulge in leisure activities
 c Jai ___
 d End an argument

HOPSCOTCHES

1 They come with reins attached
2 Yield
3 Device for mixing oxygen into a liquid
4 *View of Toledo* painter: 2 wds.
5 One withholding permission
6 Doonesbury creator Garry

7 Widespread
8 Very versatile
9 Cereal that Wilford Brimley says is "the right thing to do"
10 Language of Biblical times
11 They'll get you in the can
12 Hide, or ooze
13 Like workers in *The Grapes of Wrath*
14 Pool predator

PENCIL POINTERS

BY JULIAN OCHRYMOWYCH

In this crossword, the clues appear in the grid itself. Enter the answers in the direction of the pointers.

ANSWER, PAGE 186

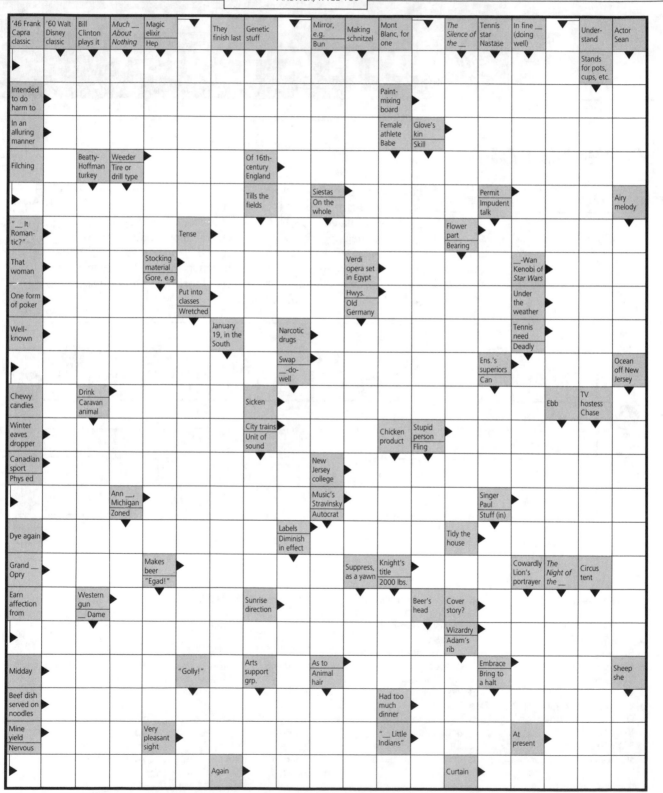

Cross Saws

BY N. M. MEYER

If "the best things come in small packages," as they say, then the nine puzzles on this page are among the best. In each one, we've taken the words of a familiar saying and joined them in a miniature crossword. Then we removed most of the letters, leaving just enough—we hope—to help you reconstruct the original saying. "He who hesitates is lost," so get to it!

ANSWERS, PAGE 186

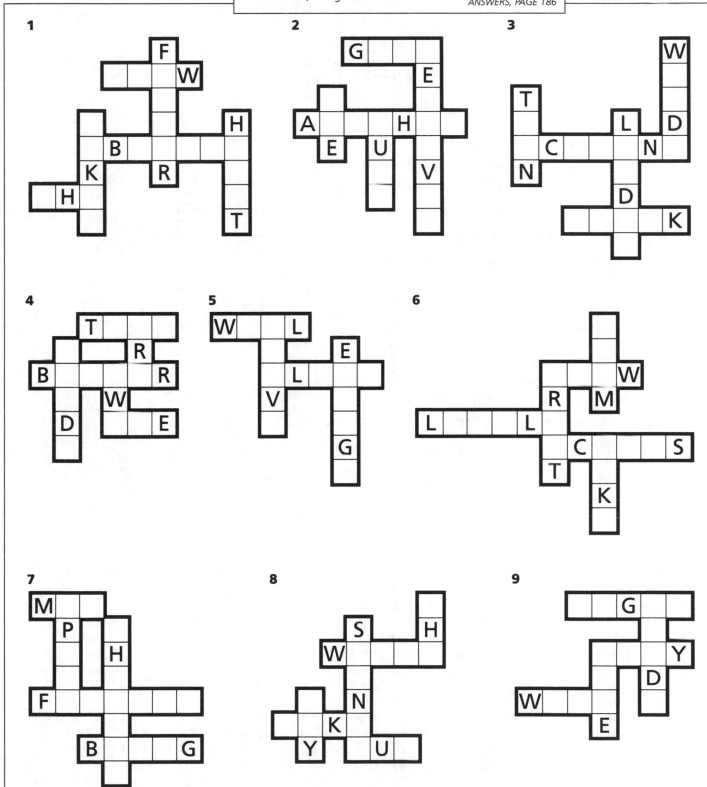

SPELL WEAVING

BY MIKE SHENK

The answers to this puzzle's clues form a continuous thread that is interwoven like a tapestry. Enter one letter per space, beginning in the top square numbered 1 and proceeding downward. When you reach an edge, make a right-angle turn, following the direction of the arrow on the corner. The first space of each answer is numbered to help keep you on the right track. Weave the right spells, and the puzzle will fill in like magic.

ANSWER, PAGE 186

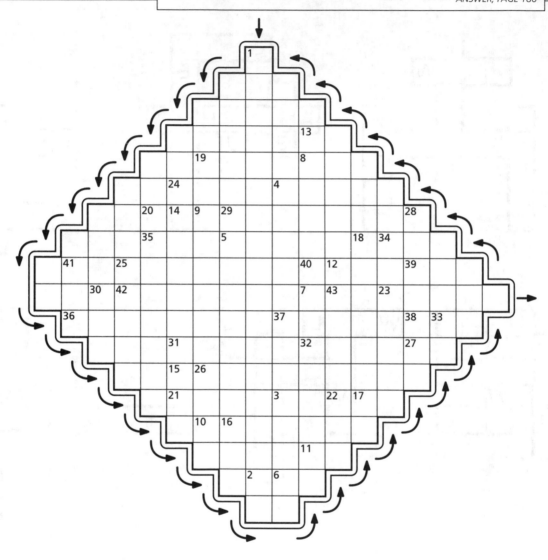

1 Sleight of hand
2 Decelerated
3 Practice for opening night
4 People with cut-and-dry jobs?
5 Ceremonies for new monarchs
6 Star of *The Bank Dick*: 3 wds.
7 Youngsters in wool coats
8 Striking

9 Jury member
10 Steak type
11 Contestant in the championship playoff
12 Golf ball feature
13 Long-range weapons
14 Overjoyed
15 Loony
16 Antiseptic tincture
17 Surrender: 2 wds.

18 Put to shame
19 Actress Miles
20 Homes of the masses?
21 Dress
22 Playing marbles
23 The Granite State: 2 wds.
24 "Sexy ___" (Beatles song)
25 Intertwined
26 Earth orbiter
27 Jerk

28 Tried hitchhiking
29 Daily diner choices
30 Guffaw
31 Shore or Manoff
32 Rid oneself, as of property
33 State-run numbers game
34 Lightly fanciful
35 State capital in the Prickly Pear Valley

36 Arthur's best knight
37 Road curves
38 Red Bordeaux wine
39 Fix
40 Jason's crew
41 Of military vessels
42 Of circulatory vessels
43 Boastful gambler

NEW DIRECTIONS

BY DAVID ELLIS DICKERSON

The answer to each clue in this puzzle begins in the correspondingly numbered space and proceeds in one of four directions—northwest, northeast, southwest, or southeast—with one letter per space. The letter in brackets after a clue gives you a start in determining the answer's direction. For example, [S] indicates the answer goes south: either southwest or southeast, which you must figure out from other answers in the grid. When you've completed the puzzle, every square will be used.

ANSWER, PAGE 186

  1 Los Angeles cagers [S]
  2 Cleanser named for a Trojan War hero [S]
  3 Kind of beer or canal [S]
  4 Lavish [S]
  5 Dexterity [S]
  6 Oscar winner James [S]
  7 Glittery fabric (2 wds.) [S]
  8 Summoned for consultation (2 wds.) [S]
  8 Frog's sound [W]
  9 Based in Washington, DC, perhaps [W]
 10 Maze obstacles [E]
 11 South Dakota's capital [N]
 12 Followed the course of [E]
 13 Keep out of the way of [N]
 14 "Star-Spangled Banner" fortifications [E]
 15 Good grade in the yeshiva? [S]
 16 One's share of the loot [W]
 17 Words to live by [W]
 18 Sign in a store window [E]
 19 Thin cut [W]
 20 Possible choices [N]
 21 Extremely long time [E]
 22 Tennis star Gabriela [E]
 23 Salad components [S]
 24 Mixed with another metal [W]
 25 Russian drinks [E]
 26 Indianapolis team [S]
 27 Adjective for modern publishing [W]
 28 It's wicked [N]
 29 Hailed vehicles [N]
 29 Thorax [N]
 30 How a bold hero often acts [N]
 31 Has longings [W]
 32 Sources of wild laughter? [N]
 33 Uses an aerosol can [W]
 34 Florida city [W]
 35 Writer France from France [N]
 36 Baloney [N]
 37 Toys that come with strings attached [N]
 38 *Rising Sun* star Wesley [N]

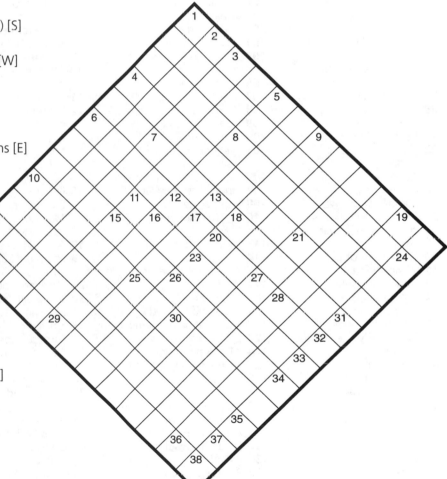

JUMBO CROSSWORD

BY COLIN GALE

ANSWER, PAGE 186

ACROSS

1 Summer wear
7 Breakfast treat
14 Emulates Cousteau
20 Popular dance in colonial America
21 Offer oneself for a job: 2 wds.
22 Report card signer
23 Sour beerlike drink of Britain
24 How good sentries do their jobs
25 Existing from birth
26 Laura Petrie's hubby
27 Traveled like Huck Finn
29 Comfort in times of sorrow
31 Pebble Beach peg
32 Common cause of drinking
35 Arizona river
36 Not written, as a test
37 Island east of Java
38 "Behold, a virgin shall conceive, and bear ___": 2 wds.
39 Gotten out of bed
41 Vampire attack
42 Dusk, poetically
44 Was briefly, suddenly bright
45 Champagne bucket
46 Targets of some suburban dogs
47 Weather map line
48 Takes the tiller
50 Life story, briefly
51 One kind of salts
53 Runs with an easy gait
55 "It's a ___ tell a lie": 2 wds.
57 Slaves away
58 Detergent ingredient
59 Bro's sibling
62 Ellipse section
64 Animated movie frame
65 Meet
67 Misfortunes: 2 wds.
71 Ribbed pants, for short
72 Roughly, in dates
73 French article
74 Clinton's alma mater
75 Rhino feature
76 You, now
77 Dance lesson part
79 Queen Guenevere's beloved: 2 wds.
83 Forty days after Ash Wednesday
84 So far: 2 wds.
86 Longing
87 Crooked
89 Avail oneself of
90 English architect Jones
91 Tiny amount in a recipe
93 Robert Louis Stevenson novel
95 Darwin's century
97 Blue
98 Actor Wallach
99 Comic's offering
100 Serpentine
101 Meeting for public discussion
103 Like a haunted house
107 Singing cowboy Gene
108 Football field feature
110 ___ roll (doing well): 2 wds.
111 Garlicky shrimp dish
114 Port sealers
115 Avoidance ploys, in Britain
117 O. Henry creation
118 Notorious Alphonse et al.
121 Beau's bow: 2 wds.
122 Fraternal order members
123 Shakes off, as a tail
124 "The Real Thing"
125 Twiddling one's thumbs
126 Sigher's cry
127 Just
128 '60s hit for Dion and the Belmonts: 2 wds.
131 Alice and Flo's boss
132 Dueler's assistant
134 Provoke
135 Prospector's find
136 Kinetoscope inventor
138 Attack verbally: 2 wds.
140 Aid for a hothead?: 2 wds.
142 Become depleted: 2 wds.
143 Comes into view
144 Gourmand's joy
145 Sorcerer's creations
146 Cart choice
147 Adds bias to

DOWN

1 Desert Storm weapons: 2 wds.
2 City in the shadow of Mauna Loa: 2 wds.
3 First ten-digit number: 2 wds.
4 Toupee, in slang
5 Onion slicer's output
6 General's ploy
7 Stand for knickknacks
8 Actress Quinn of *Annie*
9 Savage and Dryer
10 Chemin de ___ (casino game)
11 Real estate purchases
12 Praiser of the dearly departed
13 Chic
14 Mr. Clean competitor: 3 wds.
15 Chaplin prop
16 Ornate vase
17 Emma Thompson's *Much Ado About Nothing* role
18 Animal that's over the hill?
19 Four-time Super Bowl champs
28 Stocking type
30 In the direction the wind's blowing
33 Small brook
34 Perm palaces
36 Awards for off-Broadway shows
40 Summoned the butler
43 1960 Brenda Lee hit: 2 wds.
44 Job extra
47 Goes barnstorming
49 Company of "the man who wears the star"
52 Gym storage
53 Deafening
54 Hockey great Bobby et al.
56 Notebook section marker
58 Carried
59 Offer: 2 wds.
60 Church scenter
61 Kicked off
63 Bring to a halt
65 Olympics symbol
66 Steel plant
67 Going over 21
68 *My ___* (Willa Cather novel)
69 Transferring property
70 "Prince ___" (*Aladdin* song)
71 Twisted seashell
75 Submarine door
76 *Sliver* star Sharon
78 Congressional aide
80 Covered with fuzz
81 In the hospital: 2 wds.
82 Like Methuselah
85 Adds: 2 wds.
88 Color-mixing board
91 Bartlett, for one
92 Very black
93 Marx and Malden
94 Bakery buy
96 Lures
97 Enjoys a bubble bath
101 Deer's home
102 Island on which Father Damien worked
104 Contest in which everyone plays everyone else: 2 wds.
105 Close-minded
106 Subjects of spring searches: 2 wds.
107 In ___ (disordered): 2 wds.
108 Vanished
109 Time of *The Waltons* and Watergate
111 Old excursion boats
112 Phoned: 2 wds.
113 Long-lasting battery type
114 Spy's alias: 2 wds.
116 Migrant worker
119 Opposite of *sans*
120 Conditionally released
121 Cheap
124 Basketball or football player
129 Door feature
130 Model car sticker
132 Aretha's music
133 Clothing colors
137 Impresario Hurok
139 1040-publishing org.
141 Greek vowel

THE SPIRAL

BY WILL SHORTZ

This puzzle turns in two directions. The spiral's Inward clues yield a sequence of words to be entered counterclockwise in the spaces from 1 to 100. The Outward clues yield a different set of words to be entered clockwise from 100 back to 1. Fill in the answers, one letter per space, according to the numbers beside the clues. ANSWER, PAGE 186

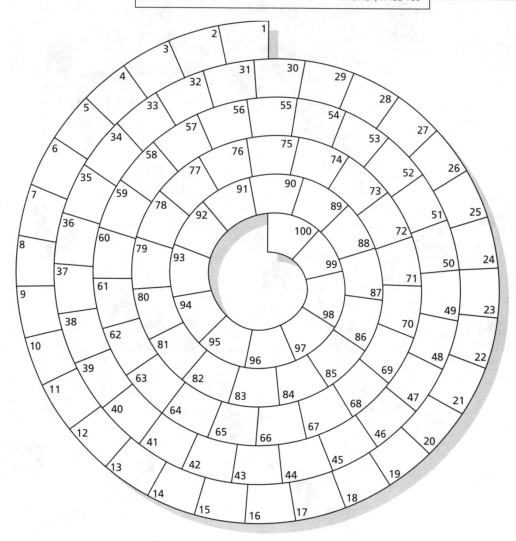

INWARD

1-5 "A Visit from St. Nicholas" poet Clement
6-11 It's attractive in a field
12-21 Opportune quality
22-30 Not true believers
31-35 English racetrack site
36-41 "The Last Frontier"
42-47 Washington city named for an Indian tribe
48-54 Old car named for a French explorer
55-58 Italian seaport
59-64 Catherine de ___ (wife of Henry II)
65-70 Cousin of the guinea pig
71-78 Without a social engagement
79-83 Rand-McNally product
84-87 Tiny hill-dwellers
88-94 Alfresco (hyph.)
95-100 Boxing sites

OUTWARD

100-96 More logical
95-90 French-built rocket that competes with NASA
89-81 ___ drip
80-73 Miniature pendant of threads, as on a Shriner's cap
72-68 Speak extemporaneously (hyph.)
67-60 Murder of a king
59-51 Popular women's fashion magazine
50-45 Deli meat
44-39 Eskimo canoes
38-33 Los ___, New Mexico
32-28 Actor Joe of *My Cousin Vinny*
27-21 Former presidential aspirant whose middle name is Ephemios
20-15 Mentally over the hill
14-9 Fingerless glove
8-1 Pinball arcade (2 wds.)

Petal Pushers

BY WILL SHORTZ

This flower is to be filled with 32 six-letter words answering the clues below the grid. Enter the words inward from the tips of the petals to the heart of the blossom, one letter per space. Half the words will proceed clockwise, the other half counterclockwise. Work from both sets of clues for a full bloom.

ANSWER, PAGE 186

CLOCKWISE

1 '60s TV western set at Fort Courage (2 wds.)
2 Star that shares its name with Orion's dog
3 Person who's "up" for a baseball game?
4 Poisonous, in a way
5 Perform, as a service
6 Prisoner's wish
7 *Vulpes vulpes* (2 wds.)
8 Closet item
9 Knitted in reverse stitches
10 Navigated a river, perhaps
11 Traveler's woe (2 wds.)
12 Pied Piper's follower
13 Al ___, major league's youngest-ever batting champion
14 Country singer Lyle
15 "Anything you want" (2 wds.)
16 Child's shooter

COUNTERCLOCKWISE

1 Incite
2 Popular spring break site, informally (2 wds.)
3 Swedish soprano Nilsson
4 "Groovy" (2 wds.)
5 Limit food supplies
6 Suppressed, as the emotions (hyph.)
7 Missile sites
8 Cattle tender
9 Like some cells or expense accounts
10 Seek, as political office (2 wds.)
11 Bureaucratese, e.g.
12 Knee jerk, for one
13 He taught the "sweathogs" on TV
14 Scooped soup
15 Gas pump sign (2 wds.)
16 Making a road

HELTER-SKELTER

BY JULIAN OCHRYMOWYCH

Helter-Skelter is a crossword variation in which the answers interlock in eight different directions. To solve, write the answer to each clue beginning in the grid square corresponding to the clue number and proceeding in a straight line toward—and, if necessary beyond—the next consecutive number. The first two answers—TOPAZ and ZEAL—have been entered in Helter-Skelter #1 as examples. When each puzzle is completed, every square in the grid will be filled.

ANSWERS, PAGE 187

HELTER-SKELTER #1

11			4	10		3 L
	17				16	A
12		20	21		15	E
			1 T	O	P	A Z
5	18		7			8
		19				22
			25	9		
13	14		6	24		23

HELTER-SKELTER #2

6			5	15		14
7					8	
	21		22			1
		23		24	12	13
	20				19	
3			4			
10		11				25
9		2		17	16	18

1 November birthstone
2 Enthusiasm
3 From the neighborhood
4 Set one's sights on, as a target: 2 wds.
5 Very soft mineral
6 Bartender's concoction
7 Palindromic boat
8 One-time New York mayor Ed
9 Like British crosswords
10 Friend of Hobbes, in the comics
11 Football's "Broadway Joe"
12 "Chances Are" singer
13 Don Quixote's squire ___ Panza
14 Dogpatch creator: 2 wds.
15 Expert
16 French resort area
17 40th President
18 Actor David ___ of *Rhoda*
19 Poem part
20 Ship's pole
21 Bridge
22 Siesta
23 Eeyore's friend
24 Storytelling dance
25 Home of the Bruins, for short

1 Made sound
2 Loud noise
3 New-fangled
4 Pink-purple flowers
5 Boom type
6 Require payment of, as a loan: 2 wds.
7 Peach's kin
8 Israeli city: 2 wds.
9 Milk shake choice
10 Buenos ___
11 Horse controller
12 Badminton need
13 Defrost
14 Holmes's chronicler
15 Pedicure targets
16 Broadway dog
17 Poisonous snakes
18 Planned undertaking
19 Game played on a fronton: 2 wds.
20 Kin of PDQ
21 Pond scum, usually
22 Fed: Hyph.
23 Eeyore's creator
24 Vientiane's country
25 Foot, to a fathom

SIAMESE TWINS

BY MIKE SHENK

This puzzle gives you two grids for the price of one. And two sets of clues to go with them, so you can work both crosswords at the same time. What's the catch? Each clue number is followed by two different clues to two different answers. The puzzle is to figure out which answer goes in which grid. The answers to 1-Across have been filled in for you.

ANSWERS, PAGE 187

ACROSS

1 Bart Simpson's dad ...
... and his mom
6 Filled with NaCl
Indiana hoopsters
12 Labor group
Puccini creation
13 African nation in the news, 1993
German baker's treat
14 Popular
Ready to drop
15 One way to be mad
Winter breakfast
16 "How sweet ___!" (Gleason line): 2 wds.
Crumb carriers
17 California's Big ___
Toothpaste type
18 Wise person
Party spread
19 Yon woman
Good name, for short
20 Word in many whodunit titles
Baseball Hall-of-Famer Ernie
22 Abel, to Adam
Drunk
23 Steering-wheel-to-wheel link: 2 wds.
Immediately: 3 wds.
26 Navy commandos
Irrationally extreme
27 Smart guy
Pentagon bigwigs
30 Polaris's place: 2 wds.
Fainted: 2 wds.
33 Singer Cole
Capitol worker, for short
36 Gin-flavoring berries
Pumps, e.g.
37 "___ you sleeping?"
Be in arrears
38 Refinery rocks
Showy flower
40 Bankroll
Print units
41 For men only
Blueprint
42 Cockpit worker
Cookie contents
44 Magician's word
Spanish hero: 2 wds.
45 Estevez et al.
Politician's aide
46 Treaty grp., 1954-77
Kind of ear or tube
47 Fume: 2 wds.
Like top players
48 Goaded on
Fancy sheet material

DOWN

1 *Far and Away* director
Stubborn
2 Daytime TV's ___ *World*
Starting bids
3 Product from Mrs. Lovett, in *Sweeney Todd*: 2 wds.
Where the fashionable French swim
4 Blunders
Leaves
5 Football lineman
Bob's partner
6 In the raw: 2 wds.
The Color of Money props: 2 wds.
7 Guitarist's aid
Curator's concern
8 Milliner's wares
Sugar serving
9 Brainstorms
Inventor Howe
10 "Swell!"
Fab Four drummer
11 Bob of TV's *Full House*
Actress Burstyn
13 Clip
Healthy
17 Is approved: 3 wds.
Man's cologne fragrance
20 Tries to save the boat
Sandwich shops
21 Puts on the payroll
Boot parts
24 Wane
Kilmer of *The Doors*
25 Catch, as crooks
Tie the knot
28 Jazz fan: 2 wds.
Usher's duty
29 Much-liked cake brand: 2 wds.
Persian Gulf nation native
31 Copier need
Paint layers
32 Sinew
Look upon
33 Furniture store buys
More pleasant
34 Wear down
Kitchen come-on
35 Audacity
Basketball score
39 Pajama material
Jail, in slang
41 Lennon-McCartney creation
Entreaty
43 Tall tale
Exploit
44 Lisper's problem
Be a contender

RIDDLE-DEE-DEE

This puzzle, dear friends, from a crossword departs; so heed this before you attempt any starts. No black squares appear, but instead heavy bars to show where the words go—the puzzle's true stars. The clues are all riddles of more than one kind—old-fashioned for one; some with wordplay you'll find. We hope you'll enjoy this and utter no curse, as you go through our riddles from not bad to verse!

BY PATRICK BERRY

ANSWER, PAGE 186

ACROSS

1 Skinny and of common stock;
Afraid of scissors but not of rock.

5 A ceremony, I am guessin',
That's many a child's first swimming lesson.

11 Voices without mouths or throats or lungs,
They know no language but answer all tongues.

13 I am the bridge from night to day,
Where live men go and dead men stay.

14 Above the feet, below the head,
It's where we keep our daily bread.

16 A "T" at the front of this word causes fright;
Remove it again—that doesn't seem right.

17 A way of referring at once, if you know it,
To the two grand sons of Ezra, the poet.

18 A world of wonder and surprise
Seen only when you close your eyes.

20 It's illegal to do this wherever you roam,
And simply impossible while you're at home.

21 What cannot be given or taken away,
Yet everyone has it, and has more each day?

22 If you don't walk to get to school,
You could do this—and be a fool.

24 This food provokes a bit of thought—
Is it a bread or is it knot?

26 This softheaded fellow's a pleasure to meet;
Ignore him, he'll cry, but kiss him, he's sweet. (2 wds.)

30 On either side of a wall stands a brother;
They look all around, but can't see each other.

33 Bridge of light from sun to ground;
In notes, precedes me with its sound.

34 Not chefs and not waiters, this much I can tell,
You'll find they still serve many hams very well.

36 Small stout man with hand on hip,
Big on mouth but thin on lip.

37 To succeed at this task, you'll have to try
To see with your fingers—and pull with your eye!

40 I'm a silvery metal with low value rating,
I'll always be used to make coating and plating.

41 Unlike the door in a riddle of fame,
When I'm halfway open, I'm still just the same.

42 Two by two by two—my word!—
Had some snacks, or so I've heard.

43 Keeper of the gold of kings
Embraces death as pain she brings.

44 I catch the fish but never eat them,
Have no kids but often beat them.

45 I'm king of my lands with a huntress for bride,
And she and my children are truly my pride.

46 I keep what you see, what you hear, what you say;
But to have it again, you must ask me to play.

47 Who knows everything and nothing at all;
Doesn't feel pain and stands fifty feet tall? (2 wds.)

48 My head is large, my feet are small,
Nothing can stand where my tiny feet fall.

DOWN

1 I'm a bug that bugs, or a noise that annoys,
Or a crow that crows as your crops it destroys.

2 We may die a thousand deaths; we may break a thousand hearts;
It's never cause for worry: We live our lives in parts.

3 Be they gloomy or cheerful, restrained or verbose,
It's how people talk when they're not very close.

4 If you can do this, then you're doing it now;
If you can't and you're this far, I don't quite see how.

6 We're trees of the forest, yet set us aflame,
And when it's all over, we'll still be the same.

7 It's the greatest persuader I ever have heard,
Small wonder it's known as a true magic word.

8 We're tiny but still we can cause quite a fuss:
If we're in your house, then your house is in us.

9 What is riddled with holes, Yet holds water like bowls?

10 Inventor of code with a small bit of lunch;
Not much to chew, and not much to munch.

12 On your knee or your arm it can cause biting pain;
Take off the end and not much will remain.

15 What's not a game, yet may be played;
Is never seen, but often made?

19 This word describes Susan, who likes to move 'round,
And many a loafer, or so I have found.

20 A figure builders often ignore,
Which leads to a building that's missing a floor.

23 I'm part of a riddle, an organ, a cell,
A map or a room in a run-down motel.

25 I am the child of the storm and the sun,
Irish folk know there's a pot where I'm done.

27 A place that's truly filled with sin,
Where many lose and few can win.

28 I'm the chains of a ghost, the toy of a child,
The warnings of serpents who live in the wild.

29 It's the ruination of human bliss—
The man who has everything often wants this.

31 I'm one of but seven, and these are the others:
Biggest and smallest, cold, dark, and two brothers.

32 Deadly widow, dressed in black,
Keeps her children in a sack.

35 Your hands have ten, and ten has two,
And two has one—and *that's* your clue.

36 Though I sound like a proof mark or food for a bunny,
I'm really a measure of stones—and of money.

38 Bedeviled and beaten, often named for a spy,
Yet to birds there is nothing essential as I.

39 The answer to this one is rather sublime,
But you'll figure it out; it's a question of time.

41 Some say we've made an odd alliance:
We share an Apple with a horde of Giants.

SHORT STUFF

BY PATRICK BERRY

Ready to challenge your IQ? All the answers in this small crossword puzzle are acronyms, abbreviations, initials, and other short all-capital-letters stuff. Consider yourself a VIP if you can fill in the entire grid without help; if you get stuck, though, looking at the answers is OK.

ANSWER, PAGE 187

ACROSS

1 President Ford's economic plan
4 England, Wales, Scotland, and Northern Ireland
6 First state admitted to the Union
8 George Bush once headed it
9 Murphy Brown's news show
11 Disease of the central nervous system
12 Sign at a packed theater
14 Closing for an invitation
16 Pronto
18 Zone between Pacific and Central
19 Home of the Rams
20 Sprint rival
22 School bake sale sponsor, often
25 Regulatory agency for business
27 Jim Bakker's The ___ Club
29 Army duty often meted out as punishment
30 Club for club users?
32 Kind of party thrown by cheapskates
34 Fictional Cincinnati radio station
36 TV station on The Mary Tyler Moore Show
37 Rating of The Age of Innocence
38 Organization symbolized by a caduceus
40 Method of payment
43 Blood type

44 Company that puts out Superman comics
45 Tooth care group

DOWN

1 Rest room
2 in old Rome
3 Endeavour's launchers
4 Alien transport
5 "Derby" state
6 Place to wait for a license
7 Clairvoyance
10 April collectors
13 Platter speed unit
15 Brand of motor oil additive
16 Sitcom featuring an extraterrestrial creature
17 College entrance exam
18 New England school noted for math and science
21 Professional bookkeeper/ auditor
23 Boxing bout outcome
24 "Calling all cars ..." announcement
26 Lifesaving technique
28 Creator of "The Great Society"
31 4.0, for a college whiz
33 Village People song
34 New Deal agency
35 Soviet spy agency
36 Military female
39 Physician
41 Take too much of a drug
42 Prosecutor for the people

THE WORLD'S MOST ORNERY CROSSWORD

BY MIKE SHENK

Variety Pack

The crossword on this and the next two pages has two independent sets of clues: "Hard" and "Easy." First, fold this page back on the dashed line so the clues below face the solving grid on page 39. If you use only the Hard Clues (appearing below and continuing under the grid), you'll find the puzzle uncommonly challenging. If you want help, or prefer a less severe challenge, open to the Easy Clues (tucked in beneath your fold on page 146).

FOLD THIS PAGE

HARD CLUES

ACROSS

1 I Don't Give a Darn, in a comedy routine
10 "Man partly is, and wholly ___ be": Browning
17 Gas thief's aid
23 She played Glinda in The Wiz
24 Ste. Thérèse's birthplace
25 Designer's edge
26 Ahead
27 "The Far Side" cartoonist et al.
28 A Current Affair reports
29 Gen. Bragg's org.
30 Slavery
32 Short-winded
33 Start of an encyclopedia's Volume 1 title
34 Stewbum
35 1988 Olympics host
37 Mah-jongg piece
38 Rundown place
39 Stirs
41 Organic compound ending
42 Selma Lagerlöf hero
43 Warning sign
44 Planetary track
46 All there
47 Superman's Krypto
48 Made bad news less traumatic
51 Apt. coolers
52 Astronaut's quaff
53 Forte of Belli and Bailey

54 ___ Palmas (largest city in the Canary Islands)
55 "Stop already!"
57 Suffers a crush
58 Supergiant of the summer sky
62 Pauline's lot
64 Con man, at times
66 Institute
67 Lively, to Leinsdorf
69 Arthur et al.
70 Queen Victoria wasn't
74 Escort offerer
75 Ring need
76 Complete 180
78 Get mad
79 London's ___ of Court
80 Fabrics derived from wood pulp
81 Flophouse bed, in Britain
82 Fiedler's command, 1930-79
83 Road curve
84 AAA map abbr.
85 Speed-the-Plow playwright
86 Doll's cry
88 Dugout, e.g.
89 Louvre entrance designer
90 Central
91 Ned Beatty's Superman role
92 Sub's kin
93 It's just under a cup
95 Present accessories
96 Nureyev and Baryshnikov
98 Cheesy treat

99 Mensa offering
100 Military group
101 La Motta's portrayer
102 Eccentric fellow
103 "Cheers 'n' Jeers" publisher
105 Ouzo flavoring
106 Collector's interest
108 Spode and Staffordshire
109 Corrupt
111 Finishing strokes
114 Eight-time Peter Lorre role
116 Member of Lenny Wilkens's team
117 Unsweetened
118 Tickbirds
119 Hairdo holder
120 Arrangement in Gray and Black No. 1
127 Speedway area
128 The Harlequin's Carnival artist
129 Opposite of presto
130 Dune duke
131 Writer Jaffe
132 Marilu on Evening Shade
133 Bank
135 Boom or mast
136 Bride's wear
137 Probably gonna
139 Hoss's pa
140 Out of sorts
141 Become unruly
143 Foist
145 Unprocessed
146 Put up
148 TV spokestuna
150 Unfashionable
152 Groups
153 American League MVP of 1988

THE WORLD'S MOST ORNERY CROSSWORD (CONTINUED)

Don't Peek Until You Read Page 145!

ANSWER, PAGE 187

EASY CLUES

ACROSS

1 Infielder between second and third base
10 Has aspirations toward: 2 wds.
17 Draining tube
23 "Stormy Weather" songstress: 2 wds.
24 French lace-making city (NON-LACE anag.)
25 Skirt's edge
26 Out front: 3 wds.
27 "The Far Side" cartoonist Gary and family
28 Uncovers
29 Jefferson Davis's side: Abbr.
30 *Of Human ___* (Maugham novel)
32 Concise
33 From ___ Z: 2 wds.
34 Drunkard
35 Where *M*A*S*H* took place
37 Bathroom floor piece
38 Garbage truck destination
39 Noisy commotions
41 Direction opposite WSW
42 Rocker Lofgren
43 Sign of things to come
44 Travel around a planet
46 Not crazy
47 Poodle or Peke
48 Made a shock less severe: 3 wds.
51 Cooling appliances: Abbr.

52 Distinctive flavor
53 TV's *L.A. ___*
54 ___ Vegas
55 Sufficient amount
57 ___ on (is overly fond of)
58 Star in the summer sky (RAN EAST anag.)
62 Dangers
64 Swindler
66 Discovered
67 Lively, in music (IOTA MAN anag.)
69 Actresses Benaderet and Arthur
70 Entertained
74 Model T maker
75 Alternative to mittens
76 Driver's reversal of direction
78 Brush part
79 Taverns
80 Synthetic fabrics
81 British flophouse (SODS anag.)
82 Bursts, as a balloon
83 Lisper's problem letter
84 Highway: Abbr.
85 Playwright David
86 Daddy's wife
88 Indian's boat
89 Architect I.M.
90 Center: Prefix
91 Singer Redding
92 Protagonist
93 Flying ___ (UFO)
95 Ribbons
96 They leave countries for political reasons
98 Melted cheese or chocolate dish
99 Intelligence exam: 2 wds.
100 Mile or meter

101 Actor Robert of *Cape Fear*
102 Strange old geezer
103 Magazine for viewers: 2 wds.
105 Licorice-flavored herb
106 Painting or sculpture: 2 wds.
108 Tea services
109 Polluted
111 Finishes a golf hole
114 Japanese detective of books and films: 2 wds.
116 Cleveland basketballer, for short
117 Arid
118 Black cuckoos
119 Toothpaste type
120 Famous painting of a woman in a chair: 2 wds.
127 Cherry seed
128 Painter Joan
129 Slowly, in music
130 Mother of Artemis and Apollo (TOLE anag.)
131 Columnist Barrett
132 Actress Gardner
133 Accumulate
135 Practice boxing
136 Bride's face covering
137 ___ be (likely): 2 wds.
139 Kingsley or Vereen
140 Sick
141 Misbehave: 2 wds.
143 Dispose of by fraud: 2 wds.
145 Uncooked
146 Built
148 Movie great Chaplin

150 Old-fashioned
152 Puts into categories
153 Baseball slugger Jose
154 Miami resident
155 Views again
156 Have lunch delivered: 2 wds.
157 Nickel's value: 2 wds.

DOWN

1 Oil spill
2 Muppets creator Jim and family
3 Toronto's province
4 Cheering word
5 John Jakes historical novel: 2 wds.
6 Song for one
7 New Jersey's capital
8 Stop ___ (come to a quick halt): 3 wds.
9 Propelled a bike
10 Patriot Nathan
11 Ending for "plug" or "pay"
12 Bother
13 Small musical groups
14 Arachnid with a stinging tail
15 Great weights
16 Beginning
17 Church maintainers
18 Place, as a fine
19 Arafat's group: Abbr.
20 Made derisive sounds to, as a villain: 2 wds.
21 Two-person basketball game
22 Moneys saved for future use: 2 wds.
25 Aspirin's target

31 ___ *Prefer Blondes*
36 Regions inhabited by sprites
38 "Nice and easy ___": 2 wds.
40 Mock orange trees
45 Half-price tickets
49 Ram's mate
50 Badgering
52 Donut shape, in geometry (ROUTS anag.)
56 ___ Bator, Mongolia
57 Death
58 Declared as true
59 Midday
60 Went to bed: 2 wds.
61 Deli meats
62 Rotate about a point
63 Obnoxious braggart
65 Homeowner's place to park
68 Poet Alfred
69 Phone's in-use sound: 2 wds.
71 "Speed up": 3 wds.
72 Differently
73 Ceased
75 Annoy: 2 wds.
77 Newsman Brokaw
78 Plant used in folk cures (NO BEETS anag.)
82 Walked about nervously
85 Finicky feline
87 Fort ___, California
88 "The first ___ the deepest": 2 wds.
92 Nocturnal bird: 2 wds.
94 Aftershave brand: 2 wds.

95 Short skating leap: 2 wds.
97 Presents
98 Shape
102 Poet William ___ Williams
104 Actor Mature
105 ___ controller (control tower worker)
107 Green gems
108 Place to keep change: 2 wds.
110 *Much ___ About Nothing*
111 Goldilocks tried his porridge: 2 wds.
112 Astronomy subject
113 Female giant of myth
115 Stephen King book reissued with extra material: 2 wds.
119 Lime-gin drinks
121 Page-fastening gadget
122 Tell quickly: 2 wds.
123 They lead to responses
124 ___ cocktail (explosive)
125 Get on the express
126 Machine gun sound
128 ___ d' (restaurant employee)
134 Vanzetti's partner
138 Country singer Buck
142 Burn on the outside
143 Lowly worker
144 Aft's opposite
147 Track star Sebastian
149 Here: Fr.
151 Ike's monogram

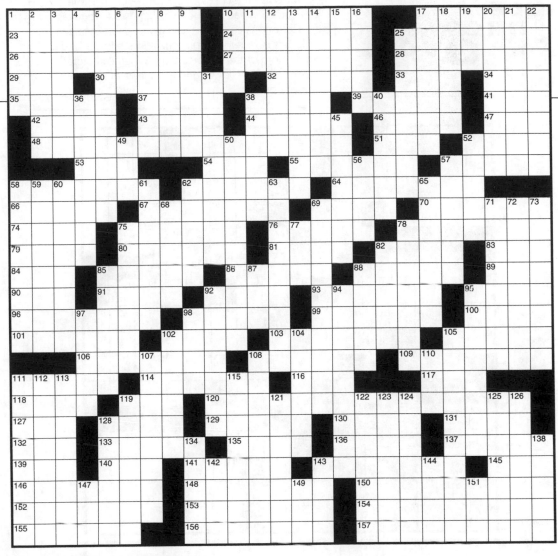

HARD CLUES (CONTINUED)

154 Disney World employee, e.g.
155 Sits through a second showing of
156 Get a pizza, perhaps
157 Inscription beneath Monticello

DOWN

1 Glossy mag
2 Jim ___ *Muppet Babies*
3 Second-largest province
4 Sidelines cry
5 First book in the Kent Family Chronicles
6 Without help
7 U.S. capital in 1790

8 One way to stop
9 Rode a Schwinn
10 Golfer Irwin
11 Wave, to Juan
12 Unsettle
13 Coordinated outfits
14 Desert stinger
15 Cargo measurement
16 Inception
17 Church bell ringers
18 Be a nuisance
19 Grp. recognized by the U.N. in 1976
20 Greeted, as a villain
21 1977 Robby Benson movie
22 IRAs, e.g.
25 Inconvenience
31 They hold doors

36 Mythical realms
38 "Nobody ___ Better"
40 Inedible oranges
45 Special offers
49 Sheared she
50 Vexation
52 Inner tube, geometrically
56 Red, in Mongolian
57 End
58 1978 Triple Crown winner
59 When shadows are shortest
60 Fingered
61 Greek island, site of a 480 B.C. battle
62 Turning point
63 Blowhard
65 House adjunct

68 "The Highwayman" poet
69 Caller's bane
71 "Hurry!"
72 On the other hand
73 Stopped
75 Irritate
77 Huck's pal
78 Tea-making plant
82 Showed nervousness
85 Old pantomime dance
87 Like first, third, etc.: Abbr.
88 Skin layer
92 Haunted forest resident
94 "Thanks—I needed that" brand
95 Figure-skating leap

97 Donations
98 Application blank
102 Villain in Ludlum's Bourne books
104 Champion
105 Control tower concern
107 Most valuable gems
108 Change place
110 ___ Annie (*Oklahoma!* character)
111 Hard bed occupant
112 Cosmology study
113 Rhea or Mnemosyne
115 Stephen King epic
119 Citrus cocktails
121 Desk accessory

122 Recite rapidly
123 Incentives
124 Stalin colleague
125 Board the Metroliner
126 Tommy gun sound
128 ___ de ballet (dance trainer)
134 Codefendant Nicola
138 1936 Olympics track star
142 Flat cleaner
143 Field worker
144 Cry at St. Andrews
147 Tucker ___ (Donald Westlake pseudonym)
149 Not *là*
151 HST successor

DOUBLE DROP QUOTE

BY TIMOTHY TEBBE

As you solve the crossword below, you'll find there's one square in each of the 16 columns that requires two letters instead of the usual one. Drop each pair of letters in order into the square in the lower grid at the bottom of the same column. When completed, the letters in the lower grid will spell a quotation by Andy Rooney.

ANSWER, PAGE 188

ACROSS

1 Optimally
7 Harvard and Yale, for example
12 Short flight
15 *The Challenge to Liberty* author
16 Intimate
17 Top draft status
18 Wheaties endorser, typically
19 Gangster's gat
20 Umbrella part
21 Hospital units
22 Liable
24 A million to one, e.g.
26 Instruction sheet item
27 Garbage bag layer
28 Like Felix Unger
29 Nickel cigar
33 Go downhill, in a way
35 Blindly imitate
37 Mischievous boy of the comics
39 Hill makers
41 Kuwaiti, e.g.
44 *Candid Camera* creator
46 Poorly
48 Towel inscription
50 "L'etat," to Louis XIV
51 Letter from the Thessalonians
52 Widespread
54 Jodie Foster role
56 Roderick Usher's creator
58 Reign of the glaciers
59 Check-cashing needs
61 Gum amount
63 Provides with funding
64 Standards
67 Rave's opposite
69 Young & Rubicam output
71 Takes care of
73 Bart's sister
74 Baker's dozen
78 Append
79 Shop sight
81 Give a new look to
83 Mint punch
84 They make lots
85 Writer Leonard
86 Lawn section
87 Electrician's target
88 Performed camels

DOWN

1 Starbuck's captain
2 Sweets-sweet link
3 Intrepid
4 Nights, in classifieds
5 Match part
6 Pick up the tab
7 Helms position?
8 Flying formation
9 In the least
10 Jermaine's sister
11 Ferry tail
12 Multitude
13 Silverware brand
14 Blue Ribbon company
23 Livens (up)
25 Dead duck
26 Show "about nothing"
27 Cream purchase
29 Bait-and-switch, e.g.
30 Eagle ___ (car make)
31 North, familiarly
32 Collapse
34 Krazy ___
36 Resplendent residences
38 Fruitcake
40 Peppermint Patty, to Marcie
42 Leading
43 Game that's called
45 Carpet feature
47 Son of Jacob
49 Crockpot concoctions
52 Shell game need
53 Broadway's Cariou
55 Shopping aid
57 Hold
60 Common quiche ingredient
62 Lecturer hall feature
64 *The Masai,* e.g.
65 Call for backup, perhaps
66 Watched over
68 Elroy's pet
70 Challenges
72 Sighed word
73 For fear that
74 Kenneth's wife
75 No-show in a 1952 play
76 *Sommersby* star
77 Winter glider
80 Yon ship
82 Red deer's kin

Marching Bands

BY MIKE SHENK

The words in this puzzle march around the grid in two ways. In one formation ("Rows"), words march across—two words for each numbered line, reading consecutively from left to right. The dividing point between these answers is for you to determine, except in row 7, where the words are separated by a black square. In the second formation ("Bands"), words march around each of the six shaded and unshaded bands, starting at the lettered squares (A, B, C, D, E, and F) and proceeding in a clockwise direction, one word after another. For example, Band A, when filled, will contain seven consecutive words (a through g) starting in square A and reading around the perimeter of the grid. Band B will contain a series of six words (a through f) starting in square B. Again, the dividing points between these answers are for you to determine. All clues are given in order. When the puzzle is completed, each square in the grid will have been used once in a Row word and once in a Band word.

ANSWER, PAGE 188

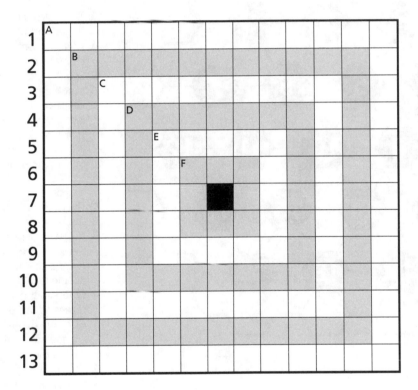

ROWS

1 a Jacket joint
b Spiral galaxy close to our own
2 a Composer who loved George Sand
b More garish
3 a Singer/ songwriter James
b Wireless inventor
4 a Jeans material
b Ontario, e.g.
5 a Persian Gulf princes
b Playwright Rattigan and others
6 a Turn for Kasparov
b Greenpeace scientist
7 a Watches for
b Role originally played in the movies by Pal
8 a Ziggy Marley's music
b Twist's creator

9 a Proverb
b Clear and unmistakable
10 a Discussion groups
b They deal in checks and balances

11 a For real
b Rates
12 a Painter's protector
b Blind alley: Hyph.
13 a Go by
b Salk discovery

BANDS

A a Tar
b Caravan critters
c Midterms, e.g.
d Like the Grand Canyon

e Spelunking sites
f Most ashen
g Ambulance worker
B a Longing
b Theater groups
c Boosted
d Gambler's asset
e Buddy
f 19th Amendment beneficiaries
C a English class concern
b Dictionary writer's skill
c School paper
d Moon goddess
e MacLeod of *The Love Boat*
D a On the mend
b Chef's pans
c More likely to become a Rockette
E a Platter player
b Book before Romans
c Brainstorm
F a Crashes

HEX SIGNS

BY MIKE SHENK

Each answer in this puzzle is six letters long. These six letters are to be entered into the six hexagons surrounding the appropriate number in the grid, reading clockwise or counterclockwise. The direction and the starting space are for you to determine. Each clue consists of a sentence from which the consecutive letters of the answer have been removed and replaced with a star. The object is to reinstate the missing letters (supplying spacing as needed) to complete a sensible sentence. For example, the answer to #1 is ALMOST, which completes the sentence "In the king's reALM, OSTentatious displays are nearly always forbidden." As a bonus hint, each clue also contains a synonym or short definition of the answer (like "nearly" in the example).

ANSWER, PAGE 188

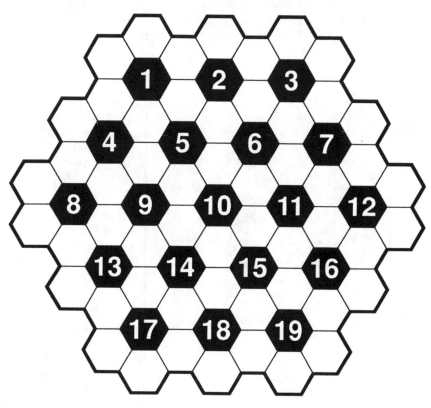

1 In the king's re★entatious displays are nearly always forbidden.
2 The wi★ks lecture on piety to their less educated brethren.
3 The newspa★d to be read more before the advent of TV.
4 An argumentative person's li★pically shorter than a good-natured person's.
5 Scoring a home r★e way to bring togetherness to the team.
6 While celebrities may need to travel incognito, those of us lacking acclaim sh★lasses indoors.
7 If a naughty boy is staying with you, it may be smart to lock yo★a cupboard.
8 For a culinary treat, try asking the ch★ortoni.
9 Tom Sawyer's natural friendliness put Huck F★ase.
10 A new artilleryman is likely to find all the shootin★ving.
11 An aristoc★eneral won't associate with people in a lower social class.
12 When visiting New Del★ajah always comes to this place.
13 After the game, the winning players left the aren★phantly to meet their fans in the courtyard.
14 This pottery glaze was created years ago by som★ess artisan.
15 You can bet that people who say they seldom make an erro★ing.
16 An uncooperative patient can be somewhat difficult fo★apist.
17 I like any flavor of bubb★xcept perhaps peanut butter.
18 If you want to con★ricists when they're blue, you only need to praise their songs.
19 During the Gold Rush, you'd find many prospector★ing favor with claim office workers.

SPLIT ENDS

BY WILL SHORTZ

Each clue in this crossword has been cut into two parts, and the parts have been given numbers from 1 to 78. To solve the puzzle, find and rejoin each matching pair of clue parts to produce the original clue. Enter the answer to each clue at the grid space indicated by the sum of the numbers of the clue's two parts. For example, #50 and #38 below combine to form the clue "Part of/A jigsaw puzzle." The answer, PIECE, is filled in at #88 (50 + 38). Either part of the clue may appear first in the numbered list. Every part will be used exactly once in the completed puzzle.

ANSWER, PAGE 188

CLUES

1 Rabbit's	21 Tracks	41 To a typesetter	60 Elevator
2 A "Santa"	22 Famous in horseracing	42 Painting time	61 Turkey's
3 On a traffic light	23 Art of shaping	43 Drug	62 Baseball Hall-of-Famer
4 Wife (hyph.)	24 Women's attire	44 Figure	63 A Harley
5 The hula	25 "Sightings"	45 The capital of Peru	64 A "sneak"
6 Bean named for	26 To get on with things	46 Alpha	65 A unicycle
7 They fly in a	27 Person who might do	47 Bottom line	66 Of an addition
8 Snack	28 Egg	48 Trees	67 Woody
9 Assignment	29 Eggs	49 Preliminary	68 A son's
10 Eight-and-a-half	30 It sank	50 Part of	69 Subject of many
11 Middle color	31 Eager	51 Or Czech, for example	70 Enclosure
12 English class	32 Pole	52 Musial	71 Nationality
13 Criminal who's	33 That catches insects	53 Doubled	72 Inventor
14 Consolidation	34 Sex or status	54 Sticky surface	73 Where words of a feather
15 Tennessee	35 Egg-shaped	55 It immediately follows	74 Smoked in a pipe
16 *Star Trek*'s Uhura	36 Film director	56 High-priced fish	75 Has one
17 Person who rides	37 Flock together	57 Rank for	76 Saddam Hussein's
18 Muslim	38 A jigsaw puzzle	58 Leave as is,	77 Location, mostly
19 Corporate	39 Zoo	59 The *Titanic*	78 Word after
20 V	40 ___ Ford		

RULE BREAKING

BY FRANK LONGO

ANSWER, PAGE 188

ACROSS

1 Navigator Islands, now
6 Wasn't stingy
12 Shows pain
20 Grad school exams
21 Power of the movies
22 Fonda's *Julia* costar
23 Schmeling beater of 1938
24 Noble aspirations
25 Provided the means?
26 Like this entry
29 *Seven Beauties* director Wertmuller
30 What children should be
31 Output of dirty tricks departments
32 Bar workers: Abbr.
33 Sinuous swimmer
34 Range groups
35 Record book datum
37 Beatles beater
39 Robert's love in *The Great Gatsby*
40 St. Andrews goal
43 Less doubtful
46 Israelites' home in ancient Egypt
48 Fido's offering
51 Steed with speed
53 Best Picture of 1968
56 *Daddy Long Legs* star
58 Like this entry
63 Go over the missed spots
64 Welcomes
65 Get ready for surgery
66 Sacramento-to-L.A. heading
67 Rest of the Mexicans?
70 Old-time hamlet
73 Artful
74 Wasn't colorfast
75 Rock band named for a radio pioneer
78 Painter Chagall
80 Leaping leporids
83 LAX abbr.
84 "Waterloo" singers
87 Phrase tacked on for emphasis
91 Shoshonean people
92 Like this entry
95 June 1944 battle site of northwest France
96 Having simple, straight lines
98 Paul Hogan, for one
99 Ewoks' home moon in *Return of the Jedi*
100 Diver's attachment
101 *Paper Moon* costars
102 Embarrassing outburst
103 Contest hopefuls
104 Serves the bisque
105 Cast

DOWN

1 Goes it alone
2 ___ *With a View*
3 Lilac's kin
4 Baseball's Tony and family
5 Declares
6 Calaboose
7 Nine-headed monster slain by Hercules
8 "Give it ___!"
9 Comical tributes
10 Sign up
11 Proud papa of January, 1953
12 The deer and the antelope, on the range
13 Party
14 Nice thought?
15 Team leader: Abbr.
16 It's on the border between Kazakhstan and Uzbekistan
17 More shrewd
18 Tied up
19 Coupes' big brothers
27 Hirsute twin
28 Japanese plane of WWII
34 Heloise offerings
36 ___ l'oeil (optical trick)
38 Reach accord
39 Private meal?
40 Figure skating division
41 April Fools' Day sign
42 Employee's request
44 Popular street name
45 Hoop part
47 Two-passenger carriage
48 Marina structures
49 Staggering
50 Like a five-hanky movie
52 Yuppie's wheels
54 Bettor's mecca
55 For all time, in verse
57 Egyptian headdress symbol
59 Western elevations
60 ___ *Kampf*
61 Court divider
62 Ultimate
68 Advances
69 Hatcher of *Lois and Clark*
71 Go on and on
72 March, maybe
74 Cobbler, at times
76 California's ___ Beach
77 Lowered
79 Wrap up, as a championship
80 '70s dance
81 Reach
82 Raise again
83 Emissary
85 Kind of metabolism
86 Crony?
88 Downy duck
89 Snack for teatime
90 Propeller type
92 Show amusement
93 Reading, for example
94 Home for a monster
97 Ending for pay or plug

Going Too Far

BY MIKE SHENK

Some of the answers in this crossword puzzle are one letter too long for their spots in the grid. These words go "too far" by extending into an adjacent shaded square, either at the beginning or the end. Each shaded square will be used exactly once. When the grid is complete, the letters in the shaded squares will spell a quotation by William Blake.

ANSWER, PAGE 188

ACROSS

1 Entire range
5 Children's card game
10 Humorist Bombeck
14 Have a Vegas wedding, perhaps
15 Key without sharps or flats
16 Thin bed of coal
17 Souchong and oolong
18 Go too far
19 Rate of speed
20 Big top securer
22 Gets off the Metroliner
24 Winter cap feature
26 Cool
27 Beetle's boss
30 Its motto is "Union, Justice, and Confidence"
35 *A Fish Called Wanda* star
36 "Smoke Gets in Your Eyes" composer
37 Battle souvenir
38 The Jungfrau, for one
39 Ring win
41 Use the dotted line
43 Witness's oath
44 Oats eaters, in a silly song
46 Construct
48 Murdered
50 Trade show?
52 Showing fallibility
53 Marine shocker
54 Appearance in *The Player*, for many
57 Crazy ___
61 Coming down in buckets
65 Tablet
66 Parking pro
68 Drive
69 McClurg and Adams
70 Smoothed out
71 1968 U.S. Open winner
72 Fashionably nostalgic
73 Prepare leftovers
74 Roulette bet

DOWN

1 Contact
2 Away from the wind
3 Express one's agony
4 Surpassed professionally
5 Courtroom rappers
6 Psi follower
7 Natural needle source
8 Encyclopedia volume
9 Restful
10 Like many summer movies
11 Memento
12 Stephen King's state
13 Rock concert needs
21 The magic word
23 Olympian warrior
25 "The Gold Bug" author
27 Oodles
28 Uncultivated
29 21st Amendment topic
31 Dunaway's *It Had to Be You* costar
32 Turning litmus red
33 South African writer Gordimer
34 Dorothy Lamour costume
36 1988 Olympics setting
40 Fall down unexpectedly
42 Nobelist Sakharov
45 Grade school book
47 List-ending abbr.
49 Term for a triathlete
51 Catty remark
55 Bowl
56 Alma ___
57 School essay
58 Comment to the audience
59 Stepped down
60 Basilica part
62 ___ facto
63 Radar's soda, on *M*A*S*H*
64 Lascivious looker
67 Took wing

SQUARE DEALING

BY HENRY HOOK

Each of the five missing Across clues (18-, 31-, 50-, 63-, and 83-Across) is a single five-letter word. These words, arranged in the proper order, can be filled into the smaller grid to make a word square (with the same five words reading across and down).

ANSWER, PAGE 188

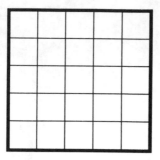

12 Cross words?
13 Lewis or Sullivan
14 No backers, they
17 He said "Th-th-that's all, folks"
19 Tone of many 1940s movies
20 Circus performer
26 Pink-slip
28 Triangular sail
30 Comprehend
32 *Veni*
33 One in a million?
34 Eeyore's friend
35 Connecticut town
39 *Mystery!* hostess
40 MPs' prey
41 *The Rape of the Lock* poet
42 Lock part
43 Alternative to retsina
44 Dray pullers
46 Grand
47 Farewell
51 "___ quiet!"
52 Use a sickle
57 Dweeb
59 Motor oil additive
61 Relay runner's allotment
64 Unparalleled
65 MacLachlan of *Twin Peaks*
66 Jayne's sister
67 It may be run by a child
68 Square
69 Perhaps soon
70 Man behind the wheel
71 American rival
72 "The choice of a new generation"
77 Madonna's "La ___ Bonita"
78 Osso buco base
79 Concert pianist Gilels
81 Microscope sight
84 Pacino and Martino
85 Detroit-to-Toronto dir.
86 Teachers' org.

ACROSS

1 Horror movie reactions
6 Sequel title start
11 Goya subject
15 "... woman who lived in ___"
16 A customer follows this
17 House of Lords member
18 _____
21 Officeholder, briefly
22 Lanka lead-in
23 "I cannot ___ lie"
24 Numerical prefix
25 Mars's counterpart
27 N. modifier
29 Marx cohort
31 _____
36 XXV times XII
37 Port ringer
38 Mouth, in slang
42 Water pipe

45 Mell Lazarus comic strip
48 ___ Jima
49 Dumas's *La Dame ___ Camélias*
50 _____
53 Bush league?
54 Verbifying suffix
55 Prime number?
56 Ad verse
58 Brown and Silver
60 Canaanite god
62 A foot wide?
63 _____
70 There's a demand for it
73 Eviscerate
74 007 villain
75 Enzyme suffix
76 Martini extra
80 Groove on
82 Snitch
83 _____
87 Supermarket section

88 Frankie or Cleo
89 1966 hit "Walk Away ___"
90 One of Charlie's Angels
91 Strike setting
92 Ready to strangle, maybe

DOWN

1 One of the Magi
2 Having missed the boat
3 Author Aleichem
4 "___ favor, señor"
5 Match parts
6 Icosahedra, e.g.
7 ___ budget
8 Egg container
9 Will-wisp link
10 Put one over on
11 *Printemps* month

8 EXTRA-TOUGH PUZZLES FOR EXTRA-SHARP SOLVERS

THE SILVER WINDOW

BY BOB STANTON

Prince Hero stands before the silver window behind which the fair princess is imprisoned. It is a solid silver slab, one inch thick, enameled with a design of overlapping squares, as shown below. The only opening is a small hole at the center (the black square in the drawing).

The prince carries a potion that will shrink him for a short time; the more he drinks, the smaller he'll become—but if he gets *too* small the potion's effect will become permanent and he won't return to full size. Thus, the prince must figure out exactly how small to become. He knows from ancient legend that the window contains 508 cubic inches of silver. From this, he must determine the exact dimensions of the hole in its center.

What size *is* the hole?

ANSWER, PAGE 188

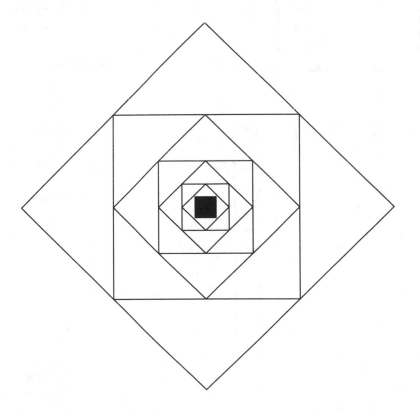

THINK TWICE

BY RAYMOND YOUNG

You'll need to think twice to solve this puzzle—that's because it's actually two crisscross puzzles in one. The 23 five-letter words below can be filled into the grid in crossword fashion in two different ways. To start you off, we've put one word into each grid. Can you find the solutions?

ANSWERS, PAGE 189

MIND FLEXERS

BY ROSALIE MOSCOVITCH

In each of these puzzles, match each item on the left with one on the right based on similar or related meanings. The relationships are disguised by use of double meanings or altered spacing within words. For example, the answer to the first item in Puzzle 1, "Blusher," is C, "Redone" (red one). Psychology professor Morgan Worthy, who invented "Mind Flexers" 18 years ago to test and improve mental flexibility, says, "Do not take them too seriously, and you will quickly improve at seeing the relationships."

ANSWERS, PAGE 189

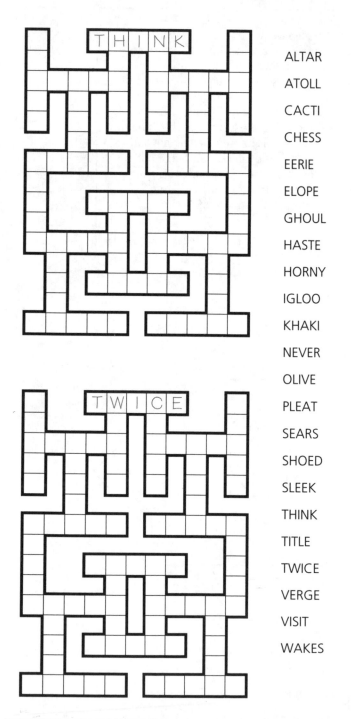

ALTAR
ATOLL
CACTI
CHESS
EERIE
ELOPE
GHOUL
HASTE
HORNY
IGLOO
KHAKI
NEVER
OLIVE
PLEAT
SEARS
SHOED
SLEEK
THINK
TITLE
TWICE
VERGE
VISIT
WAKES

PUZZLE 1

____ 1. Blusher
____ 2. Flathead
____ 3. Minuteman
____ 4. Penchant
____ 5. Tiny pen

A. Oink, oink, oink
B. Microbic
C. Redone
D. Dwarf
E. Landlord

PUZZLE 2

____ 1. Rigor mortis
____ 2. Holster
____ 3. Autoharp
____ 4. Hearing aid
____ 5. Beaten

A. Backseat driver
B. Rate like Bo
C. Armrest
D. Solid state
E. Gavel

PUZZLE 3

____ 1. Loaded gun
____ 2. Feathered
____ 3. Endanger
____ 4. Vanguard
____ 5. Split decision

A. Divorce
B. Bumper
C. Bulletin
D. Cool down
E. Bearing down

PUZZLE 4

____ 1. Spot remover
____ 2. Scrabble piece
____ 3. Low blows
____ 4. Rustler
____ 5. Current

A. Stocktaker
B. Dogcatcher
C. Kennel fee
D. Dirty socks
E. Utile

PUZZLE 5

____ 1. Slipcover
____ 2. Appendix scar
____ 3. Backward
____ 4. Tenure
____ 5. At ease

A. Sideline
B. Fire prevention
C. Correction fluid
D. Coquette
E. Orthopedic department

CROSSNUMBER PUZZLE

BY MIKE SHENK

Instead of filling the grid below with letters, place one digit from 0 to 9 in each space. You'll need to use a little logic and a lot of basic arithmetic to correctly solve the puzzle—and a calculator sure wouldn't hurt. If you'd like help beginning, a starting hint appears on page 186.

ANSWER, PAGE 189

ACROSS

1 Reverse of 20-Across
6 Multiple of 50-Across
10 Product of 42-Across and 63-Across
14 Multiple of 16-Across
15 A perfect square
16 Product of 57-Across and 3-Down
17 Multiple of 42-Across
18 Sum of 50-Across and 11-Down
20 Perfect square in which each digit is greater than the preceding digit
22 Total number of 8s and 9s in the completed grid
23 Factor of 32-Down
25 1-Across minus 1-Down
27 Three consecutive digits of 49-Down
28 Multiple of 42-Across
29 Product of 22-Across and 33-Across
31 Product of 10-Down and 88-Down
33 A perfect square
35 Half the product of 22-Across and 86-Down
37 Twice the product of 84-Down and 86-Down
39 Reverse of 42-Down
42 Square root of 63-Across
44 Square of 61-Across
46 Product of 42-Across and 26-Down
48 Product of 17-Across and 6-Down
50 Reverse of 10-Down
51 Multiple of 63-Across
52 Sum of 3-Down and 10-Down

53 Cube of 88-Down
55 Product of 22-Across, 11-Down, and 86-Down
57 Square root of 7-Down
58 15-Across minus 17-Across
59 Multiple of 35-Across
61 Average of 17-Across and 19-Down
63 A perfect square
65 Product of the first two digits of 67-Across and the last two digits of 67-Across
67 Sum of 42-Across, 50-Across, and 73-Down
70 Half the product of 22-Across and 84-Down
72 Product of 22-Across and 42-Across
74 19-Down minus 11-Down
76 Palindromic number
77 Multiple of 42-Across
78 Product of 42-Across, 3-Down, and 11-Down
80 Multiple of the first two digits of 40-Down
82 Two consecutive digits of 68-Down
83 A perfect square
85 Product of 22-Across and 76-Across
87 Product of 42-Across, 57-Across, and 80-Across
89 Sum of 10-Across and 33-Across
90 Sum of 40-Down and 41-Down
91 Product of twice 61-Across and twice 88-Down

DOWN

1 A perfect square
2 26-Down minus 42-Down

3 Square root of 5-Down
4 21-Down minus 10-Down
5 A perfect square
6 Digit sum of 6-Across
7 A perfect square
8 Square of 50-Across
9 Rearrangement of the digits of 12-Down
10 Square root of 20-Across
11 Digit sum of 68-Down
12 Multiple of 62-Down
13 Product of 57-Across and 86-Down
19 Rearrangement of the digits of 55-Down
21 Twice 33-Across
24 Sum of 7-Down and 10-Down
26 Number in which each digit is one less than the preceding digit

28 Product of 6-Across and 88-Down
30 Rearrangement of the digits of 4-Down
32 Multiple of 23-Across
34 Sum of 22-Across and 55-Down
36 Rearrangement of the digits of 12-Down
38 29-Down minus 23-Across
40 Product of 57-Across and 56-Down
41 Product of 23-Across and 42-Across
42 Product of 63-Across and 6-Down
43 Product of 3-Down and 84-Down
45 Sum of 5-Down and 56-Down

47 Product of 42-Across and 7-Down
49 Rearrangement of the digits of 26-Down
51 Multiple of 36-Down
54 Product of 57-Across and 84-Down
55 Three consecutive digits of 46-Across
56 Sum of 33-Across and 11-Down
60 Cube of 17-Across
62 Sum of 22-Across and 32-Down
64 A perfect cube
66 35-Across minus 42-Across
68 87-Across minus 35-Across
69 Product of 22-Across, 57-Across, and 6-Down
70 Rearrangement of the digits of 6-Across

71 Product of 17-Across and 64-Down
73 Rearrangement of the digits of 5-Down
75 Sum of 12-Down and 88-Down
78 Average of 42-Across, 52-Across, and 76-Across
79 Product of 17-Across and 42-Across
81 Sum of 28-Across and 64-Down
84 Two consecutive digits of 72-Across
86 Square root of 83-Across
88 Two consecutive digits of 38-Down

SOLITAIRE HANGMAN

BY R. WAYNE SCHMITTBERGER

WORDS TO BE GUESSED

I. ___ ___ ___ ___ ___ ___ ___ ___
   1   2   3   4   5   6   7   8

II. ___ ___ ___ ___ ___ ___ ___ ___
    1   2   3   4   5   6   7   8

III. ___ ___ ___ ___ ___ ___ ___
     1   2   3   4   5   6   7

IV. ___ ___ ___ ___ ___ ___ ___
    1   2   3   4   5   6   7

V. ___ ___ ___ ___ ___ ___ ___
   1   2   3   4   5   6   7

VI. ___ ___ ___ ___ ___ ___ ___ ___
    1   2   3   4   5   6   7   8

VII. ___ ___ ___ ___ ___ ___ ___
     1   2   3   4   5   6   7

VIII. ___ ___ ___ ___ ___ ___ ___ ___
      1   2   3   4   5   6   7   8

IX. ___ ___ ___ ___ ___ ___ ___ ___
    1   2   3   4   5   6   7   8

X. ___ ___ ___ ___ ___ ___ ___
   1   2   3   4   5   6   7

XI. ___ ___ ___ ___ ___ ___ ___ ___ ___
    1   2   3   4   5   6   7   8   9

XII. ___ ___ ___ ___ ___ ___ ___ ___ ___
     1   2   3   4   5   6   7   8   9

LETTERS MISSED

As in the two-player version of Hangman, the object of this solitaire challenge is to guess the identity of a word before being "hanged."

To begin, choose any letter of the alphabet that you think might be in word I below. Suppose you pick T. Go the Letter Chart on the facing page and find the number listed in row T of Column I (because you are working on word I). The number is 75; you now look in box number 75 in the Position Chart (to the right of the Letter Chart) and find the number 4. This means the letter T occurs in the fourth position (and nowhere else) in word I. If a letter occurs more than once in a word, the Position Chart will show all its locations.

If you find from the Position Chart that a letter appears in position 0, then that letter does not appear in the word. As a penalty for an incorrect guess, you must draw part of a stick figure below the scaffold beside the word blanks. On your first incorrect guess, draw the head; on the second, the body; and on the next four, the arms and legs. If you complete the figure (that is, make six incorrect guesses) before identifying the word, you are "hanged."

If you can identify 8 of the 12 words before being hanged, either you're psychic or you have a remarkable gift for words.

ANSWERS, PAGE 189

LETTER CHART

	I	II	III	IV	V	VI	VII	VIII	IX	X	XI	XII	
A	4	46	100	2	50	98	89	88	42	59	56	45	A
B	21	6	44	91	14	78	19	63	33	94	77	76	B
C	56	59	83	65	92	91	30	79	27	5	15	9	C
D	78	11	27	45	56	52	83	46	54	44	93	14	D
E	83	52	28	63	86	6	31	61	23	58	32	46	E
F	33	71	50	52	83	42	21	6	98	63	19	59	F
G	42	93	31	11	29	61	56	18	65	21	33	78	G
H	31	3	14	6	57	46	23	95	22	50	99	13	H
I	16	24	99	35	27	43	3	71	53	91	6	61	I
J	50	91	56	93	23	35	5	81	52	95	27	11	J
K	29	89	61	46	95	65	11	44	93	31	42	38	K
L	80	5	81	89	34	44	33	14	100	78	68	65	L
M	82	63	29	71	31	69	78	19	35	61	83	89	M
N	37	12	95	78	20	81	27	84	19	71	21	35	N
O	44	53	25	33	17	27	98	89	84	65	58	29	O
P	15	9	21	59	19	14	47	11	46	81	95	23	P
Q	23	98	8	5	89	29	42	56	11	96	71	63	Q
R	81	65	19	84	93	59	49	97	6	92	91	56	R
S	19	60	39	21	59	10	50	31	89	47	44	87	S
T	75	67	42	61	81	64	70	83	4	98	52	27	T
U	58	35	55	81	21	73	52	78	29	74	28	40	U
V	95	42	33	44	5	63	59	76	14	11	50	93	V
W	35	87	5	51	71	40	91	59	7	23	98	96	W
X	27	23	98	42	63	95	65	29	56	14	81	21	X
Y	61	19	23	18	33	50	72	41	83	46	34	71	Y
Z	14	33	59	98	44	71	29	5	81	52	31	83	Z
	I	II	III	IV	V	VI	VII	VIII	IX	X	XI	XII	

POSITION CHART

1 9	**2** 2,5	**3** 6	**4** 3	**5** 0
6 0	**7** 1	**8** 3	**9** 8	**10** 1,5
11 0	**12** 4	**13** 4,6	**14** 0	**15** 1
16 5	**17** 6	**18** 3	**19** 0	**20** 7
21 0	**22** 4,5	**23** 0	**24** 7	**25** 5
26 1,4,5	**27** 0	**28** 2	**29** 0	**30** 1,7
31 0	**32** 9	**33** 0	**34** 5	**35** 0
36 2,6	**37** 6	**38** 9	**39** 1	**40** 2
41 8	**42** 0	**43** 3,7	**44** 0	**45** 7
46 0	**47** 4	**48** 9	**49** 2	**50** 0
51 1,4	**52** 0	**53** 2	**54** 8	**55** 4
56 0	**57** 3	**58** 7	**59** 0	**60** 5
61 0	**62** 9	**63** 0	**64** 8	**65** 0
66 1,6	**67** 1	**68** 8	**69** 4	**70** 5
71 0	**72** 3	**73** 6	**74** 3,6	**75** 4
76 1	**77** 3,4	**78** 0	**79** 7	**80** 2
81 0	**82** 8	**83** 0	**84** 6	**85** 2,4,7
86 1,4	**87** 3	**88** 2,5	**89** 0	**90** 9
91 0	**92** 2	**93** 0	**94** 1	**95** 0
96 5	**97** 4	**98** 0	**99** 6	**100** 7

500 RUMMY

BY JACK SCHNEIDER

Can you score 500 or more points in Word Rummy hands from the card spread below?

ANSWERS, PAGE 189

	A	2	3	4	5	6	7	8	9	10	J	Q	K	
♠	O	B	S	C	H	R	N	O	Q	U	E	E	M	♠
♥	B	A	N	H	O	S	E	I	T	R	I	L	A	♥
♦	A	T	R	A	N	T	M	G	E	E	N	T	W	♦
♣	C	R	O	N	B	I	E	M	U	Z	F	I	R	♣
	A	2	3	4	5	6	7	8	9	10	J	Q	K	

♠ HOW TO PLAY

Find as many common seven-letter words as you can whose cards form Word Rummy hands. A Word Rummy hand is a seven-letter word whose letters appear on cards that make up one **set** (three or four cards of a kind, like 7 7 7 or K K K K) and one **sequence** (three or four cards of the same suit in numerical order, like ♥ A 2 3 or ♣ 9 10 J Q). Either the **set** or the **sequence** may come first. The letters of a **set** may be used in any order; the letters of a **sequence** must be used in the left-to-right order given in the grid. The same card cannot be used twice in one hand. Sets and sequences, however, may be repeated in other words. Proper names and foreign words are not allowed, but plurals are fine.

♥ SCORING

Each card in a Word Rummy hand scores its face value. A 6 scores 6 points, for example. Aces are low and count 1 point each. Jacks, queens, and kings count 10 points each.

♦ EXAMPLE

In the puzzle at right the word OBSCENE forms a Word Rummy hand. The ♠ A 2 3 4 are a sequence with the letters O-B-S-C; the ♥ 7 ♠ 7 ♣ 7 are a set with the letters E-N-E. The cards used have values 1 2 3 4 7 7 7, for a total of 31 points.

♣ RATINGS

Knock: 350 points (good game)
Gin: 500 points (winning game)
Gin-off: 878 points (our best score)

CARDS & WORDS — POINTS

O	B	S	C	E	N	E	31
A	2	3	4	7	7	7	

COLUMN 2 TOTAL

COLUMN 1 TOTAL

COLUMN 1 TOTAL

TOTAL SCORE

WORD GAMES

BY DAVID ELLIS DICKERSON

This puzzle is really four games in one. The clues are presented in four sections, each posing a different challenge. We've given an example in each category below. First answer as many of the clues as you can. Then enter the letters of the answers into the diagram, as indicated by the letter/number pairs. (Thus, A1 represents the upper left corner square, R8 the lower right corner square, etc.) Many squares are used in more than one answer, so every clue you solve will provide some help toward others. When the puzzle has been completed, you will find a bit of original light verse reading across the diagram, line by line, beginning in square A1.

ANSWER, PAGE 189

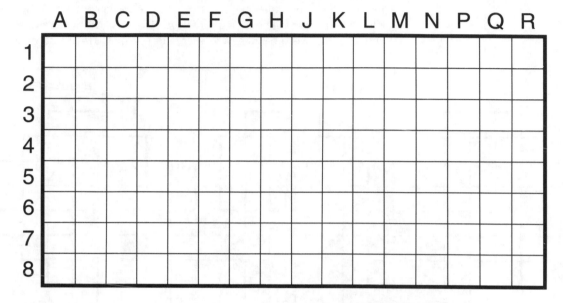

MISSING LINKS

Ex. drum _____ call: ROLL
 1. mouth _____ meal: F6 R7 B2 Q3 P8
 2. light _____ hitter: M1 F3 J6 E8 P6 L5
 3. stir _____ quilt: N2 R1 D7 Q8 B4
 4. draw _____ table: L2 J5 M6 E3 K8 L1
 5. feather _____ lifter: G6 H4 H8 J7 B1 H3
 6. top _____ service: N7 D6 N5 G2 R2 H1
 7. work _____ play: G8 B3 Q1 K2 F5
 8. bean _____ intelligence: C8 Q6 Q5 N6 A1 R3 F4

OPPOSITES

Ex. black: WHITE
 1. in: G5 P1 R8 J4 D3
 2. truth: A6 D7 E5 C1
 3. sharp: K1 H2 A8 C2
 4. gun: E7 B5 C6 M7
 5. land: N4 E1 R6 H7 F8 L5
 6. open: J1 J8 F2 G3 K4 D8 B7 L3 P5 N6 A5 K6
 7. dry: L8 P7 E6 M5 H1
 8. mountain: Q4 M8 M4 L6 G8 A2 A8 R5

DOUBLE DEFINITIONS

Ex. carries; animals: BEARS
 1. plunged; peacenik: K3 P5 M3 B2
 2. eat in a field; scratch: C7 J5 E1 Q8 B8
 3. polished; increased: P7 P2 L7 G4 D2
 4. sulked; scooter: Q2 Q6 F6 F5 D2
 5. felling trees; clumsy:
     M4 Q5 D1 A4 K7 C3 L4 J8 E4
 6. babysitter; delicate: B7 D4 F7 E3 M7 P3
 7. glass; gymnast: K4 R6 N1 A3 K6 J2 E5
 8. used; clock feature:
     R4 E2 N5 D5 F1 K3 H6 D8 F7 C4

RATIOS

Ex. car : land :: boat : SEA
 1. war : piece :: left : G6 C3 L3 E8 E2
 2. father : thereafter :: mother :
     K5 Q7 D4 Q1 N8 N3 Q2 K7 C5 J2 P3
 3. peel : spare :: live : B6 M2 L7 P4 K2 A1
 4. move slowly : imploded :: dinner neckwear :
     G3 K1 A3 P4 A4 D6 C2
 5. fill : wanter :: sprung : R4 J6 D1 N8 H4 R1
 6. unnecessary : needles :: hoping :
     P1 R8 G5 M6 A7 H2 F1
 7. humorous : fully :: join : C8 D5 N4 C6 R3 N2 K5
 8. Superman : Luthor :: J3 B3 R5 Q4 G4 L8 :
     N1 H5 A7 G7 P2 G2 C5 G1

PENTATHLON

BY MICHAEL SELINKER

Welcome to the Cryptolympics! Representing 57 countries, the entrants—the answers to the clues to this cryptic crossword—are about to compete in the pentathlon, a series of five track and field events, each represented by one of the rings of the grid. Each clue answer must be altered before being entered into the grid, according to the appropriate ring's event; where a word crosses one of the shaded squares shared by two rings, either event may apply. Both clue answers and grid answers are words (including some proper names and abbreviations).

The five events are (not necessarily in order): **Long Jump:** the answer's first letter jumps to the end—e.g., DEMOTE becomes EMOTED; **Javelin:** the answer throws out one javelin (the letter I)—e.g., MARTINIS becomes MARTINS; **Shot Put:** the answer throws out one ball (the letter O)—e.g., LASSOES becomes LASSES; **Hurdles:** one letter hurdles over the next—e.g., MARTIAL becomes MARITAL; **Pole Vault:** the answer vaults over a bar (a new interior letter)—e.g., OUTAGES becomes OUTRAGES.

ANSWER, PAGE 189

Event 1: _____   Event 3: _____   Event 5: _____

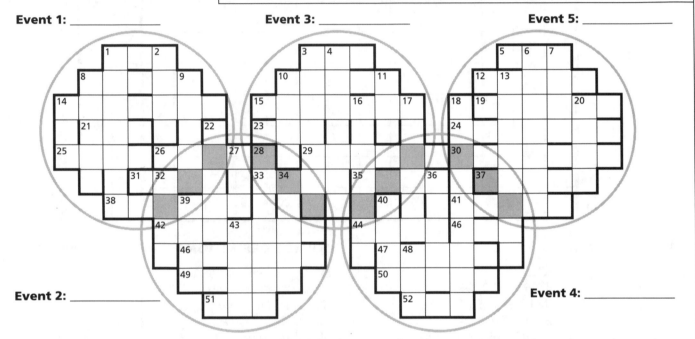

Event 2: _____   Event 4: _____

ACROSS

1 Gave money to Paraguay's leader to help out
3 Reportedly feel sick from United Kingdom beverage …
5 … such as found in Senegal
8 Zambia's establishment holds prejudices
10 Read the letters of south Latvia's premier, enrapt by favorite
12 Lake in Ireland reflected
14 U.S. Marine assaulted Guyana's neighbor
15 Arise from sending back letter from Greece delegate
19 Vice-president takes in front of Ghana ravine
21 Egypt divinity lives twice
23 Study Denmark without grade
24 Last trio from Philippines and Senator Kennedy made a home
25 Fibs about Pakistan's last securities
26 Central Mali disrupted declaration
29 The GI stumbling around Hungary's top elevation
30 Locating peaceful protest at Gambia's capital
31 Head of Finland food store returned, put papers away
33 Close to Nepal, forgetting chum (a Republican)
35 Arches circle most of Canada birds

37 Transported stew from Portugal to the Americas, for example
38 Guards confiscating lid from Luxembourg ointments
41 Shakespearean king's exiling English guy in Norway
42 Poland's top judge with eastern court minister
44 Alert Romania with no rage to exploit
45 Author of much poetry in eastern part of Lebanon
46 Pouch, ruddy like a cow in India
47 Ermines original to Switzerland, perfectly small
49 Made attempts, even around middle of Australia
50 Worked with Ness back at Djibouti's capital
51 Rearmost third of Cameroon's cricket side
52 He hops to eastern half of Chad

DOWN

1 Twosomes butchered Iran pigs
2 Aide corrupted Liechtenstein's first model
3 Thin poster showing Lithuania's capital
4 Dessert from appliance company, with words from Italy
6 Gabe Kaplan's role: Kenya's first river dweller

7 Nickname for a male general on Israel's borders
8 Occupies tops of barracks under siege in El Salvador
9 Yes, in Mexico distance is something comparable
10 Spain is missing one bridge
11 Direction in the Seychelles
13 Sort Niger out in recovery
14 Small product of Iraq dirt
16 Reel for men only, at Germany
17 Usher of China, for one, with endless term
18 Called a Turkey unlisted exchange
20 Take $1000 and quarter from Ethiopia
22 Bush and Communist in *Cuba: The Returning*
27 United States accepts military's first hesitations
28 Transpose Singapore's last two lines that rhyme
32 In France, the Pyrenees' peak is azure blue
34 Russia's premier easily scored *Ran*
36 Back half of Laos duck is bony
39 They're experienced in both sides of Venezuela arguments
40 Japan's inauguration to displace contest
43 Style for a hairdo from Botswana?
48 Yugoslavia leader given to holding it

PROCRUSTEAN BED

BY EMILY COX & HENRY RATHVON

Like the bedroom guests of the legendary Procrustes, every clue answer in this cryptic crossword must be shortened or stretched to fit into its resting place in the diagram. Every alteration is made by dropping or adding a single letter at the front or back of an answer, always forming a new word to be entered into the grid. In all, 20 answers are lengthened and 20 are shortened. One of the newly formed words is a proper name.

ANSWER, PAGE 189

ACROSS

1 European saint entertains company
5 Not easy keeping drill sheltered
10 Member of the clergy tries to open top of tin
11 Top 100 finished
12 Hurried, carrying one saw
13 Party was next to yacht, perhaps
14 Shot snipe in trees
15 Happy story recalled by editor
16 Exercises inside house sometimes
19 Tries redistributing share
22 Lunatic thinks about grand, chivalrous men
25 Blueprint left in vessel for cooking
27 Place for a knife cook kept in silence
30 Limits sound made by lodgers
31 Permit everything that hurts
32 Bugs makes an escape, we hear
33 Go astray with $1000 commercial
34 Maintain public relations Reeves improved
35 Controls spider's weaving around middle of web
36 Boxed, having energy, and quit

DOWN

1 Trying for snake with one coil
2 Turn drinks upside-down
3 Dances in movie segments
4 Part-time worker encountered upcoming chief of police
5 I search all over for a store employee
6 Listen to stringed instrument intended for a low place
7 Soar after changing propellers?
8 Worst dressed in vest, I left
9 Sell off some lengths
14 Cereal Fido ate inside
17 Wise guy, taking medicine, sloshed stuff
18 Spacy rock: Dotty adores it
20 Lassie has topless parties
21 Emphasized sweet dishes in return
23 Sheet misrepresented the ones here
24 Fools with golf clubs
25 Flip reviews keyboard element
26 Finally, AT&T collects Spanish article (2 wds.)
28 Times for hurlers' stats
29 First Lady has a hangover?

PET PROJECT

BY SUZIE ELLIOTT

ANSWER, PAGE 189

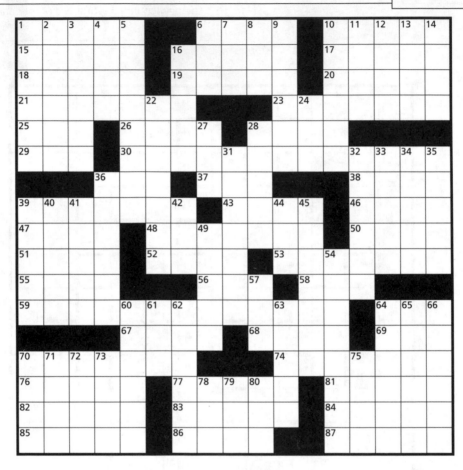

ACROSS

1 Grouch
6 Strawberry stats
10 PBS premiums, often
15 Capital on the Songka River
16 Drill leader
17 Likeness
18 Tired city?
19 Two trios and a duo
20 Lively dance
21 Hillary, for one
23 K2's neighbor
25 Beer bash need
26 Algerian port
28 Nero's way
29 Computer setup, for short
30 How Sandburg's fog comes in
36 Saint-Tropez's busy season
37 Upsilon follower
38 All-night dance party
39 Sanctuary site, sometimes
43 "___ Three Ships"
46 Salt Lake City players
47 Yves's eve

48 Dorothy's pick-me-up?
50 Polite chap
51 Shetland's gait
52 Hidden hindrance
53 ___ terribles
55 Imprecation
56 Gist
58 ___ Aviv
59 Engage in a sportive pursuit
64 Ambulance worker: Abbr.
67 Potter's buy
68 Ground-floor apt.
69 Fleur-de-___
70 In the wrong part
74 "Let ___" ("I need to consider")
76 Paragon
77 "___ man with seven ..."
81 Is lacking
82 "___ the Girls I've Loved Before"
83 Leek kin
84 Cultural character
85 Designer Perry
86 High time
87 Wright flight site

DOWN

1 Crude cabins
2 Annie of western fame
3 Strips ships
4 Space
5 Hero of a Perrault story
6 Huge bird of myth
7 Cricket club
8 Puck's place
9 Small Jewish community of Europe
10 Ocelot, e.g.
11 Barbra's Funny Girl costar
12 Fabrication
13 Ids' rivals
14 Half of quatorze
16 Pinkish yellow
22 Borgnine and Hemingway
24 Flying formation
27 Tuck's partner
28 "___ far, far better thing ..."
31 Watchamacallit
32 Thrifty
33 All gone
34 Episode
35 Tries out

36 Ribald
39 Halt, legally
40 Fable finale
41 Flora plus fauna
42 That one thar
44 Fables in Slang author
45 "You ___ Me" (Beatles song)
49 Country's Travis
54 Ante up
57 Halloween cry
60 Derisive shouts
61 Unser and Oerter
62 State
63 Destroy the courage of
64 Otis of elevator fame
65 Gilligan's boat
66 "Shame on you!"
70 Small sum
71 Graven image
72 Zoo barker
73 L.L. Cool J's "Going Back to ___"
75 "___ not a Jew eyes?": Shylock
78 6, on a phone
79 A-U link
80 Whole heap

GAMES, MAGIC, & THINGS TO DO

Die Jest

BY LUTHER WARM

Welcome to the world of magic. I have a hunch that you like to play games. A pretty amazing guess, right? OK, maybe you're not impressed yet. However, if you read on, I'll perform a trick that will prove my powers beyond doubt.

Most people believe that dice games are purely games of chance, but I will now demonstrate that I can foresee the number on top of a die that is totally within your control.

First, find a die in a junk drawer or game box. Next roll the die so that it lands on this page. Use any technique you like: Throw it from under your leg, behind your neck, or while vigorously rubbing it and humming.

Move the die into the square below, aligning the edges of the die with the edges of the square. Now, if the number showing on top of the die is even, give the die a quarter-turn to the right, as indicated by the arrow. If the top number is odd, give it a quarter-turn toward the top of the page instead.

Now look at the new number showing on top of the die. If it's even, again turn the die a quarter-turn to the right; if it's odd, turn it toward the top. Repeat this procedure (*turning* the die—don't rethrow it) five more times.

The die is now warmed up. Continue turning it, according to the arrows, until a six appears on top. Then turn it one more time in the indicated direction, and remember the number on top.

I have a hunch about that number. So strong a hunch, in fact, that I've written it in the Answers, page 190.

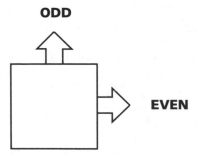

Max—
A Two-Player Game

BY CHARLES WEAVER

Your goal in this two-player game is to accumulate a higher point total than your opponent after two rounds of play. To play Round One, choose which player will take Rows and which will take Columns. The Row player goes first by crossing out any number from the row containing the star. The Column player then crosses out any number in the *column* containing the first player's previous move. Taking turns, play continues in this way, with each player playing in the row or column of the other player's previous move. The round ends when one of the players cannot make a legal move. On each turn, the number a player crosses out is added to that player's score (or subtracted from the score if the number is negative). For Round Two, the players switch roles (Row and Column), and play proceeds with the second grid. After two rounds, the player with the higher total score wins. You'll need to plan ahead carefully to reach the max. (We've provided two pairs of grids below, enough for you to play two complete games—of course, you can make copies of this page if you'd like to play more.)

GAME ONE

2	9	1	−7	4	5	−2	−3
7	−9	9	−4	3	8	−2	1
−2	−5	4	6	3	−6	4	6
1	−6	−2	−4	15	−6	1	5
10	−1	−1	8	−1	5	−3	7
0	2	3	★	4	−1	0	2
−1	−5	1	0	2	3	2	3
0	−4	−3	0	5	7	0	2

ROUND ONE

2	9	1	−7	4	5	−2	−3
7	−9	9	−4	3	8	−2	1
−2	−5	4	6	3	−6	4	6
1	−6	−2	−4	15	−6	1	5
10	−1	−1	8	−1	5	−3	7
0	2	3	★	4	−1	0	2
−1	−5	1	0	2	3	2	3
0	−4	−3	0	5	7	0	2

ROUND TWO

2	9	1	−7	4	5	−2	−3
7	−9	9	−4	3	8	−2	1
−2	−5	4	6	3	−6	4	6
1	−6	−2	−4	15	−6	1	5
10	−1	−1	8	−1	5	−3	7
0	2	3	★	4	−1	0	2
−1	−5	1	0	2	3	2	3
0	−4	−3	0	5	7	0	2

ROUND ONE

2	9	1	−7	4	5	−2	−3
7	−9	9	−4	3	8	−2	1
−2	−5	4	6	3	−6	4	6
1	−6	−2	−4	15	−6	1	5
10	−1	−1	8	−1	5	−3	7
0	2	3	★	4	−1	0	2
−1	−5	1	0	2	3	2	3
0	−4	−3	0	5	7	0	2

ROUND TWO

WHITE HOUSE STARS

BY MAX MAVEN

Do the stars guide us? The Reagan administration seemed to think so: It's rumored that some presidential decisions were aided by astrology. Whether or not you're a believer, I guarantee that the stars will influence a presidential decision you are about to make, mainly: Who you would select as your ideal president. Skeptical? Then explain away this: By using the secrets of astrology, I will predict just which president suits you best!

First, put your finger on the circle that contains your astrological sign. Now, spell out the name of that sign, one letter per circle, by moving your finger clockwise around the outer circles, beginning with the next clockwise circle.

Where you've landed, only you know. From this new location, move inward (following the line) to the nearest inner circle. Now, spell the name of the president, moving your finger clockwise again around the inner circles.

Now, you are on another inner circle, located by your stars. Remember the name of that president—turn to page 190 for my prediction.

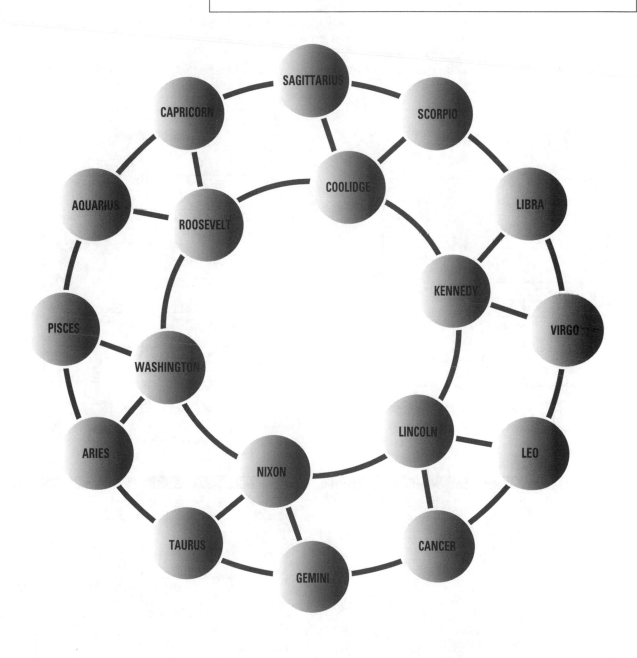

BOUNCE

BY STEPHEN SNIDERMAN

In this pencil-and-paper game for two players, you can happily tell your opponent where to go!

How to Play Using the grids below (or facsimiles), you and another player take turns placing your chosen symbol—either X or O—in any space that doesn't already contain that symbol. Use one grid for the X's, the other for the O's. The first player to get four of the same symbol in a row either vertically or horizontally (but not diagonally) wins the game.

One player begins by placing an X anywhere in the X-grid. The other player then decides whether to play X or O for the rest of the game. The O player now places an O in the column or row of the O-grid indicated by the letter or number in the space used by the first player. For example, if the first player has put an X in the square B2 (two squares from the left and two squares from the top), the second player must play in any square in column 3, which is the number that appears in square B2. Let's say the second player, who has chosen to play the O's, now places an O in square E3 (in the O-grid). The first player now must play an X somewhere in row A of the X-grid.

Players continue placing their symbol in the row or column indicated by their opponent's previous move until one player gets four symbols in a row.

Variations You can alter the length or complexity of the game by changing the size or shape of the grids, and you can label the individual squares either randomly or in some systematic way. You can shorten the game by requiring only three in a row, lengthen it by requiring five or six in a row, or vary it by requiring completion of a two-by-two square. As long as both you and your opponent agree to a variation and it works, do it!

Puzzles Two puzzles appear at the bottom of the page. You may want to try them to get a feel for the strategy of Bounce before playing an actual game.

ANSWERS, PAGE 190

PLAYER X

	1	2	3	4	5	6
A	B	C	D	E	F	1
B	2	3	4	5	6	A
C	D	E	F	2	A	B
D	4	5	6	C	1	3
E	F	6	A	B	C	D
F	3	4	E	1	2	5

PLAYER O

	1	2	3	4	5	6
A	B	C	D	E	F	1
B	2	3	4	5	6	A
C	D	E	F	2	A	B
D	4	5	6	C	1	3
E	F	6	A	B	C	D
F	3	4	E	1	2	5

PUZZLE 1

O's last move was in space F3, so it's X's turn to play somewhere in row E. With the right play, X can win in three turns. Can you find the correct moves?

PUZZLE 2

O's last play was in space D5, so it's X's turn to play somewhere in column 1. X can win in five turns with the right series of moves. Can you find it?

Stifle

BY JIM WINSLOW

A TWO-PLAYER STRATEGY GAME

EQUIPMENT The Stifle board at right and two contrasting sets of four playing pieces each (coins, beans, etc.).

SETUP Players put their pieces on the four dotted intersections at their respective ends of the board, one piece per intersection. The dots merely indicate the starting position and have no function during play.

PLAY In turn, players move one of their own pieces in any direction along an unobstructed straight line to an unoccupied intersection. A piece may neither jump over nor capture another piece of either color.

MOVEMENT The number of intersections a piece must move is exactly equal to the number of other pieces it is adjacent to *of either color in any direction* when it starts its move. For example, a piece adjacent to four other pieces may move only to the fourth intersection in any direction. If it can't, that piece may not move at all. A piece adjacent to only one other piece may move only to the nearest unoccupied intersection. (Note that an isolated piece may not move at all, and neither may a piece that is adjacent to five or six other pieces.) A player must move a piece if there is a legal move; passing is not allowed.

WINNING A player wins by preventing the opponent from moving.

SCORING For tournaments, play four games, with players alternating having the first move. Score one point for winning, plus one point for each opponent's piece that is isolated at game's end. Highest total wins the tournament.

STRATEGY Isolate an opponent's piece by moving away an adjacent piece of your own color; or increase the mobility of an opponent's piece by placing one of yours next to it, forcing it to move far away and isolate itself.

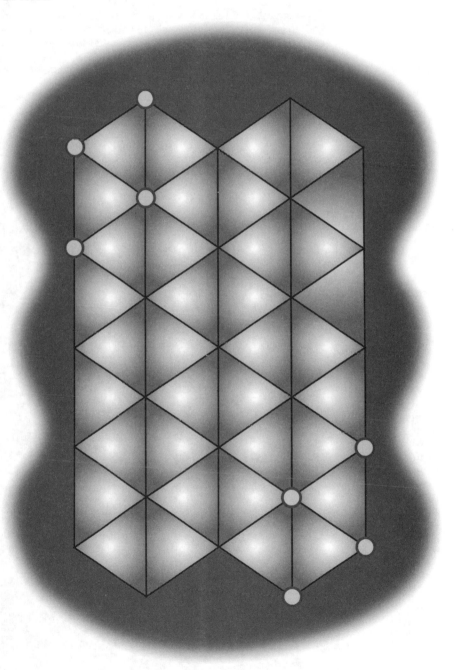

Heads Up!

A stranger sidles up to you at a bar and hisses: "$50 says you can't solve two simple coin puzzles." Care to take him on?

HINTS, PAGE 186
ANSWERS, PAGE 190

MAGIC MONEY

Place one or more coins in each box at right so that each row, column, and corner-to-corner diagonal has the same value. You may use only the standard American coins: penny, nickel, dime, quarter, half dollar, and dollar. No box in the completed square may be empty, and no two boxes may contain exactly the same coins or combination of coins. The top center box contains only one coin—a nickel—which has been placed for you.

What is the smallest number of coins that will complete the magic square?

COIN FLIP

Place a penny, nickel, dime, and quarter in the spaces below. The object is to reverse their order—that is, to get them in the sequence quarter, dime, nickel, and penny—in the fewest possible turns. In each turn, move a coin one square to the left or right. You may move a coin only into an empty square or onto an adjacent coin of higher value (e.g., a penny can move onto a nickel, but not vice versa). Only the top coin of a stack may move. What is the smallest number of turns necessary to effect the switch?

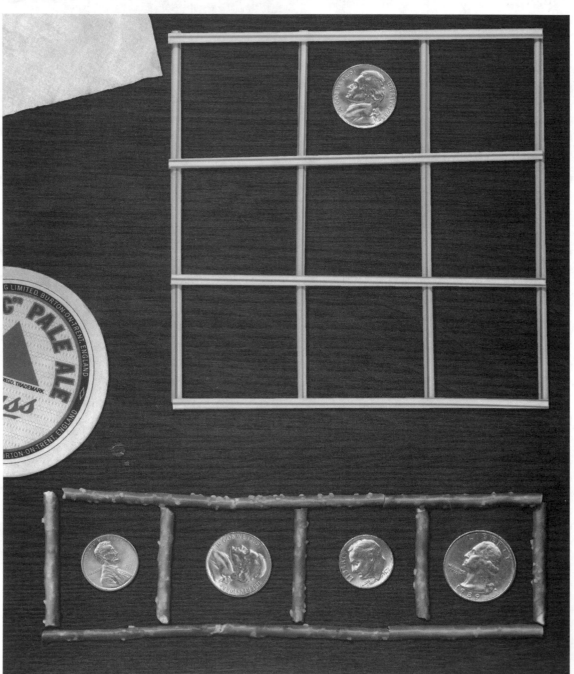

FIELDS OF ACTION

BY SID SACKSON

A TWO-PLAYER STRATEGY GAME

EQUIPMENT

A checkerboard and two contrasting sets of 12 pieces each (such as 12 light checkers and 12 dark checkers). Each set of pieces must be numbered 1 through 12 (we recommend using circular stickers).

SETUP

Place the pieces on the board as shown in the diagram. Choose who will go first in any convenient manner.

PLAY

In turn, each player moves one of his or her pieces in any direction (horizontally, vertically, or diagonally). A piece must move exactly as many spaces as there are pieces (of either color) next to it at the start of its turn.

While moving, a piece may pass over pieces of either or both colors. A piece may not land on a friendly piece; but it may land on an enemy piece, which is then captured and removed from play.

EXAMPLES

In the starting diagram, White's 9 piece, which touches only one other piece, can move to any of the spaces marked A. White's 12, touching three pieces, can move to B, C, D, or E. After moving 12 to C, where it touches two pieces, White would threaten to capture Black's 11 (though Black's 11 could capture at C first). After moving 12 to E, White threatens to capture Black's 8.

ISOLATED PIECES

A piece that does not have any pieces next to it is free to move any number of spaces in any direction, provided that:

   (i) it does not make a capture, and

   (ii) it lands next to at least two pieces (which may belong to either or both players).

WINNING

A player wins by capturing five pieces that are in numerical sequence, such as 3-4-5-6-7. (The order in which the captures were made is unimportant.) A player also wins if the opponent has no legal move when it is the opponent's turn.

VARIATIONS

For a change of pace, Fields of Action can be played with other opening setups. We recommend that pieces occupy the same set of squares, with only the numbers rearranged; but players may find other setups that work well.

ANSWERS ANSWERS ANSWERS

SECTION ONE

7 MORE BUTTONS

The correct button 15 is the one that was incorrectly numbered 8. The original order of buttons is as shown:

14	13	12	11
15	16	9	10
6	7	8	1
5	4	3	2

8 SQUARE DANCE

1. D4
2. H3
3. B8
4. G7
5. E2
6. A10
7. J1
8. H9

9 SUM OF THE PARTS

The six categories and their respective parts are:

SHIP: bow (A), bridge (D), cabin (J)
CAR: hood (B), horn (G), trunk (Q)
COMPUTER: mouse (E), keys (K), RAM (M)
PANTS: fly (F), cuffs (I), pocket (P)
BOOK: leaves (H), spine (O), jacket (R)
WRISTWATCH: band (C), hand (L), crystal (N)
One reader found another solution for C, L, and N:
BASEBALL: players (C), wave (L), and diamond (N).

12 THE LOST PICTURE SHOW

1. *Pat and Mike*
2. *The Cotton Club*
3. *The Hand That Rocks the Cradle*
4. *The Man in the Iron Mask*
5. *Kiss of the Spider Woman*
6. *Ice Station Zebra*
7. *Blade Runner*
8. *City Slickers*
9. *Horse Feathers*
10. *Top Gun*

(Your order of 7–10 may be different.)

11 ONE, TWO, THREE

C	HO	ICE	■	PRE	S	SU	RE	■	MIC	ROW	A	VE
H	US	SK	■	PS	AL	M	S	■	KEY	HO	L	E
OR	DIN	ATE	■	CH	E	AT	ER	■	M	USE	UM	S
D	I	R	TYP	OOL	■	RA	VE	N	OUS	■	■	■
■	■	■	ES	S	EX	■	■	AST	E	RO	ID	S
S	CAR	L	ET	■	P	EA	R	Y	■	B	EA	N
TAP	W	A	TER	■	A	RR	EST	■	MET	ER	MA	ID
LEG	A	TE	■	MA	ND	ING	O	■	A	TO	N	E
UN	SH	R	OU	DED	■	RE	MA	P	■	■	■	■
■	■	■	TO	O	THA	CHE	■	INS	HOR	TOR	DE	R
AC	CO	UNT	FOR	■	T	RI	VE	T	■	TI	M	ED
REA	D	IE	D	■	CHE	SH	I	RE	■	L	OTI	ON
GE	Y	S	ER	■	R	ING	L	ET	■	LA	NG	E

10 FILM DIRECTION

The movie MISSING is missing from the grid.

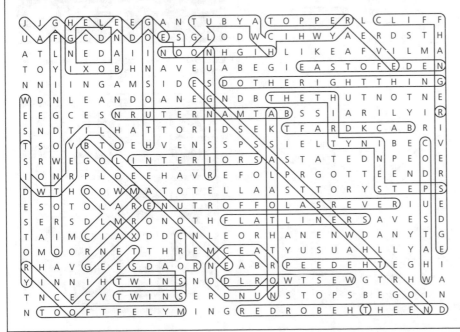

14 CHANGING CHANNELS

The shows were mixed as follows.

Name of show	In the style of
Coach	M*A*S*H
M*A*S*H	Jeopardy!
Jeopardy!	Cheers
Cheers	Star Trek
Star Trek	The Simpsons
The Simpsons	Family Feud
Family Feud	Quantum Leap
Quantum Leap	Mission: Impossible
Mission: Impossible	Northern Exposure
Northern Exposure	I Love Lucy
I Love Lucy	The Twilight Zone
The Twilight Zone	Bonanza
Bonanza	48 Hours
48 Hours	LA Law
LA Law	Nightline
Nightline	Coach

26 CRACKING UP HINT

1-Across starts in the eighth box of the top row.

16 ANALOGRAMS

1. IRIS is to EYE
2. SQUASH is to RACKET
3. ACROSS is to DOWN
4. SPOKE is to WHEEL
5. ROOSTER is to COMB
6. CUCUMBER is to GREEN
7. STAIRS is to ESCALATOR
8. WIND is to WOUND
9. DIE is to CUBE
10. BOO is to BECKONED (rhymes of a number—one and two—and its ordinal form—first and second)
11. MORTAR is to BRICK
12. FLY is to WEB
13. NEWSCAST is to ANCHOR
14. RANGE is to ARRANGE (added AR)
15. SCRATCH is to RECORD
16. LATVIAN is to VALIANT (anagrams)
17. POOL is to SINK
18. OURS is to THYME (homophones of units)
19. WITCH is to BROOM
20. SWALLOW is to PLUG (reversals of synonyms)

17 "B" HIVE

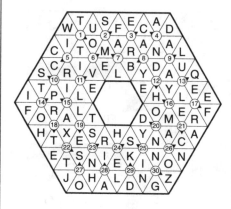

18 ODDS & ENDS

The pairings (in alphabetical order) are:

Bait & switch
Block & tackle
Chips & dip
Duck & cover
Head & shoulders
Horse & carriage
Movers & shakers
Nuts & bolts
Part & parcel
Safe & sound
Show & tell
Surf & turf

22 ILLUSTRATED EXCLAMATIONS!

1 – h ("Duck!")
2 – e ("Hail!")
3 – i ("Check!")
4 – b ("Pop!")
5 – c ("Match!")
6 – a ("Present!")
7 – g ("Hut!")
8 – f ("Fire!")
9 – j ("Ring!")
10 – d ("Safe!")

25 STAMP OF DISAPPROVAL

The remaining letters (across and then down) spell "BAD TASTE"

20 BORDERLINE INSANITY

The "new states" and the states that were pieced together to make them are as follows. (Names are hyphenated to show where the names were spliced together.)

1. INE-AH (Maine + Utah)
2. VIRGINIA-DA (West Virginia + Florida)
3. NE-WEST (Nebraska + West Virginia)
4. NEWYO-UT (New York + Utah)
5. CALI-BRASKA (California + Nebraska)
6. FLORI-ANA (Florida + Louisiana)
7. ALA-FORNIA (Alabama + California)
8. OKLAH-AHO (Oklahoma + Idaho)
9. BAMA-NIA (Alabama + Pennsylvania)
10. LOUISI-MA (Louisiana + Maine)
11. OMA-RK (Oklahoma + New York)
12. PENNSYLVA-ID (Pennsylvania + Idaho)

26 CRACKING UP

SECTION TWO

27 LEAPIN' LIZARDS

24 ONE FOR THE BOOKS

Based on an idea by Linda Shepard

28 MENTAL EXERCISE

1. Fencing
2. Hurdles
3. Pommel horse (gymnastics)
4. Cycling
5. Swimming
6. Rowing
7. Javelin throw
8. Pole vault
9. Uneven bars (gymnastics)
10. Archery
11. Equestrian
12. Weightlifting

29 MAKING THE ROUNDS

1–B
No Smoking sign

2–L
Pepsi logo

3–E
Volkswagen logo

4–F
Yin/Yang symbol

5–C
Westinghouse logo

6–A
CBS logo

7–D
Smiley face

8–J
General Electric logo

9–K
Prudential logo

10–I
Bell System logo

11–G
Peace symbol

12–H
Charlie Brown

32 SHADOW PLAY

1. U.S. Capitol, Washington, D.C.
2. Arc de Triomphe, Paris
3. Statue of Liberty, New York
4. Leaning Tower, Pisa
5. Taj Mahal, Agra, India
6. Stonehenge, Salisbury, England
7. Empire State Building, New York
8. Space Needle, Seattle
9. Transamerica Building, San Francisco
10. Colosseum, Rome
11. Tower Bridge, London
12. Gateway Arch, St. Louis
13. Sydney Opera House, Sydney
14. Ancient statues, Easter Island

34 WHAT'S LOOKIN' AT YOU, KID?

1. Goldfish
2. Mouse
3. Bat
4. Rabbit
5. Dolphin *or* porpoise
6. Cat
7. Groundhog
8. Dog
9. Rat

30 WHIRLED LEADERS

1. Fidel Castro
2. Margaret Thatcher
3. Yasir Arafat
4. Mao Tse-tung
5. Mikhail Gorbachev
6. Idi Amin

7. Golda Meir
8. Nelson Mandela
9. Ayatollah Khomeini
10. Winston Churchill
11. Indira Gandhi
12. Saddam Hussein

13. Anwar Sadat
14. Bill Clinton
15. Joseph Stalin
16. Franklin Roosevelt
17. Corazon Aquino
18. Lech Walesa

Photos: Castro, Arafat, Mandela, Khomeini—Jerry Ohlinger's; Churchill—New York Public Library; Hussein, Clinton, Stalin—Globe Photos; Roosevelt—Movie Star News

36 PARADING YOUR DIFFERENCES

The differences are circled:

37 ARTIFACT—OR FICTION?

The piece not stolen was the bowl on the table at right (though the thief apparently mistook it for an ashtray and left cigarette butts in it). The other pieces were incorrectly forged as follows (from left to right): the swordsman has no sword; Cupid has shot his arrows; Franklin is not wearing glasses; the soup is Tomato instead of Chicken Noodle; the face on the urn is smiling instead of frowning; the banana is peeled; the woman's hands are crossed differently; the abstract pattern goes in the wrong direction; the girl is holding a puppy instead of a kitten; the Thinker is on a different pedestal; the carriage is facing the wrong direction; the man is wearing a tie.

38 OUT OF THIS WORLD

1. Jupiter, Florida
2. Venus Bay, Australia
3. Sun River, Montana
4. Moon Lake, Utah
5. Le Planet, France
6. Mars, Pennsylvania
7. Meteor Crater, Arizona
8. Mercury Island, New Zealand
9. Star, North Carolina
10. Neptune, New Jersey
11. Satellite Bay, Canada (Northwest Territories)
12. Earth, Texas

24 ONE FOR THE BOOKS AUTHORS

Burr—(Gore) VIDAL
Emma—(Jane) AUSTEN
Giant—(Edna) FERBER
Roots—(Alex) HALEY
Exodus—(Leon) URIS
Lolita—(Vladimir) NABOKOV
Candide—VOLTAIRE
Ivanhoe—(Sir Walter) SCOTT
Lord Jim—(Joseph) CONRAD
Ulysses—(James) JOYCE
Jane Eyre—(Charlotte) BRONTË
Moby-Dick—(Herman) MELVILLE
The Trial—(Franz) KAFKA

Tom Jones—(Henry) FIELDING
Kidnapped—(Robert Louis) STEVENSON
Native Son—(Richard) WRIGHT
White Fang—(Jack) LONDON
Animal Farm—(George) ORWELL
East of Eden—(John) STEINBECK
Ethan Frome—(Edith) WHARTON
Little Women—(Louisa May) ALCOTT
Steppenwolf—(Hermann) HESSE
War and Peace—(Leo) TOLSTOY
Frankenstein—(Mary Wollstonecraft) SHELLEY
The Good Earth—(Pearl S.) BUCK

40 TWICE TWISTED

The lowest-scoring route is 66, passing through (in order) 7, 6, 19, 12, and 22.
One such path is shown below.

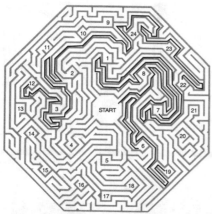

43 MIX & MATCH

R	U	S	T	L	E	S		E	A	R	T	H	E	N
E		T		A		T		A		E		E		O
C	A	R	E	D		A	S	S	I	S	T	A	N	T
I		E		D		T		Y		O		R		I
P	R	E	S	I	D	E	S		R	U	S	T	I	C
E		T		E		M		T		N				E
S	A	C	K		R	E	P	R	O	D	U	C	E	S
		A		M		N		A		S		O		
P	E	R	S	I	S	T	E	N	T		G	A	P	S
R				N		S		S		K		S		E
O	O	D	L	E	S		M	I	N	I	S	T	E	R
T				R		K		E		S		L		P
E	D	U	C	A	T	I	O	N			S	N	I	D	E
S				L		L		L		C		E		N
T	R	E	A	S	O	N			E	A	R	N	E	S	T

48 TO THE NINES

1. Philately
2. Challenge
3. Panoramic
4. Think over
5. Penalized
6. Anacondas
7. Fundament
8. Relatives
9. Complaint
10. Manifesto
11. Saltpeter

"I have a memory like an elephant. In fact, elephants often consult me."—(Noël) Coward

44 LESS IS MORE

1. Contemplate
2. Mountain
3. Crudity
4. Reinforces
5. Masochism
6. Tournament
7. Catalog
8. Chocolate
9. Primrose
10. Generally
11. Travesty
12. Ingenuity
13. Placebo
14. Maestro
15. Anchovies
16. Doorstop
17. Seashore
18. Beneath
19. Asylum
20. Chemist
21. Sequence
22. Orchestra
23. Stranger
24. Beguile
25. Unified
26. Debris
27. Soloist
28. Frontier
29. Campaign
30. Identify
31. Complain
32. Primate
33. Anteater
34. Subtle
35. Gymnastic
36. System
37. Clanked
38. Mnemonic

"Television has proved that people will look at anything rather than each other."—Ann Landers

48 COMMON STOCK

1. Presidents: Polk (potluck); Harding (heart-rending); Taft (steadfast); Carter (caretaker)
2. Fruits: lime (eliminate); apple (appliance); pear (predator); plum (petroleum)
3. Planets: Mars (comparison); Saturn (saturation); Venus (cavernous); Pluto (pollution)
4. Birds: quail (quadrillion); robin (probation); egret (belligerent); raven (gravestone)
5. European countries: Greece (greengrocer); France (fragrance); Italy (immortality); Spain (inspiration)
6. Metallic elements: gold (eightfold); copper (clodhopper); iron (improving); lead (lemonade)

42 NOT MY TYPE

The typefaces are mixed as follows:

The name:	is set in:
Giddyup	Digital
Digital	Mesquite
Mesquite	Umbra
Umbra	Shotgun
Shotgun	Moulin Rouge
Moulin Rouge	Nuptial
Nuptial	American Typewriter
American Typewriter	Mythos
Mythos	Mystery Black
Mystery Black	Parisian
Parisian	Shanghai
Shanghai	Lemonade
Lemonade	Pointille
Pointille	Elektrik
Elektrik	Stencil
Stencil	Old German
Old German	Arriba-Arriba
Arriba-Arriba	Paintbrush
Paintbrush	Rock A Billy
Rock A Billy	Quake
Quake	Tigerteeth
Tigerteeth	Kells
Kells	Collegiate
Collegiate	Countdown
Countdown	Shatter
Shatter	Hairpin
Hairpin	Giddyup

82 SUM-BUDDY SPECIAL

Alley cat	Crystal ball	Marshal Dillon
Birdcage	Field day	Murphy Brown
Blacksmith	Fox hunt	North Star
Brooks Brothers	Greenhorn	Petty cash
Candy cane	"Hail, Caesar!"	Rosebush
Car chase	Heartburn	Strawberry
Churchill Downs	Hollywood	Fields
Clay pigeon	Lord Nelson	*Torn Curtain*

45 SUNDIAL

46 CARTOON BEBUSES

1. Barbados (bar-bay-dose)
2. Soupy Sales (Sioux-peace-ales)
3. Gatorade (gate-a-raid)
4. Kay Kyser (cake-eyes-er)
5. Roger Clemens (rah-jerk-lemons)
6. *Where's Waldo?* (wears-wall-dough)
7. Springfield, Illinois (spring-feel-dill-annoy)
8. Bilbo Baggins (bill-bow-bag-inns)
9. *Steinfeld* (sign-felled)
10. Tampa Bay Buccaneers (tam-pub-A-buck-a-nears)
11. Rhoda Morgenstern (row-dumb-organs-turn)
12. Henry Mancini (hen-ream-Anne-scene-E)
13. Rutger Hauer (rut-grrrrr-how're)
14. Prosciutto (pro-shoot-O)

SECTION THREE

49 THINK-A-LINK MAZE

The word chain is as follows: Box spring, spring fever, fever pitch, pitch-black, blackball, ballpark, park bench, bench press, press-on, on tap, tap water, water ski, ski pole, polecat, cat box. The path is shown in grey:

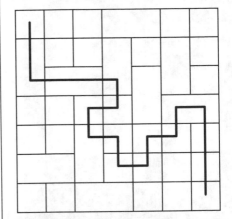

50 BRAGGING RITES

1. H and K	**6.** H and O	**11.** J and L
2. E and I	**7.** F and L	**12.** K and N
3. B and F	**8.** C and M	**13.** E and G
4. D and O	**9.** A and C	**14.** B and N
5. J and M	**10.** A and G	**15.** D and I

52 SNOWFLAKE

53 ROWED SIGNS

AT AN EXPLOSIVES FACTORY

I	N	C	U	R	S	O	R	C	A
S	E	L	E	C	T	R	I	C	E
O	F	F	S	E	T	T	E	R	I
R	E	H	E	A	T	H	E	R	B
R	E	A	P	S	H	A	W	K	S
P	E	K	I	N	G	P	I	N	E
D	E	A	R	T	H	L	Y	R	E
C	O	N	I	C	H	E	R	D	S

"In case of fire, break speed records."

IN THE WINDOW OF A BURGLAR ALARM STORE

M	I	N	K	W	E	L	L	E	R
C	H	I	N	S	U	L	T	A	N
D	I	S	C	U	S	T	O	M	E
I	D	E	A	T	H	R	O	W	S
P	R	O	P	E	R	M	I	T	T
E	A	R	E	N	A	C	T	E	D
B	A	S	T	E	R	I	S	K	Y
I	C	O	N	T	A	I	N	T	S
E	M	A	N	A	T	E	E	L	F

"Merchandise is protected by itself."

54 SIGN A SONG

1. "Bowlin' in the Wind" ("Blowin' in the Wind")
2. "A Horse With No Mane" ("A Horse With No Name")
3. "Baby Café" ("Baby Face")
4. "Cork Around the Clock" ("Rock Around the Clock")
5. "The Rates of a Clown" ("The Tears of a Clown")
6. "China Gang" ("Chain Gang")
7. "File in the Fast Lane" ("Life in the Fast Lane")
8. "Dealer of the Pack" ("Leader of the Pack")
9. "I've Got You Under My Sink" ("I've Got You Under My Skin")
10. "Band on the Urn" ("Band on the Run")
11. "I Host the Sheriff" ("I Shot the Sheriff")
12. "Lady of Pains" ("Lady of Spain")

56 CROSSHATCH

A	B	S	T	R	A	C	T		C	E	R	A	M	I	C	S
L		T		A		C		A	E		O					
T		I	M	P	A	S	T	O		N		L		E	T	C	H
A		L		H		T		L		V		I		L			A
R		L		O		C	O	L	L	A	G	E		L			S
P	A	L	E	T	T	E		R		S		F		L			S
I		I		O		M	G			P			P	R			S
E		F	I	G	U	R	I	N	E			I		R			
C		E		R			N		N		E	X	H	I	B	I	T
E			H	A	N	D	I	C	R	A	F	T		M		C	
	F			P		P		A		E			M	I		A	
B	R	U	S	H		T		P		S	T	Y	L	E		L	
A		T			S	C	U	L	P	T	O	R		I		V	
M	A	T		R	A	S	S							V		P	
A	E	S	T	H	E	T	E		I		T	E	M	P	E	R	A
R		U			U		N		E			R		R		T	
T	O	N	E		C	U	R	A	T	O	R		O	I	L		R
		I					E		E				N				O
P	A	S	T	E	L		P	O	R	T	R	A	I	T		I	N	K

57 THE TROUBLE WITH TRIPLES

1. Chill, child, chili
2. These, theme, there
3. Four, hour, tour
4. None, gone, zone
5. Liner, liver, liter
6. Here, herd, hero
7. Decide, decode, decade
8. Father, bather, rather
9. Point, paint, print
10. Deft, dent, debt
11. Chords, chorus, chores
12. Mayor, major, manor
13. Irises, arises, crises
14. Buoy, busy, bury
15. Squire, squirt, squirm
16. Concept, concert, conceit
17. Deluxe, delude, deluge
18. Mobster, monster, moister
19. Paltry, pastry, pantry
20. Tries, trios, trips

58 LINEAR THOUGHT

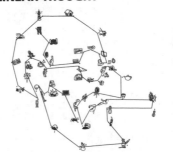

59 QUOTE BOXES

1. Harpists spend ninety percent of their lives tuning their harps and ten percent playing out of tune.
2. Television is an invention that permits you to be entertained in your living room by people you wouldn't have in your home.
3. There are few more charming ways to spend an afternoon than to sit, surrounded by fine china and friends, wolfing down scones and bringing up epigrams.

60 STAINED GLASS

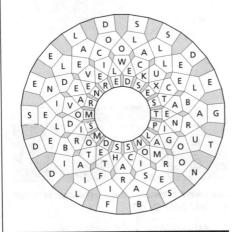

61 WACKY WORDIES REVISITED

1. A house divided	15. Midnight *or* middle of the night
2. Crossed wires	
3. The mind's eye	16. Six of one, half dozen of the other
4. High seas	
5. Wide-awake	
6. Unbalanced	17. On the outside looking in
7. Tilting at windmills	
	18. G-men
8. Jailbreak	19. Grandstanding
9. The lesser of two evils	20. United States
	21. Big cheese
10. Back to basics	22. American Revolution
11. Enlightening	
12. Tightwad	23. Lickety-split
13. End in itself	24. Blockhead
14. Parting of the ways	

GAMES readers offered a number of alternative answers. "A house divided" could also be "open house" or "housebroken." "High seas" could also be "seize up," and "parting of the ways" could be "two-way split."

62 DIAL "M" FOR MIX-UP

1. Bridge Clubs
2. Weight Loss Centers
3. Paper Hangers
4. Dating Services
5. Boxing Instruction
6. Diamond Setting
7. Rubber Stamps
8. Squash Courts
9. Dancing Schools
10. Stocks and Bonds
11. Antique Dealers
12. Paging Services
13. Muffler Repair
14. Computer Services
15. Private Investigators

64 DOUBLE CROSS

A.	COTTON	**N.**	DOWNING
B.	HABITAT	**O.**	FOX TROT
C.	ROCK CANDY	**P.**	INSECT
D.	INSIDIOUS	**Q.**	LION IN WINTER
E.	BOTANY BAY	**R.**	LUGUBRIOUS
F.	ACTIVE	**S.**	OUTCRY
G.	LIGHT IN AUGUST	**T.**	FOOT
H.	TOOTHPASTE	**U.**	MOUSSORGSKY
I.	HOWE	**V.**	ENTWINED
J.	EBBETS FIELD	**W.**	MOTTO
K.	LIBIDINOUS	**X.**	OSIRIS
L.	ANN RICHARDS	**Y.**	ROUT
M.	NEST EGG	**Z.**	YAKUTSK

It's not dramatic ... but pretty Wisconsin is one of those girl- or guy-next-door states. Not your first choice to ask out, but if New York is busy, you might think about giving [it] a call. Wisconsin knows it's being called on the rebound, and is good-natured about it.—C. (J.) Hribal, "The Land-fill of Memory, (The Landscape of the Imagination)"

SECTION FOUR

65 WATCH OUT!

Outer dial (in clockwise order):
1. A minute marker (line) is missing between the 3 and 4
2. Too many minute markers appear between the 6 and 7
3. The five-minute marker next to the 7 is not dark

Main dial (in clockwise order):
4. A minute marker (dot) is missing between the 1 and 2
5. Too many minute markers appear between the 3 and 4
6. The 2 and 5 are switched and inverted
7. The 6 is upside-down
8. The 8 is reversed (the heavy stroke should curl from the upper left to lower right)
9. The 10 and 11 are switched
10. One of the digits in the 11 is missing a lower serif

Inner dial (in clockwise order):
11. The 5 is tilted
12. The 20 is in Roman numerals
13. The five-second marker next to the 40 is a square instead of a circle
14. Too many second markers appear between the 55 and 60

Also:
15. "Synchronized" is misspelled
16. The fat end of the hour hand is not straight
17. The pivot on the second hand on the inner dial is not centered
18. The two kinds of minute markers (dots and lines) are not aligned
19. The watch lid is attached backward (the concave portion is on the wrong side)
20. The watch shows an impossible time (the hour hand could not point directly to the 9 with the minute hand between the 2 and 3)

68 ALL DOLLED UP

1. Alec Guinness, Obi-Wan Kenobi, *Star Wars* (series)
2. Harrison Ford, Han Solo, *Star Wars* (series)
3. Billy Dee Williams, Lando Calrissian, *Star Wars* (series)
4. Michael Keaton, Batman, *Batman* (series)
5. Robin Williams, Peter Pan, *Hook*
6. Sylvester Stallone, John Rambo, *Rambo* (series)
7. Leonard Nimoy, Mr. Spock, *Star Trek* (series)
8. Frank Morgan, the Wizard, *The Wizard of Oz*
9. Kevin Costner, Robin Hood, *Robin Hood: Prince of Thieves*
10. Kurt Russell, Col. Jack O'Neil, *Stargate*
11. Kiefer Sutherland, Athos, *The Three Musketeers*
12. Arnold Schwarzenegger, Jack Slater, *Last Action Hero*
13. John Goodman, Fred Flintstone, *The Flintstones*
14. Jane Curtin, Prymaat Conehead, *Coneheads*
15. Michelle Pfeiffer, Catwoman, *Batman Returns*
16. Dustin Hoffman, Captain Hook, *Hook*
17. Laura Dern, Ellie Sattler, *Jurassic Park*
18. Jeff Goldblum, Ian Malcolm, *Jurassic Park*
19. Malcolm McDowell, Dr. Soran, *Star Trek Generations*
20. Jack Nicholson, the Joker, *Batman*
21. Warren Beatty, Dick Tracy, *Dick Tracy*
22. Dan Aykroyd, Beldar Conehead, *Coneheads*
23. Kyle MacLachlan, Cliff Vandercave, *The Flintstones*
24. Michael Keaton, Betelgeuse, *Beetlejuice*
25. Kyle MacLachlan, Paul Atreides, *Dune*
26. Whoopi Goldberg, Guinan, *Star Trek Generations*
27. Sylvester Stallone, John Spartan, *Demolition Man*
28. Dennis Hopper, King Koopa, *Super Mario Bros.*
29. Rosie O'Donnell, Betty Rubble, *The Flintstones*
30. Sting, Feyd Rautha, *Dune*
31. Keanu Reeves, Ted, *Bill and Ted's Excellent Adventure*
32. Paul Reubens, Pee-wee Herman, *Pee-wee's Big Adventure*
33. John Belushi, Jake Blues, *The Blues Brothers*
34. Madonna, Breathless Mahoney, *Dick Tracy*
35. Dana Carvey, Garth Algar, *Wayne's World* (series)
36. Hattie McDaniel, Mammy, *Gone With the Wind*
37. Vivien Leigh, Scarlett O'Hara, *Gone With the Wind*
38. Mike Myers, Wayne Campbell, *Wayne's World* (series)
39. Clark Gable, Rhett Butler, *Gone With the Wind*
40. Dan Aykroyd, Elwood Blues, *The Blues Brothers*
41. Patrick Stewart, Capt. Jean-Luc Picard, *Star Trek Generations*
42. Judy Garland, Dorothy Gale, *The Wizard of Oz*
43. Bela Lugosi, Dracula, *Dracula*
44. Danny DeVito, the Penguin, *Batman Returns*
45. Marilyn Monroe, Lorelei Lee, *Gentlemen Prefer Blondes*

66 FISH STORY

1. Angelfish
2. Fish and chips or game fish
3. Selfish
4. Fish for compliments or fish line
5. Starfish
6. Fish out of water
7. Fishwife
8. Fish-eye lens
9. Other fish to fry
10. Cold fish
11. Goldfish
12. Shooting fish in a barrel
13. Oafish
14. Passion fish
15. Bluefish
16. Monkfish
17. Fish tank
18. Go Fish or game fish
19. Neither fish nor fowl
20. Shellfish
21. Fish farm
22. Fish sticks
23. Fishbowl
24. Fish scales

72 LAST NAME FIRST

1. James Dean Martin
2. Little Richard Pryor
3. Elton John Lennon
4. Babe Ruth Westheimer
5. Bob Hope Lange
6. Meg Ryan O'Neal
7. Aretha Franklin Roosevelt
8. Eddie Albert Einstein
9. John Glenn Close
10. Ron Howard Cosell
11. John Wayne Newton
12. Raul Julia Roberts
13. George Harrison Ford
14. Steve Martin Sheen
15. Diana Ross Perot

Photo credits: Babe Ruth, Ruth Westheimer, John Glenn, Diana Ross, Ross Perot—Globe Photos; all others—Movie Star News

70 TRIPLE PLAY

Top row: Lobster tank—water (battleship) and tanks (military tank); Tom Cruise and Dustin Hoffman in *Rain Man*—Toms (Tom and Jerry ties) and precipitation (Snow White); *The Paper Chase* videotape—tapes (tape dispenser) and paper (paper clips); pipe cleaner—pipes (bagpipe) and cleaners (vacuum cleaner)
Bottom row: Barney and Betty Rubble from *The Flintstones* movie—Barneys (Barney the dinosaur) and *The Flintstones* (Dino from the TV series); Jack Nicklaus—Jacks (jack of diamonds) and clubs (ace of clubs); diamond ring—diamonds (baseball diamond) and rings (Olympic rings); *The Phantom of the Opera* CD—masks (surgeons) and operas (soap opera)

Photos: Battleship, military tank, tape dispenser, bagpipe, vacuum cleaner, Olympics, diamond ring, Nicklaus—New York Public Library; Barney the dinosaur, The Flintstones movie—Movie Star News; surgeons—Charles Thatcher/Tony Stone Images; General Hospital—Capital Cities/ABC; lobster tank—Stark Products; Rain Man—Jerry Ohlinger's

74 LIQUID ASSETS

1. Honey [generic brand]
2. Dishwashing liquid—Palmolive
3. Aftershave lotion—Aqua Velva (Ice Blue)
4. Shampoo—Johnson's Baby
5. Cranberry juice cocktail—Ocean Spray
6. Eyedrops—Visine
7. Nail polish remover—Cutex
8. Syrup—Log Cabin
9. Mineral water—Perrier
10. Mouthwash—Listerine Antiseptic
11. Household cleaner—Murphy Pure Vegetable Oil Soap
12. Soap bubbles—Jack & Jill
13. Mouthwash—Scope (Original Mint)
14. Beer—Michelob

76 PLUMB LOCO

1–H; 2–G; 3–I; 4–D; 5–F; 6–C; 7–B; 8–E; 9–A

84 SHIP-WRECKED

The items and packaging match as shown.

78 SITE SEEKING

In order from left to right, the clues go with the following countries:
1st row: Ecuador, Japan, Italy, Australia, Egypt, France
2nd row: Italy, France, Ecuador, Egypt, Japan, Australia
3rd row: Australia, Egypt, France, Japan, Italy, Ecuador
4th row: Japan, Italy, Australia, France, Ecuador, Egypt
5th row: Egypt, Australia, Japan, Ecuador, France, Italy (the surrounded states are San Marino and Vatican City)
The city names formed from the first letters of each country's clues are Perth (Australia), Quito (Ecuador), Cairo (Egypt), Paris (France), Milan (Italy), and Osaka (Japan).

Photo credits: Olivia de Havilland—Movie Star News; Punic Wars, Dutch sailing ships—The Bettmann Archive; tortoise and cleaner—UPI/Bettmann.

58 LINEAR THOUGHT LIST

The pictured items, in order, are:

blue jeans	pinwheel	tone arm
blueprint	wheelchair	armpit
fingerprint	rocking chair	cockpit
index finger	rocking horse	peacock
index card	sea horse	peanut
postcard	seashell	nutcracker
postmark	band shell	firecracker
bookmark	hatband	fireman
pocketbook	hatbox	snowman
pocket watch	mailbox	snowball
watchdog	mailbag	golf ball
doghouse	tea bag	golf club
lighthouse	teapot	club sandwich
headlight	flowerpot	sandwich
headline	sunflower	board
clothesline	sundial	blackboard
clothespin	dial tone	black widow

80 SYMBOL LOGIC

Alphabets & Codes
a. 52	**e.** 25	**i.** 18
b. 13	**f.** 15	**j.** 7
c. 29	**g.** 35	
d. 24	**h.** 51	

Astronomy & Astrology
a. 2	**c.** O in "Symbol"
b. 30	**d.** M in "Symbol"

Cattle Brands
a. 54	**b.** 36	**c.** 19

Family & Medicine
a. 4	**c.** 28	**e.** 17
b. 10	**d.** 1	**f.** 37

Game Symbols
a. 9	**d.** 14	**g.** 34
b. O in "Symbol"	**e.** 27	**h.** 20
c. 33	**f.** 40	

Hazards
a. 57	**c.** 11	**e.** 8
b. 6	**d.** 12	

Hobo Signs
a. 22	**b.** 45	**c.** 53

Manufacturing
a. 60	**d.** 26	**g.** 42
b. G in "Logic"	**e.** 46	
c. 39	**f.** 50	

Maps
a. 23	**c.** 56
b. 55	**d.** 43

Mathematics
a. 3	**c.** 44
b. 31	**d.** 32

Meteorology
a. 5	**b.** S in "Symbol"
c. 58	

Money
a. C in "Logic"	**b.** L in "Logic"
c. Y in "Symbol"	

Music
a. 49	**b.** B in "Symbol"
c. L in "Symbol"	

Traffic & Cars
a. 38	**c.** 16
b. 59	**d.** 48

Travel
a. 21	**c.** I in "Logic"
b. 47	**d.** 41

In case you were wondering, the group of sticks figures on the piece of paper on page 81 is a substitution cipher from the Sherlock Holmes story "The Adventure of the Dancing Men." Deciphered, it reads THIS IS NOT THE HIDDEN CONTEST, a reference to a frequent feature in GAMES.

88 SNOWPLACE LIKE DOME

1. Hollywood
2. Chicago
3. Alcatraz
4. Indiana
5. Plymouth
6. Atlanta
7. New Orleans
8. San Francisco
9. Montreal, Canada
10. San Antonio
11. Baltimore
12. Long Beach (the ship is the *Queen Mary*)
13. Arizona
14. Seattle
15. Kentucky
16. Reno
17. Utah
18. Philadelphia
19. Sydney, Australia
20. London, England

86 TIME AFTER TIME

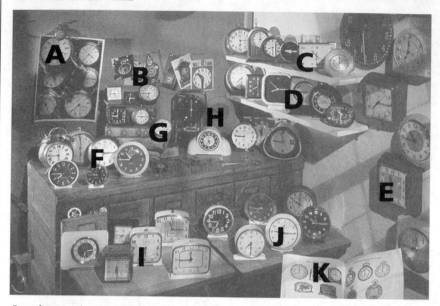

For reference, the 11 groups are lettered A through K as shown. The solution is as follows: A-5:00, A-5:45, G-5:45 (G-6:15 can be inserted here but isn't necessary), G-6:45, J-6:45, J-7:30, D-7:30 (D-8:00 can be inserted here but isn't necessary), D-8:15, A-8:15, A-8:45, H-8:45, H-9:30, B-9:30, B-9:45, F-9:45, F-10:45, E-10:45, E-11:30, K-11:30, K-12:00.

82 SUM-BUDDY SPECIAL NAME LIST

Row 1 (left to right)
Clint Black
Jane Curtin
Sally Field
Rip Torn
David Byrne
Winston Churchill
Penny Marshall
Mary Hart
W.C. Fields
Natalie Wood
Row 2
Nicolas Cage
Chevy Chase
James Brown
John Candy
Buddy Holly
Sid Caesar
Johnny Cash
Bob Dylan
Row 3
Tom Petty
Mel Brooks
Walter Pidgeon
George Bush
Darryl Strawberry

Kirstie Alley
Lorne Greene
Jaclyn Smith
Row 4
Susan Dey
Eddie Murphy
Dr. Joyce Brothers
Michael J. Fox
Lena Horne
Willie Nelson
Hugh Downs
Ringo Starr
Larry Bird
Billy Crystal
Row 5
Jack Lord
William Katt
Helen Hunt
Michael Caine
Barbara Hale
Oliver North
Deborah Kerr
Andrew Dice Clay
Lucille Ball
Pete Rose

Photos: Winston Churchill, Tom Petty—Globe Photos; all others—Movie Star News and Jerry Ohlinger's

92 PUT YOUR FEW CENTS IN

1. Skee-Ball
2. Car wash vacuum
3. Heart/stress analyzer
4. Storage locker
5. Cigarette machine
6. Slot machine
7. Gumball machine
8. Pinball machine
9. Parking meter
10. Photocopier
11. Arcade game
12. Bowling ball polisher
13. Postage stamp vending machine
14. Jukebox
15. Scenic binocular viewer
16. Pay phone
17. Newspaper vending machine
18. Clothes dryer
19. Compressed air machine (at a service station)

90 MAKE ROOM FOR DADDY

1–g, Tim Allen as Tim Taylor, *Home Improvement*
2–p, Danny Thomas as Danny Williams, *The Danny Thomas Show* (formerly *Make Room for Daddy*)
3–j, Andy Griffith as Andy Taylor, *The Andy Griffith Show*
4–l, Bob Saget as Danny Tanner, *Full House*
5–o, Dick Van Dyke as Rob Petrie, *The Dick Van Dyke Show*
6–k, James Avery as Phillip Banks, *The Fresh Prince of Bel-Air*
7–h, Fred MacMurray as Steve Douglas, *My Three Sons*
8–b, John Goodman as Dan Conner, *Roseanne*
9–a, Bill Cosby as Cliff Huxtable, *The Cosby Show*
10–f, Michael Landon as Charles Ingalls, *Little House on the Prairie*
11–e, Dan Lauria as Jack Arnold, *The Wonder Years*
12–i, Ozzie Nelson as himself, *The Adventures of Ozzie and Harriet*
13–n, Dick Van Patten as Tom Bradford, *Eight Is Enough*
14–d, Brian Keith as Bill Davis, *Family Affair*
15–c, Robert Reed as Mike Brady, *The Brady Bunch*
16–m, Ralph Waite as John Walton, *The Waltons*

Photos: 2, k, m—Globe Photos; all others Movie Star News

94 SEW WHAT?

The sets of 1, 3, 4, and 5 matching buttons are shown.

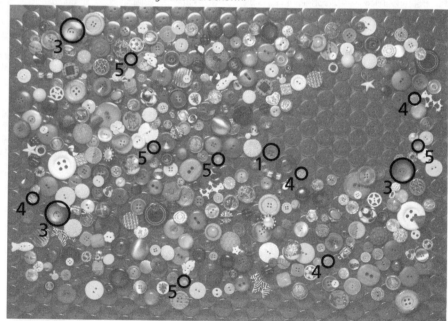

96 AGE DISCRIMINATION

1. 4	**4.** 7	**7.** 5	**10.** 6½
2. 2½	**5.** 2	**8.** 5½	**11.** 3
3. 6	**6.** 1½	**9.** 4½	**12.** 3½

SECTION FIVE

97 POOLING RANK

	Mon	Tue	Wed	Thu	Fri
Driver	Yancy	Wendy	Vlady	Ziggy	Xanny
Passengers	Vlady	Xanny	Wendy	Vlady	Vlady
	Wendy	Yancy	Yancy	Wendy	Yancy
	Xanny	Ziggy	Ziggy	Xanny	Ziggy
At Home	Ziggy	Vlady	Xanny	Yancy	Wendy

Since the same three people want to be passengers on Monday and Thursday (clue 1), the drivers on Monday and Thursday must work at home on Thursday and Monday, respectively. The Monday and Thursday drivers/stay-at-homers cannot include Vlady, since he wants to work the day before he drives (clue 2). Therefore, Vlady must work at home on Tuesday and drive on Wednesday.

The day that Xanny drives must be the day that Wendy works at home, since Wendy would refuse to be a passenger that day (clue 4) (and since each person must drive exactly once and stay home exactly once). Therefore, since Wendy cannot be at home on Tuesday (because Vlady will be), Xanny cannot be the driver on Tuesday; and since Xanny cannot be the driver on Wednesday (because Vlady will be), Wendy must not be at home on Wednesday.

For Yancy to stay at home the day after Xanny does (clue 3), Yancy cannot stay at home Monday, nor Xanny on Friday. Since Yancy does not want to be at home on Friday, the only successive days on which Xanny and Yancy could be at home are Wednesday and Thursday. Being home on Thursday, Yancy must be the Monday driver; and since Xanny will not be home on Monday, she cannot be the Thursday driver, and must therefore be the driver on Friday (since we have already ruled out her driving on Monday through Wednesday). That must be the day that Wendy will be home, leaving Ziggy to stay home on Monday and be the Thursday driver. By elimination, Wendy must drive on Tuesday.

98 CROSS MATH

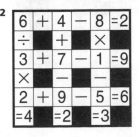

98 GEOGRAPHY SQUARES

```
1.    175     2.    437     3.    843
    x 175         x 437         x 843
    -----         -----         -----
      875          3059          2529
     1225          1311          3372
      175          1748          6744
    ------        ------        ------
    30625        190969        710649
```

99 THE ANTIQUES THIEF

Turn the page 90° clockwise and you'll see the thief's name spelled out.

100 PAINT BY NUMBERS

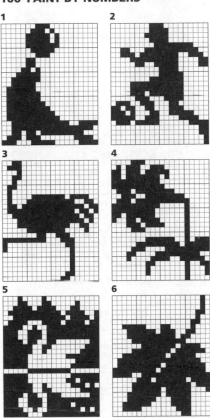

104 THE CAPE DIAMOND THEFT

When Hawk removed the extortion note from the typewriter and put it on the desk, *it lay perfectly flat* (picture #4). If it had been typed the prior evening, when the robbery supposedly occurred, it would have been curled from being in the typewriter roller. Therefore, the note must have been typed shortly before Hawk's arrival. Hawk realized that Carl Tyson, who was the first partner in the office that morning, must have stolen the Cape Diamond himself and typed the extortion note before telephoning the police. Tyson had also reset the clock to indicate that the time of the robbery had been the previous evening.

102 DIGITITIS

PUZZLE 1
```
            69672
     16 )1114752
         96
        ---
         154
         144
         ---
         107
          96
         ---
         115
         112
         ---
          32
          32
          --
           0
```

PUZZLE 2
```
            95117
    761 )72384037
         6849
         ----
          3894
          3805
          ----
           890
           761
           ---
          1293
           761
          ----
          5327
          5327
          ----
             0
```

PUZZLE 3
```
              300324301
    333 )100007992233
         999
         ---
         1079
          999
         ----
          809
          666
          ---
         1432
         1332
         ----
         1002
          999
         ----
          333
          333
          ---
            0
```

PUZZLE 4
```
            4205948
    243 )1022045364
         972
         ---
         500
         486
         ---
         1445
         1215
         ----
         2303
         2187
         ----
         1166
          972
         ----
         1944
         1944
         ----
            0
```

103 PUZZLE PALACE

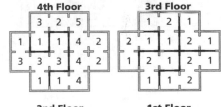

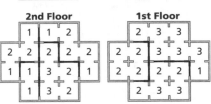

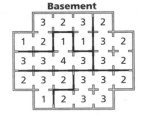

106 ACROSS TOWN

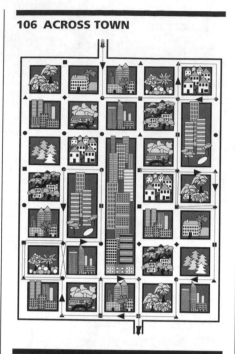

107 BALANCING ACT

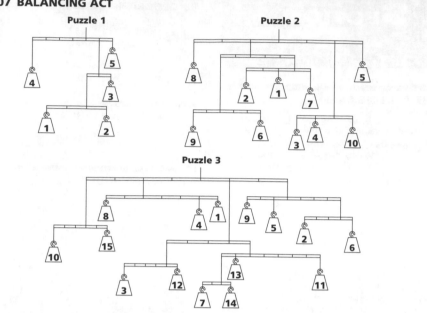

Puzzle 1

Puzzle 2

Puzzle 3

108 MY FIRST CASE

110 CONCENTRATED CHALLENGES

1. THE OLYMPI-ADD
The mirror reflection of this solution also works:

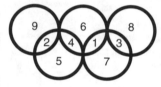

2. MATCH WITS
The circled match will ignite last.

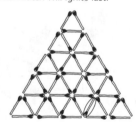

3. BEHIND CLOSED DOORS
Open the doors bearing these numbers: 10, 6, 12, and 14. Each row and column will total 20.

4. BUTTONS AND BOWS

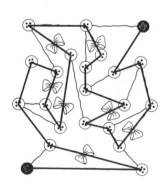

5. LOOKOUTS FOR NO. 1
Place the lookouts in the intersections marked:

6. PERFECT PERFECT VISION

7. TRIP-WIRE
Connect the pegs shown:

8. WORD WRESTLE

112 ROLE MODELS

Four actors appeared in Act I (clue 4) and the other two in Act II (clue 8). Georgie, in a male role, muffed his line in Act I, Scene I (clue 7); so Fragilica's blunder was in Act I, Scene II (clue 4). By the time the second blunder had occurred, four were already on stage (clue 4), so Senta Pokenose is one of the two whose entry was in Act II (clue 3)—and she was played by Moodie (clue 8). Since Georgie played neither Mr. Vested (clue 7) nor Titus Stint (clue 8), he played the only other male role—Mr. Pounce.

The muffs in Act III were made by Dana and Hamm (clue 6)—who must be Terry (clue 1). Terry's role, which began in Act I (clue 1), was neither Senta, Uncle Titus, nor the widow (clue 6)—so it was Mr. Vested. Robin's blunder came before Act III and Charlie's after Act I, Scene I, so: Charlie's was in Act I, Scene II (as Fragilica); Curtin's was in Act II, Scene I; Robin's was in Act II, Scene II (clue 2); and Curtin, by elimination, is Kelly. *Mr.* Spouter, then, who did not play Fragilica and whose blunder preceded Senta's Act II entry, is Robin (clue 3)—who, by elimination of male roles, played Uncle Titus. It then follows that Senta's entry was in Act II, Scene II, and that her muff was in Act III—so she was played by Dana Moodie; Senta's blunder was in Act III, Scene I, and Mr. Vested's was in Act III, Scene II (clue 5). Georgie, not Stagey, (clue 5), is Stentor. By elimination: Charlie's last name is Stagey, and Kelly played Angela Lone.

In summary, by order of blunder, we have:
Act I, Scene 1: Georgie Stentor as Mr. Pounce
Act I, Scene 2: Charlie Stagey as Fragilica Lone
Act II, Scene 1: Kelly Curtin as Angela Lone
Act II, Scene 2: Robin Spouter as Titus Stint
Act III, Scene 1: Dana Moodie as Senta Pokenose
Act III, Scene 2: Terry Hamm as Mr. Vested

113 BATTLESHIPS

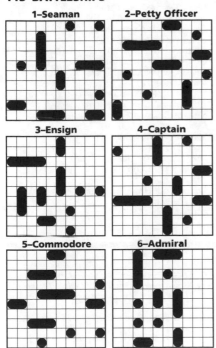

114 BOXED IN

1. STACKING BOXES

There are 141 boxes in the stack. The number of boxes in each column is given in the top view below:

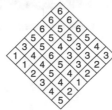

2. CUTTING BOXES

It's not possible to get 27 cubes with fewer than six cuts. Consider the center cube: All six of its faces require a cut.

3. CROSSING BOXES

It will take the fly about 2 minutes and 14 seconds. The shortest route is shown below, crossing at the midpoint of the edge at which the two faces meet, with a distance that's the square root of 5 times the length of the side.

4. TIPPING BOXES

The fourth box from the left is the original center box. If the boxes are thought of as dice with numbers on them (conventionally arranged so that pairs of numbers on opposite faces add up to 7), the sum of the numbers for the upper, front, and right faces of any of the boxes is an odd or even number according to its orientation. The orientation of a box (i.e., whether it's odd or even) changes each time the box is tipped over. This results from the fact that tipping the box leaves two of the three previous numbers, while the third is replaced by its difference from 7 and thus becomes odd if it had been even and vice versa. Now imagine the boxes are being moved on a checkerboard. If a box is odd when it's on a white square, it will always be even when it's on a black square, and always odd when on a white one. Suppose in the final arrangement the first, third, and fifth boxes are on black squares. Then they had to have been on black squares in the original arrangement, too. The second box in the final arrangement is on a white square, but it's orientation is "odd," so it must have been on a black square to start. These four boxes, all on black squares, must be the original four outer boxes. Thus, the remaining box—the fourth in line—must have been in the center originally.

115 POLISH YOUR WITS

1. ABSOLUTELY AMAZING

The route is shown:

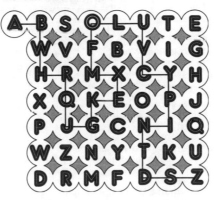

2. ORDERLY ADDITION

$$\begin{array}{r} 74 \\ 63 \\ 752 \\ + \ 641 \\ \hline 1530 \end{array}$$

3. THE TROJAN HORSE

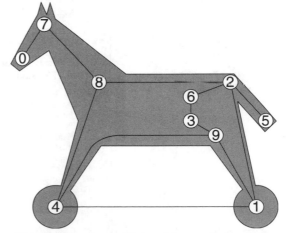

NOTE: The numbers 1, 4, and 9 can take the places of 9, 1, and 4, respectively.

116 JUEGOS ARGENTINOS

1. THE CLOCKWISE ANT

The ant spent 54 minutes on the clock. From the ant's first encounter with the minute hand to her second, the minute hand passed over 45 minute marks; in the same time, the ant passed over 105 minute marks (45 more than a complete circumference). The ratio of speeds was therefore 45/105, or 3/7. If we call the time before the first encounter X minutes, then the minute hand passed over X minute marks while the ant passed over 30 − X minute marks, so: X/(30 − X) = 3/7. Solving, we get X = 9 minutes. Thus, the total time is 9 + 45 = 54 minutes.

2. DIE PEEKING

One of the faces is the six. All the faces of a die have spots in at least one corner except for the one, which has a single spot in the center. Thus, we know none of the faces showing can be the one, and the one must be on the face opposite one of the three faces we can see. Since opposite faces of a die add up to seven, this means the six must be one of the three faces showing.

3. ASTROLOGICAL AGE

Her sign is Pisces. The only date on which the statement could have been made was February 29 (during a leap year), when the teacher's age was 29. Six days later, on March 6, her age was 30. So her birthday is one of the first six days in March.

4. MYSTERY MENU

Here's one possible solution:
First night: abberflooies, bommeljips, curwinkles, dinquapods, dinquapods (from which the travelers could determine dinquapods);
Second night: abberflooies, ecka-eckas, flop-hummers, grobvolleys, grobvolleys (from which they could determine grobvolleys and abberflooies, the only dish common to both nights);
Third night: bommeljips, ecka-eckas, hinkboos, ibbergats, ibbergats (from which they get: ibbergats; bommeljips, the only dish common to the first and third nights; ecka-eckas, the only dish common to the second and third nights; and curwinkles, flophummers, and hinkboos, each occurring only once on the first, second, and third nights, respectively).

5. MULTIPLE TOWERS

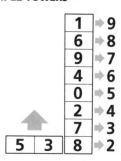

SECTION SIX

118 HIGH-LOW QUIZ

1. High. In 1993, Vatican City had a population of 800.
2. High. After singing at the German Opera in Berlin, Luciano Pavarotti once received 165 curtain calls, lasting 1 hour, 7 minutes.
3. Low. The first contact lenses were designed by a German glassblower 107 years ago, in 1887. (Plastic lenses became available about 50 years later.)
4. Low. The earliest known written reference to jigsaw puzzles appeared in 1763, 231 years ago. The oldest dated jigsaw puzzle extant—a hand-colored engraved map of England and Wales divided into their counties—was published in 1767.
5. Low. After extensive research by our staff, our count of the average number of plain M&M's in a one-pound bag is 512.
6. Low. Respectively, the Eiffel Tower and the Washington Monument are 985 feet and 555 feet high, a difference of 430 feet.
7. High. For Monopoly, Parker Brothers printed $21.5 billion worth of currency in 1993. The Bureau of Engraving and Printing issued $104.3 billion the same year.
8. High. On its first day, the original Macy's took in just $11.06. That store was located 20 blocks south of the current Macy's in Herald Square.
9. Low. The tallest unicycle ever mastered was 101 feet, 9 inches high. It was ridden a distance of 376 feet in Las Vegas in 1989 by Steve McPeak with the aid of a safety wire suspended by an overhead crane.
10. Low. King Mongkut of Siam (played by Yul Brynner in The King and I) had 9,000 wives and concubines.
11. High. Washington (as in George Washington) is the name of counties in 30 states plus one parish (Louisiana). Incidentally, there are 25 Jefferson counties, 24 Franklin, 23 Lincoln, and 23 Jackson—plus one Louisiana parish for each.
12. Low. Women in Japan were first allowed to watch sumo wrestling in 1778, 216 years ago.
13. Low. An ant queen has been known to live 13 years.
14. Low. It takes 43 muscles to frown. (To smile takes 17.)
15. High. Box turtles typically spend their entire lives within 125 yards of their birthplace.

Photos: 2, 10—Movie Star News; 6 (Washington Monument), 8, 9, 12, 13—New York Public Library; 14—Jerry Ohlinger's

122 REFERENCES ON REQUEST

1. Travel guide (*Fodor's Europe*)
2. Spanish/English dictionary (*The University of Chicago Spanish Dictionary*)
3. ZIP code directory (Dome Publishing's *ZIP Code Directory*)
4. Crossword puzzle dictionary (*The Random House Crossword Puzzle Dictionary*)
5. *Books in Print*
6. Almanac (*The Old Farmer's Almanac*)
7. Dictionary (*The Random House Dictionary of the English Language, Unabridged*)
8. Biographical reference (*Who's Who in America*)
9. Rhyming dictionary (*Whitfield's University Rhyming Dictionary*)
10. Encyclopedia (*Encyclopedia Americana*)
11. Movie guide (*Leonard Maltin's Movie and Video Guide*; the movie listing is for *The Last of Sheila*)
12. Quotations book (*Bartlett's Familiar Quotations*)
13. Abbreviations dictionary (*New International Abbreviations Dictionary*)
14. *The Guinness Book of Records*
15. Baby name book (*Name Your Baby*)
16. Atlas (*Oxford Atlas of the World*)
17. Thesaurus (*The Synonym Finder*)
18. Slang dictionary (*New Dictionary of American Slang*)

117 STATE CAPITAL 20 QUESTIONS

1. Dover, Salem
2. Augusta, Juneau
3. Sacramento, Trenton
4. Austin, Boston
5. Salt Lake City (Utah), Santa Fe (New Mexico)
6. Columbia, Columbus
7. Carson City, Jefferson City
8. Denver, Providence
9. Concord, Lansing
10. Bismarck (North Dakota), Frankfort (Kentucky), Little Rock (Arkansas), Oklahoma City (Oklahoma), Topeka (Kansas)
11. Charleston, Springfield
12. Annapolis, Cheyenne, Pierre, Tallahassee
13. Jackson, Lincoln, Madison
14. Montgomery, Montpelier, Richmond
15. Atlanta, Indianapolis
16. Baton Rouge (Louisiana), St. Paul (Minnesota)
17. Harrisburg, Hartford, Helena, Honolulu
18. Albany, Nashville
19. Boise, Des Moines
20. Olympia, Phoenix, Raleigh

123 PLACES OF NOTE

"By the Time I Get to *Phoenix*" (6)
"*Chattanooga* Choo Choo" (18)
"Deep in the Heart of *Texas*" (B)
"Do You Know the Way to *San Jose*?" (2)
"*Philadelphia* Freedom" (22)
"*Tupelo* Honey" (15)
"Hotel *California*" (A)
"I Left My Heart in *San Francisco*" (1)
"I Lost My Sugar in *Salt Lake City*" (5)
"I've Got a Gal in *Kalamazoo*" (17)
"*Tallahassee* Lassie" (19)
"*Wichita* Lineman" (10)
"Little Old Lady From *Pasadena*" (3)
"Meet Me in *St. Louis*, Louis (13)
"Moonlight in *Vermont*" (J)
"Moon Over *Miami*" (21)
"My Old *Kentucky* Home" (E)
"Okie from *Muskogee*" (12)
"*Georgia* on My Mind" (G)
"On the Atchison, Topeka, and the *Santa Fe*" (7)
"On the Boardwalk in *Atlantic City*" (23)
"Please Come to *Boston*" (25)
"*Virginia* Reel" (I)
"Shuffle Off to *Buffalo*" (20)
"Sidewalks of *New York*" (24)
"Sink the *Bismarck*" (8)
"*Pennsylvania* 6-5000" (H)
"Stars Fell on *Alabama*" (F)
"*Sioux City* Sue" (9)
"The City of *New Orleans*" (16)
"The Night *Chicago* Died" (14)
"The *Arkansas* Traveler" (C)
"Twenty Four Hours From *Tulsa*" (11)
"Viva *Las Vegas*" (4)
"*Indiana* Wants Me" (D)

120 IT'S SATURDAY NIGHT!

Who's Who
1. Howard Cosell. The "Prime Time Players" were Bill Murray, Brian Doyle-Murray, and Christopher Guest, all of whom were later regulars on *SNL*.
2. b
3. One. He appeared a few times at the beginning of the second season, but had already decided by then to leave the show for greener pastures.
4. Richard Pryor (December 13, 1975) and Andrew "Dice" Clay (May 12, 1990)
5. d
6. Andy Kaufman. Over 350,000 people voted, and he lost. He never appeared on the show again.
7. Harry Shearer
8. d
9. Peter Aykroyd, Brian Doyle-Murray, Jim Belushi
10. She won the "Anyone Can Host" write-in contest.
11. a and b
12. Buck Henry

On a Role
1. The Killer Bees
2. Mr. Bill
3. *Wayne's World*
4. It's Pat!
5. Dan Quayle
6. a-8, b-3, c-10, d-1, e-11, f-6, g-9, h-5, i-2, j-7, k-12, l-4
7. The Sweeney Sisters
8. He was born without a spine.
9. Joe Piscopo and Phil Hartman
10. Sammy Davis Jr.
11. The Coneheads
12. He's Gumby, dammit!
13. "Deep Thoughts" by Jack Handey
14. Toonces the Cat
15. Pat Sajak
16. They played U.S. presidents on the show. The list is chronological by president: Nixon, Ford, Carter, Reagan, Bush, and Clinton.
17. No coke. Pepsi.

Musical Interlude
1. The Beatles. Lennon and McCartney, watching at Lennon's home in New York City, nearly went to the studio as a gag, but they were too tired.
2. George Harrison
3. Elvis Costello
4. Steve Martin; the song was "King Tut"
5. Sinéad O'Connor
6. The Pope. The cast and crew thought she'd be holding up a picture of a Bosnian refugee child, which was relevant to the song she'd just sung.
7. Joe Cocker
8. Paul Shaffer, longtime bandleader and second banana for David Letterman
9. Barbra Streisand
10. The Blues Brothers, in which they performed as Jake and Elwood Blues

News Cast
1. Generalissimo Francisco Franco
2. Ripped open her blouse
3. Dennis Miller
4. The Hollywood Minute
5. A: Father Guido Sarducci
   B: Grumpy Old Man
   C: Queen Shenequa
   D: Roseanne Roseannadanna
   E: Operaman
   F: A. Whitney Brown

Photos: Roseanne Roseannadanna—Jerry Ohlinger's; all others—NBC Photo

124 GOING THROUGH THE MOTIONS

1. "Hello" or "Greetings."
2. c.
3. a and c.
4. a.
5. "What a pretty girl!"
6. d. The American side-to-side wave for good-bye means "no" in much of Europe. (The European good-bye is generally done by flapping the hand down and up.) If you try to catch a waiter's attention in Europe by waving, the waiter may interpret this as "I'm not wanted" and leave you alone.

   In Bulgaria, the gestures for yes and no are just the opposite of what they are in the States: Shaking the head means "yes"; nodding means "no."
7. All of them: a, b, c, and d. In Germany, the upraised thumb, not the forefinger, is used to signal "one." In a German beer hall, you'd flash the "thumbs-up" sign to order one beer. If you forget this and casually hold up your forefinger instead, it could be seen as meaning "two."

   In Japan, counting begins with the index finger indicating "one." The middle finger is added for "two," the ring finger added for "three," and the little finger added for "four." The Japanese show the upright thumb alone to mean "five." So if you order "one beer" with your thumb alone in Japan, you may get five beers.

   You may get an angry response elsewhere by using the thumbs-up. In Australia (and Nigeria, among other places), it is a way to tell someone to take a seat on that digit.
8. a.
9. All but "h." (The American Sign Language "H" is formed by adjoining and straightening the forefinger and middle finger, and pointing them directly away from you as if you're shooting a gun.)
10. b.
11. c.
12. d.
13. "Good-bye."

Based on Gestures: The Do's and Taboos of Body Language Around the World, copyright © 1991 Roger E. Axtell. Used by permission of the publisher, John Wiley & Sons, Inc. To order a copy, call 1-800-CALL-WILEY.

128 THROUGH THE YEARS

1st–G	11th–B
2nd–J	12th–M
3rd–P	13th–I
4th–E	14th–O
5th–N	15th–H
6th–Q	16th–D
7th–S	17th–C
8th–L	18th–K
9th–T	19th–A
10th–R	20th–F

130 NEWS REELS

1. *101 Dalmatians*
2. *The Godfather*
3. *A League of Their Own*
4. *Who Framed Roger Rabbit*
5. *Splash*
6. *Back to the Future Part II*
7. *The Silence of the Lambs*
8. *The Natural*
9. *Billy Bathgate*
10. *North by Northwest*
11. *Do the Right Thing*
12. *Witness*

126 MONKEY BUSINESS

PRIME-TIME PRIMATES
1. *B.J. and the Bear* (NBC, 1979-81)
2. *Mr. Smith* (NBC, 1983)
3. *The Monkees*, starring (clockwise from top left) Mike Nesmith, Peter Tork, Micky Dolenz, and Davy Jones (NBC, 1966-68)
4. *The Hathaways* (ABC, 1961-62, featuring the Marquis Chimps)
5. *Lancelot Link, Secret Chimp* (ABC, 1970-72)

RHESUS PIECES
1. h
2. d
3. b
4. a
5. e
6. f
7. c
8. g

CALL OUR BLUFF
Real expressions: 1, 2, 4, 5, 6. These genuine phrases were adapted from *Brewer's Dictionary of Phrase and Fable,* 14th edition, Harper & Row, 1989. "To eat the monkey's dinner" is the fake, although the first line of the quote from *Henry V* is genuine.

SIMIAN CINEMA
1. *The Wizard of Oz* (one of the Wicked Witch of the West's flying monkeys)
2. *Rebel Without a Cause* (James Dean)
3. *Gorillas in the Mist* (Sigourney Weaver and gorilla costar)
4. *Tarzan, the Ape Man*, or the Tarzan series (Maureen O'Sullivan, Cheetah, and Johnny Weissmuller)
5. *Raiders of the Lost Ark*, or the Indiana Jones series (Harrison Ford and monkey costar)
6. *Every Which Way But Loose*, or *Any Which Way You Can* (Clint Eastwood and Clyde)
7. *Bedtime for Bonzo*, or the Bonzo series (Ronald Reagan and Bonzo)
8. *The Planet of the Apes*, or the Planet of the Apes series (Roddy McDowall and Charlton Heston)
9. *Greystoke: The Legend of Tarzan, Lord of the Apes* (Christopher Lambert and "Silverbeard")
10. *Mighty Joe Young* (Terry Moore and Joe)
11. *2001: A Space Odyssey* (early apeman)

Photos: Eastwood, Greystoke—New York Public Library; all others—Jerry Ohlinger's

132 BULL'S-EYE 20 QUESTIONS

1. Know (no)
2. Housemaid
3. Spotlight (stoplight)
4. Affordable (Ford)
5. Tractor (protractor, contractor)
6. Patients (tie, pants)
7. Like
8. Willow (will owe)
9. Keenness
10. Aim (rim, arm, air)
11. Irritate
12. Gigolos (solo gig)
13. Topsy-turvy
14. Worse (Worth)
15. Rotates (toaster)
16. Benchmark (Ben, Mark)
17. Banjo (ferns)
18. Abhorrence (borne)
19. Tails (pintails, tailspin)
20. Cumulous

"Keep breathing"—Sophie Tucker

SECTION SEVEN

134 PENCIL POINTERS

135 CROSS SAWS

1. Absence makes the heart grow fonder.
2. One good turn deserves another.
3. Actions speak louder than words.
4. Two heads are better than one.
5. Leave well enough alone.
6. From little acorns great oaks grow.
7. April showers bring May flowers.
8. Make hay while the sun shines.
9. Many hands make light work.

136 SPELL WEAVING

133 HOPSCOTCH

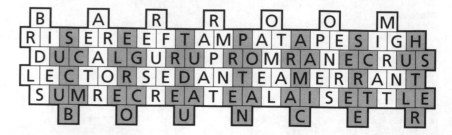

137 NEW DIRECTIONS

138 JUMBO CROSSWORD

157 CROSSNUMBER HINT

The answer to 1-Across is 65431.

170 HEADS UP! HINTS

1. Only 15 coins are needed to complete the magic square.
2. The switch can be made in 22 turns.

140 THE SPIRAL

141 PETAL PUSHERS

144 RIDDLE-DEE-DEE

142 HELTER-SKELTER

Puzzle #1

```
N I V L A C O L
A R E I V I R A
M E M A S T P E
A A Y T O P A Z
T G H K A Y A K
H A R C L R O N
I N L O U C L A
S A N C H O O P
```

Puzzle #2

```
C I N O S T A W
A P R I C O T A
L A L G A E C H
L S M I L N E T
I A L A I A J X
N O V E L I O I
A I R E S L R S
V Y D N A S P S
```

143 SIAMESE TWINS

145 VARIETY PACK

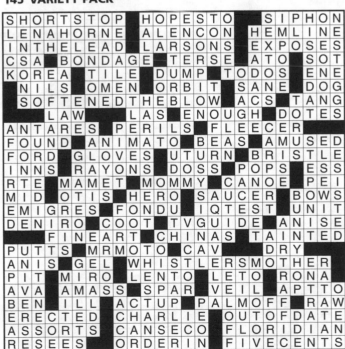

145 SHORT STUFF

What they stand for:

ACROSS:
1. Whip Inflation Now
4. United Kingdom
6. Delaware
8. Central Intelligence Agency
9. *For Your Information*
11. Multiple sclerosis 1
12. Standing room only
14. *Répondez s' il vous plaît*
16. A soon as possible
18. Mountain Standard Time
19. Los Angeles
20. No meaning, according to MCI
22. Parent-Teacher Association
25. Federal Trade Commission
27. Praise the Lord
29. Kitchen Patrol
30. Professional Golfers' Association
32. Bring your own bottle
34. No equivalent
36. No equivalent
37. Parental guidance
38. American Medical Association
40. Cash on Delivery
43. No equivalent
44. Detective Comics
45. American Dental Association

DOWN:
1. Water closet
2. Roman numeral two
3. National Aeronautics and Space Administration
4. Unidentified flying object
5. Kentucky
6. Department of Motor Vehicles
7. Extrasensory perception
10. Internal Revenue Service
13. Revolutions per minute
15. Scientifically Treated Product
16. Alien Life Form
17. Scholastic Aptitude Test
18. Massachusetts Institute of Technology
21. Certified public accountant
23. Technical knockout
24. All-point bulletin
26. Cardiopulmonary resuscitation
28. Lyndon Baines Johnson
31. Grade point average
33. Young Men's Christian Association
34. Works Progress Administration
35. *Komitét Gosudárstvennoi Bezopásnosti*
36. Women's Army Corps
39. Doctor of Medicine

148 DOUBLE DROP QUOTE

The quote is "Nothing in fine print is ever good news."

149 MARCHING BANDS

151 SPLIT ENDS

The clue parts for each answer are as follows:
9 = 1 + 8; 14 = 11 + 3; 21 = 12 + 9; 24 = 2 + 22; 27 = 7 + 20; 32 = 27 + 5; 33 = 19 + 14; 42 = 18 + 24; 51 = 6 + 45; 55 = 15 + 40; 56 = 35 + 21; 57 = 31 + 26; 63 = 10 + 53; 70 = 28 + 42; 71 = 23 + 48; 72 = 68 + 4; 73 = 57 + 16; 77 = 13 + 64; 80 = 17 + 63; 83 = 32 + 51; 85 = 56 + 29; 87 = 54 + 33; 88 = 50 + 38; 89 = 30 + 59; 93 = 49 + 44; 94 = 69 + 25; 99 = 58 + 41; 101 = 55 + 46; 103 = 36 + 67; 109 = 39 + 70; 110 = 73 + 37; 112 = 78 + 34; 113 = 47 + 66; 114 = 62 + 52; 117 = 43 + 74; 132 = 60 + 72; 138 = 61 + 77; 140 = 65 + 75; 147 = 76 + 71.

150 HEX SIGNS

The completed sentences are:

1. In the king's reALM, OSTentatious displays are nearly always forbidden.
2. The wiSER MONks lecture on piety to their less educated brethren.
3. The newspaPER USEd to be read more before the advent of TV.
4. An argumentative person's liFE IS TYpically shorter than a good-natured person's.
5. Scoring a home rUN IS ONe way to bring togetherness to the team.
6. While celebrities may need to travel incognito, those of us lacking acclaim shUN SUNGlasses indoors.
7. If a naughty boy is staying with you, it may be smart to lock yoUR CHINa cupboard.
8. For a culinary treat, try asking the chEF FOR Tortoni.
9. Tom Sawyer's natural friendliness put Huck FINN AT Ease.
10. A new artilleryman is likely to find all the shootinG UNNERving.
11. An aristocRAT IN General won't associate with people in a lower social class.
12. When visiting New DelHI, THE Rajah always comes to this place.
13. After the game, the winning players left the arenA TRIUMphantly to meet their fans in the courtyard.
14. This pottery glaze was created years ago by somE NAMELess artisan.
15. You can bet that people who say they seldom make an erroR ARE LYing.
16. An uncooperative patient can be somewhat difficult foR A THERapist.
17. I like any flavor of bubbLE GUM Except perhaps peanut butter.
18. If you want to conSOLE LYricists when they're blue, you only need to praise their songs.
19. During the Gold Rush, you'd find many prospectorS CURRYing favor with claim office workers.

152 RULE BREAKING

153 GOING TOO FAR

154 SQUARE DEALING

SECTION EIGHT

155 THE SILVER WINDOW

The size of the square hole is two inches by two inches.

Each successive square of the window, moving out from the center, contains twice the area of the previous square. (As seen here, the square can be divided into eight equal triangles, four of them within the smaller square.)

By continuing to double outward, we find that the size of the entire window is 2 x 2 x 2 x 2 x 2 x 2 = 128 times as large as the hole. So the area of the window without the hole is 128 – 1 = 127 times the area of the hole. Since the volume of silver is 508 cubic inches, and it's one inch thick, the area (without the hole) must be 508 square inches. Thus, the area of the hole is 508/127 = 4 square inches, so its width and height are each two inches.

156 THINK TWICE

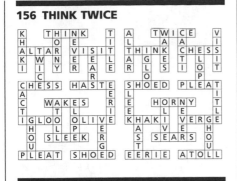

156 MIND FLEXERS

#1	#2	#3	#4	#5
1. C	1. D	1. C	1. B	1. C
2. E	2. C	2. E	2. E	2. A
3. D	3. A	3. D	3. D	3. E
4. A	4. E	4. B	4. A	4. B
5. B	5. B	5. A	5. C	5. D

157 CROSSNUMBER PUZZLE

(crossnumber grid)

158 SOLITAIRE HANGMAN

I. PLATINUM   VII. CRYPTIC
II. TOWNSHIP   VIII. VAGRANCY
III. SEQUOIA   IX. WITHHOLD
IV. WAYWARD   X. BRUSQUE
V. ECHELON   XI. CUBBYHOLE
VI. SWIMSUIT   XII. BUSHWHACK

164 PET PROJECT

(crossword grid)

160 500 RUMMY

B	A	N	Q	U	E	T	
A	2	3	9	9	9	9	42
B	A	R	O	Q	U	E	
2	2	2	8	9	10	J	43
C	A	B	O	O	S	E	
A	A	A	A	5	6	7	22
C	R	O	Q	U	E	T	
A	2	3	9	9	9	9	42
E	N	T	W	I	S	T	
10	J	Q	K	6	6	6	58
F	I	R	E	M	E	N	
J	Q	K	7	7	7	7	58
H	O	B	N	O	B	S	
5	5	5	5	A	2	3	26
H	O	S	T	I	L	E	
4	5	6	Q	Q	Q	Q	55
I	N	F	E	R	N	O	
J	J	J	J	6	7	8	61
M	A	R	Q	U	E	E	
K	K	K	9	10	J	Q	69
M	I	G	R	A	N	T	
8	8	8	3	4	5	6	42
N	O	S	T	R	I	L	
3	3	3	9	10	J	Q	48
O	B	S	C	E	N	E	
A	2	3	4	7	7	7	31
O	B	S	C	U	R	E	
A	2	3	4	10	10	10	40
O	M	I	C	R	O	N	
8	8	8	A	2	3	4	34
S	E	I	Z	U	R	E	
6	7	8	10	10	10	10	61
T	E	Q	U	I	L	A	
9	9	9	9	J	Q	K	66
T	R	A	N	S	I	T	
2	3	4	5	6	6	6	32
W	A	R	R	A	N	T	
K	K	K	3	4	5	6	48

Total Score   878

161 WORD GAMES

Missing Links   **Opposites**
1. piece   1. passé
2. switch   2. dare
3. crazy   3. mild
4. bridge   4. idle
5. weight   5. launch
6. secret   6. invitational
7. horse   7. sweet
8. counter   8. molehill

Double Definitions
1. dove   5. lumbering
2. graze   6. tender
3. waxed   7. tumbler
4. moped   8. secondhand

Ratios
1. write (homophones of opposites)
2. thermometer (same letters, used repeatedly)
3. sexist (synonym with s added to front)
4. imbibed (synonym inside im-ed)
5. simmer (seasons with vowels switched)
6. aspirin (synonym with last letter dropped)
7. collect (synonym with double-n changed to double-l)
8. Holmes : Moriarty

The Verse
The many-times-married DeVries
Became bored with divorce by degrees,
Till, I'm sad to report,
He could sleep while in court,
Gaining exes while catching some Z's.

162 PENTATHLON

THE RINGS: Event 1: Javelin; Event 2: Hurdles; Event 3: Long Jump; Event 4: Shot Put; Event 5: Pole Vault

ACROSS: 1. Paid (P + aid) 3. Ale (ail) 5. E.g. (senEGal) 8. Biases (zamBIA'S EStablishment) 10. Spelt (S + L + pet) 12. Erie (Eire) 14. Suriname (U.S. Marine) 15. Emanate (eta + name) 19. Gorge (Gore + G) 21. Isis (is + is) 23. Den (Denmark – mark) 24. Nested (nes + Ted) 25. Liens (lies + n) 26. Claim (C + Mali) 29. Height (the GI + H) 30. Siting (sit-in + G) 31. Filed (F + deli) 33. Near (Nepal – pal + a + R) 35. Ogees (O + geese – e) 37. West (stew) 38. Salves (saves + L) 41. Lars (Lear's – E) 42. Prefect (P + ref + E + ct.) 44. Rouse (Romania – mania + use) 45. Anon (lebANON) 46. Sacred (sac + red) 47. Stoats (S + to a T + S) 49. Tried (tied + r) 50. Toiled (Eliot + D) 51. Ons (cameroON'S) 52. Toad (to + ad)

DOWN: 1. Pairings (Iran pigs) 2. Ideal (aide + L) 3. Slender (sender + L) 4. Gelatin (GE + Latin) 6. Kotter (K + otter) 7. Gil (G + Il) 8. Busies (Barracks Under Siege In El Salvador) 9. Simile (sí + mile) 10. Span (Spain – I) 11. ESE (thE SEychelles) 13. Restoring (sort Niger) 14. Soil (S + oil) 16. Stagger (stag + Ger.) 17. Seater (Sea + term – m) 18. Insulted (unlisted) 20. Get (G + Et) 22. Alder (Red + la) 27. Ums (U.S. + m) 28. Reverse (re + verse) 32. Lapis (la + P + is) 34. Raced (R + aced) 36. Osteal (os + teal) 39. Vets (VEnezuela argumenTS) 40. Joust (J + oust) 43. Afro (for a) 48. Tito (to + it)

163 PROCRUSTEAN BED

(word grid)

ACROSS: 1. Scot (St. + co.) 5. Harbored (hard + bore) 10. Priest (pries + t) 11. Cover (C + over) 12. Spied (sped + I) 13. Wassail (was + sail) 14. Pines (snipe) 15. Elated (tale + ed.) 16. Uses (hoUSE Sometimes) 19. Hears (share) 22. Knights (thinks + G) 25. Plan (L + pan) 27. Sheath (heat + sh) 30. Borders (boarders) 31. Allow (all + ow) 32. Fleas (flees) 33. Gad (G + ad) 34. Preserve (PR + Reeves) 35. Presides (spider's + e) 36. Ceased (cased + E)

DOWN: 1. Aspiring (asp + I + ring) 2. Spin (nips) 3. Reels (two meanings) 4. Temp (met + p) 5. Cashier (I search) 6. Basement (bass meant) 7. Oars (soar) 8. Vilest (vest + I + L) 9. Ells (sell) 14. Oat (fidO ATe) 17. Spillage (sage + pill) 18. Asteroid (adores it) 20. Galas (gal + has – h) 21. Stressed (desserts) 23. These (sheet) 24. Putters (two meanings) 25. Spacer (recaps) 26. At last (AT&T + las) 28. Eras (ERAs) 29. Eave (Eve + a)

SECTION NINE

165 DIE JEST

The number is 3.

167 WHITE HOUSE STARS

Your stars have choosen Lincoln.

168 BOUNCE

Puzzle 1: X plays at E4. O must play at either B5 or B6 (since B2 gives X a win at B3 or F3 and B3 gives X a win at C4 or D4). In either case, X plays at A6. Any play by O gives X a win: A1 leads to a win at B3; C1 to a win at D4; D1 to a win at C4 or D4; E1 to a win at F3; and F1 to a win at B3 or F3.

Puzzle 2: X plays at D1. O must play at B4 (since D4 leads to a win for X at C2 and E4 to a win at B1). X plays at B5. O must play at B6 (since C6 leads to a win for X at B1 or B3, D6 to a win at B3, E6 to a win at D5, and F6 to a win at D5). X plays at A6. O must play at D1 (since A1 leads to a win for X at B1 or B3, B2 to a win at C2, C1 to a win at D5, E1 to a win at F1, and F1 to a win at B3). X plays at F4. Since O used the only safe play in the 1 column on the previous turn, any play will give X a win.

170 HEADS UP!

1. Fifteen coins will complete the magic square, as shown:

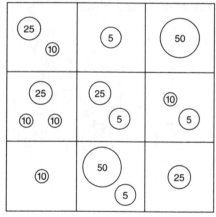

2. One way to complete the switch in 22 turns is as follows (L = left, R = right): nickel–R, R; dime–L, nickel–L, L; quarter–L; nickel–R, R; penny–R, R, R; dime–L; quarter–L; dime–R, R; quarter–L; dime–L; penny–L, L; nickel–L; penny–R, R. Another solution replaces our first eight steps with penny–R, R; nickel–L; penny–L, L; dime–L.